COMPLETE GUIDE TO HUNTING

Hunting Arms

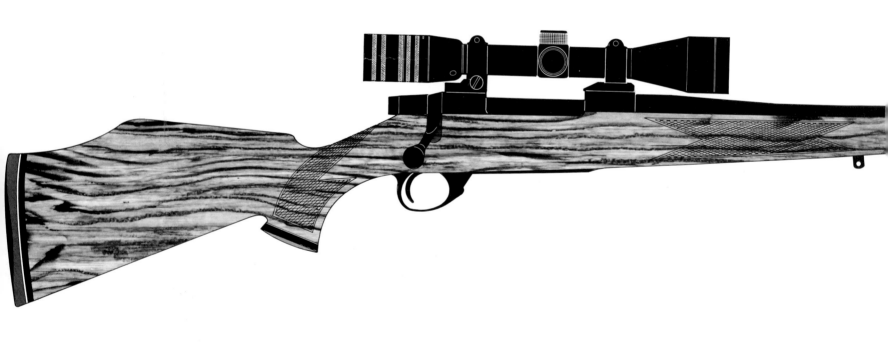

COMPLETE GUIDE TO HUNTING

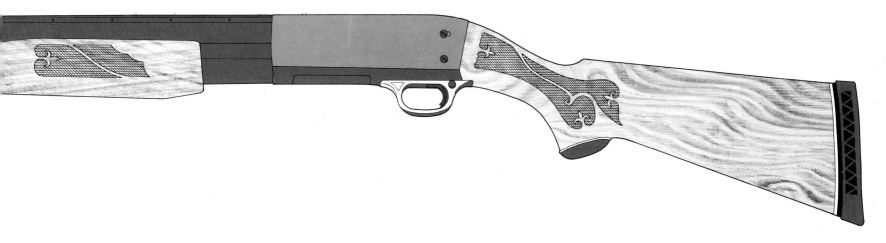

Hunting Arms

ROBERT ELMAN / *Supervising Editor*

MASON CREST PUBLISHERS, INC.

COMPLETE GUIDE
TO HUNTING

HUNTING ARMS

World copyright © 2002
Nordbok International,
P.O. 7095, SE 402 32 Gothenburg, Sweden

This edition is published in 2002 by Mason Crest Publishers Inc.
370 Reed Road, Broomall, PA 19008, USA
(866) MCP-BOOK (toll free).
www.masoncrest.com

Editor-in-Chief: Robert Elman
Cover: Nordbok

First printing
1 2 3 4 5 6 7 8 9 10
Library of Congress Cataloging-in-Publication Data on file at the Library of Congress

ISBN 1-59084-501-3

Printed & bound in The Hashemite Kingdom of Jordan 2002

Supervising Editor

Robert Elman has participated in the project from its conception, and he has worked closely with the Publisher's editorial and art departments in guiding the authors, editing their material, and collecting the illustrations. Author of over a dozen books on hunting, he has hunted widely, and, as an editor, has specialized in books on hunting and outdoors.

Contents

I Hunting Arms

Chapter 1
Shotguns

ENGLISH SHOTGUNS

J.A. Maxtone Graham

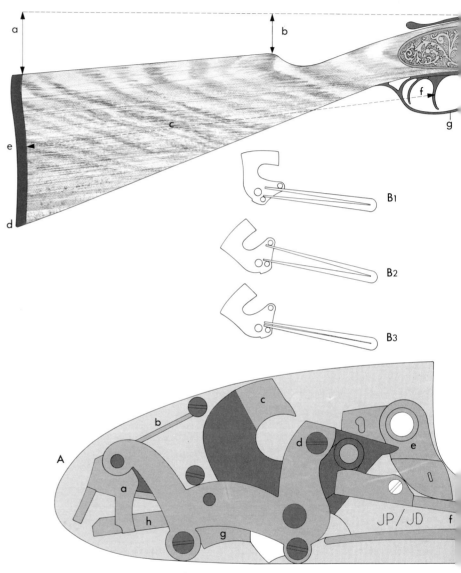

In discussing the firearms popular among European hunters, it is necessary to explain briefly what is meant by sportsmen when they speak—with some reverence—of "English guns."

In Continental Europe, as in the British Isles, double-barreled shotguns are far more popular than smoothbore repeaters. Double-barreled guns are, in fact, the rule and tradition for hunting in all of Europe. Some firms manufacture repeaters, but this is chiefly for export. However, there is an increasingly wide gap between the double guns most popular on the Continent and those most popular in Britain. In recent years, over-and-under guns have won a great many Continental admirers, whereas in Britain, the side-by-side configuration is most admired now, as it always has been.

The side-by-side is the "classic" shotgun. In the nineteenth century, this design was developed to perfection in Britain, and it alone is still closely associated with bird shooting in the British Isles. There are objective reasons why a shooter might prefer either an over-and-under or a side-by-side; these are discussed in the section on shotguns for American hunting. However, tradition and appearance of the side-by-side double are sufficient to explain the continuing British preference.

Britain imports a great many more sporting firearms of all types and levels of quality than she exports. There is a relatively new type of British shooter to be supplied: the small farmer, factory worker, businessman, and craftsman. Typically, such shooters do a bit of wildfowling now and then but never take part in grouse shoots and cannot afford the kind of double gun favored by the old aristocracy. Not even newly-rich businessmen account for many sales of the highest-quality, traditional, hand-made double guns. A man with a recently accumulated fortune, perhaps indulging for the first time in the hunting sports, is unlikely to have the patience (or intensity of interest, appreciation of the tradition, or whatever one may want to call it) to wait for a couple of seasons or more for the completion of a truly custom-built, hand-made gun.

Yet it is just such a gun that symbolizes traditional British bird shooting: a side-by-side double gun of the sort called "best" gun. This term does not mean what it might appear to mean. The finest double gun made in the United States, for example, the Winchester Model 21, is a truly excellent firearm but, in British parlance, certainly not a "best" gun; the term is used not only to specify a manufacturer's top grade—as names are used elsewhere for various grades of gun, or levels of quality—but also to specify a gun very carefully fitted to the individual buyer, and made entirely by hand. Thus, a British maker might build very fine guns and yet offer no best gun.

London has always been the center of the best-gun trade. At the end of the nineteenth century, some twenty-five makers had their shops in London, and several others were to be found in other parts of Britain.

The gunmaking firm of James Purdey and Sons was founded in London during the reign of George III. A Purdey gun is custom-made to suit the especial requirements of the individual. We show here a Purdey side-by-side shotgun to demonstrate shotgun terminology.
(*a*) Drop at heel. (*b*) Drop at comb. (*c*) Length of pull. (*d*) Toe. (*e*) Recoil pad. (*f*) Triggers. (*g*) Trigger guard. (*h*) Receiver. (*i*) Fore-end, or forearm. (*j*) Barrels. (*k*) Muzzle. (*l*) Sight.
A The famous Purdey action. (*a*) Locking sear. (*b*) Locking sear spring. (*c*) Hammer. (*d*) Bridle. (*e*) Lock lifter. (*f*) Main spring. (*g*) Main sear. (*h*) Main sear spring.
B The working principle of the action. (*1*) Gun fired and closed. (*2*) Gun open and cocked. (*3*) Gun ready to fire.

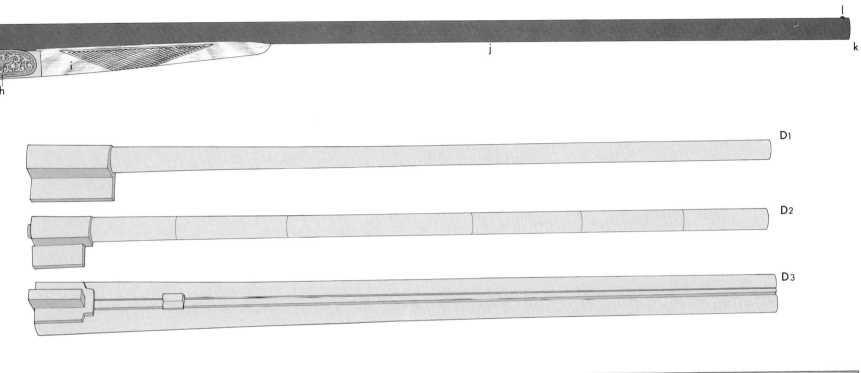

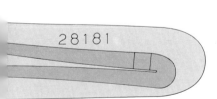

28181

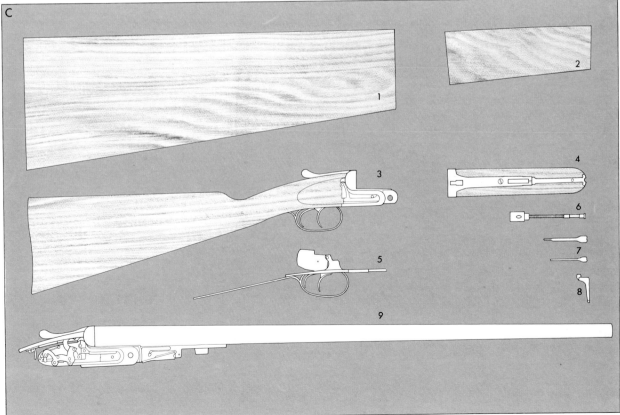

C The parts of a Purdey. *(1)* Stock blank. *(2)* Fore-end blank. *(3)* Rough-stocked gun. *(4)* The fore-end. *(5)* The furniture: trigger-plate, triggers, and trigger guard. *(6)* Fore-end snap. *(7)* Breech pin and hand pin. *(8)* Fore-end tip. *(9)* Barrels and action.
D The rough barrels *(1)* are machined from forgings of best steel. *(2)* Machined for jointing. *(3)* The barrels are brazed together and the ribs fitted.

Today, only five makers remain in the British Isles, all in London. Probably the one with the greatest reputation is James Purdey and Sons, but for reasons of tact, the following list is given in alphabetical order, and no value judgments are implied by it: Boss, Churchill, Holland & Holland, Purdey, and Rigby. During the past fifteen years, three venerable names have gone from the list: John Dickson, an old Scottish firm, have stopped making best guns; Atkin, Grant & Lang have been taken over by Churchill; and W.W. Greener have been swallowed up by Webley & Scott, who make airguns.

Best-gun makers numbers have fallen for a reason more complex than mere decline in demand. Indeed, the makers report a greater demand than they can handle: there is always a waiting list of customers, and a buyer can seldom hope to have his best gun in less than two years. Part of the reason is that the makers have always chosen to keep their best-gun operations small, almost on the scale of a cottage industry; indeed, some of the craftsmen take their work home. If the manufacture were to expand, it would no longer be elite. Another part of the reason is the difficulty and expense of obtaining some raw materials: walnut stock blanks obtained by Purdey from the Dordogne forest in France are very costly, even before they have been shaped.

Most important of all, highly skilled hand-craftsmen are in terribly short supply, and new men cannot be found or trained to replace those who retire or die. This is not an age for hand-craftsmanship. The total number of best guns produced annually does not exceed 300, and manufacturers engaged in this trade are primarily dependent for their income on guns graded as "good" guns: one without frills may be purchased for $1,000 (£500) or less, but a best gun, secondhand and in less than perfect condition, would cost much more than that, while a new one costs between $15,000 and $20,000 (£7,500 and £10,000).

Manufacture begins with a very careful fitting of the buyer, using a "try gun" which has an adjustable stock to accommodate a shooter's height, physical build, and shooting style. (Some makers have been known to send a customer to a shooting school rather than accommodate a poor shooting style.) In more than half a century, there has been little

A

B

12

change in the manufacturing technique: after fitting, the making of a best gun is basically a matter of a lot of craftsmen wearing out a lot of tools and files, for, except for boring the barrels and rough initial work, everything is done by hand.

No one would want a best gun without suitably fine engraving, nor would a maker want to diminish his reputation by releasing a gun without proper engraving. Skilled engravers are hard to find, and their work is among the most time-consuming; one estimates that his work on a gun entails 22,000 separate strokes. The actual building of a best gun—exclusive of the waiting time before the customer's name comes to the top of the list—can require a year and a half.

At one time, those who bought such guns bought them in matched pairs, and some customers still do; the sort of driven-bird shooting that demands an extra gun and a loader is now costing over $200 (£100) a day, excluding the cost of a loader and the ammunition. King George V, whose shooting career began in the 1880s, was one of the quickest and most accurate of driven-bird shots, and he used *three* matched guns and two loaders in the butts when he shot grouse. However, more and more shooters now order guns singly.

Probably at least half of these hand-made guns are still built for the "traditional" class in Britain, but the export trade has changed. At one time, it came from maharajahs and sultans, but, in recent years, American sportsmen and industrialists have become increasingly important customers, alongside such celebrated names as Nikita Krushchev, Peter Sellers, and Lord Snowdon.

For those who lack the patience to wait for a new best gun, or the money to buy it, second-hand specimens in fine condition are sometimes sold in the same shops; some are advertised by the estates of deceased sportsmen. Such guns are still costly, but not nearly as expensive as new ones, and they can be altered (without any long wait) to fit the customer—though perhaps not quite so precisely as a new one can be fitted.

The firm of Holland & Holland was founded in London in 1835 and is one of the most highly reputed gunmaking firms in the world. Many of the arms traditionally used for big game in Africa and India have come from the Holland & Holland factory, where an apprentice school ensures a supply of craftsmen capable of continuing the traditions of superb workmanship for which the company is known.
A A 12-gauge "Royal" double-barreled shotgun. The name "Royal" is used to denote the best-quality double-barreled guns.
B The magnificent engraving on the "Chatsworth" gun, a weapon made for exhibition purposes. It is so called because it was first exhibited at the Game Fair at Chatsworth in 1966.

SHOTGUNS FOR AMERICAN HUNTING

Nick Sisley

While precision is the cornerstone of basic riflemanship, shotgunning is more like an art form. Firing almost exclusively at moving targets, shotgunners must take their shots instantly. There is never any time to lie prone, take a solid rest, carefully estimate the range, or think about ballistics tables and trajectories. Among the prerequisites for an expert shotgunner are constant practice, experience, perfect stock fit, and lead judgment.

The four important types of shotguns are the slide-action, or pump, gun; the autoloader; the traditional side-by-side double; and the increasingly popular over-and-under double. In addition to these, there are two of lesser importance—the bolt-action and the break-open single-barrel types; both have limited value and merit no detailed discussion here.

Slide-action, or Pump, Guns

The double guns of Europe have never lent themselves to the mass-production techniques favored by American manufacturers. Besides, these guns hold only two shots, and, in North America, there has always been a great interest in repeat firepower in guns.

These two problems (the need for mass production in order to reduce costs and the desire for repeat firepower) were solved by the invention of the slide action, which, because of the way it works, is also known as the pump action. It worked reliably, it did not require an excessively oversized action and receiver, and it held extra shots in a tubular magazine beneath the barrel. Furthermore, its construction was such that the action could be mass produced. Winchester's Model 97 was not the first of that basic design, but it was the first really successful slide-action shotgun—an immediate hit with hunters all over the continent, and especially with wildfowlers, who could now fire at least five shots without reloading. Some market hunters even built long magazine extensions that held as many as eleven shots (this practice was later prohibited). Fowling pieces with such long magazines were poorly balanced, especially when filled to capacity; despite this, they bagged enormous numbers of ducks and geese.

Although most Europeans disdain the slide-action shotgun, it is excellent in the field. With a semiautomatic or a double-barreled gun, a shooter sometimes takes that all-important second shot too quickly, and the result is almost always a miss—or tail feathers. With the slide-action gun, however, a split second of physical activity is required to work the action, and this effectively requires the shooter to reswing the gun for the second shot, thus giving himself a much better chance of a hit.

The slide-action gun is also the least expensive shotgun that is effective on almost any moving target. It is mechanically reliable and safe. John Moses Browning designed most of the slide-action guns that were made around the turn of the century. Exposed-hammer actions came first, followed a few years later by the internal-hammer action. All of today's slide-actions are of the latter type.

The slide-action gun's tubular magazine is quickly loaded at the receiver end. A generously proportioned fore-end of wood wraps round the magazine and serves as the pump handle, or slide. Using the non-shooting hand, the shooter quickly moves this handle rearward and then forward. This extracts and ejects a fired cartridge, feeds in a fresh one, and cocks the gun. The safety catch is usually a button on the trigger guard or a slide on the top tang. The simplicity of the action and of the feeding mechanism is a blessing, especially when one is hunting in rough upland or waterfowling country. A good slide-action gun will continue to work even with bits of sand or mud in the action, whereas this would cause a semiautomatic to malfunction. Moreover, the slide-action is a

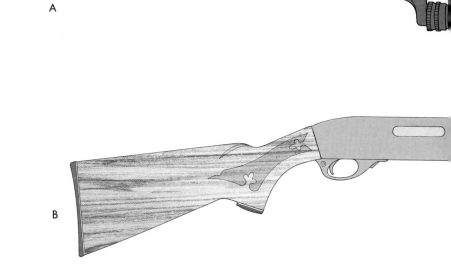

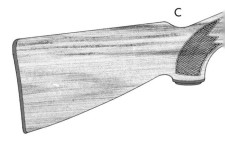

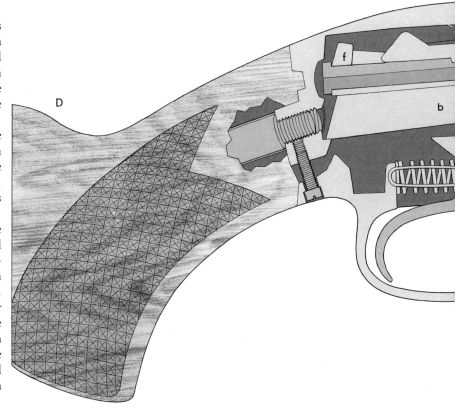

A The Ithaca Model 37 Standard Vent Rib slide-action shotgun. The ventilated rib is a raised sighting plane that allows air to disperse the distorting hot air that rises from a hot barrel.
B The Remington Model 870 slide-action.
C The Italian gunmaker Beretta's RS 200 slide-action is now being marketed in North America. As well as their two factories in Italy, Beretta have one in Brazil.

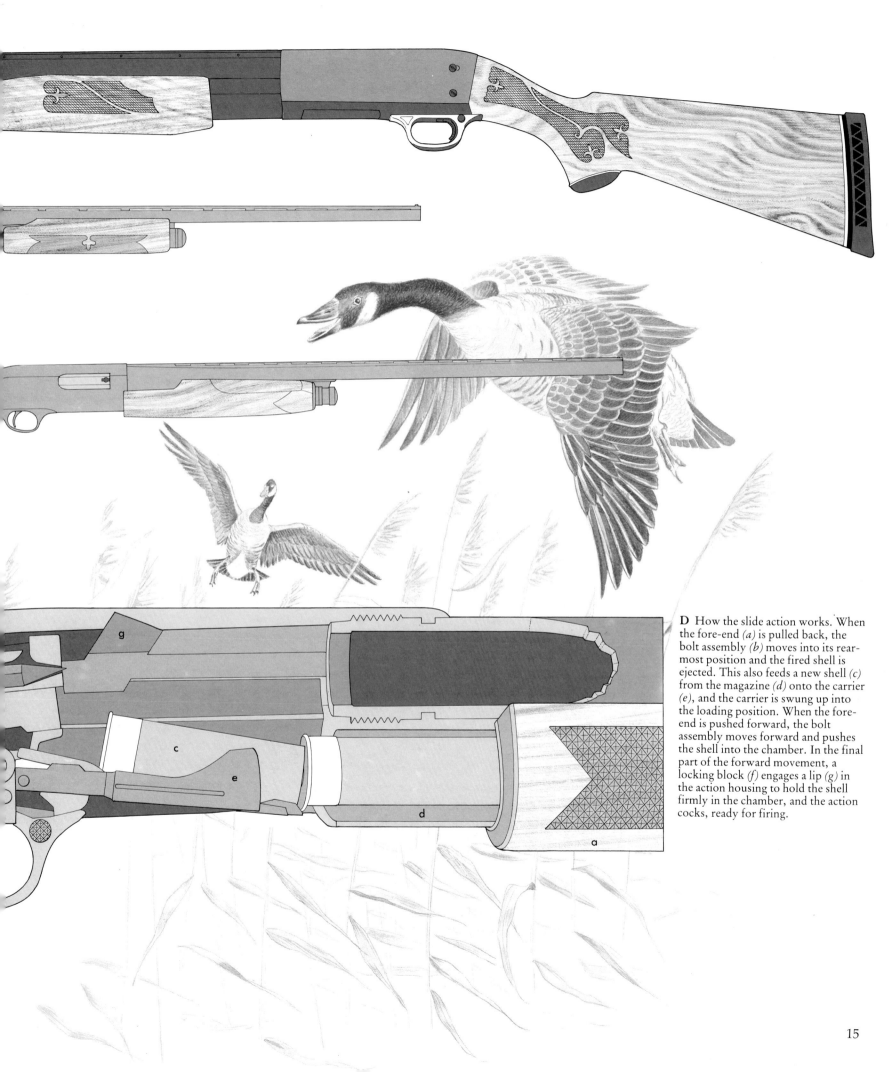

D How the slide action works. When the fore-end *(a)* is pulled back, the bolt assembly *(b)* moves into its rearmost position and the fired shell is ejected. This also feeds a new shell *(c)* from the magazine *(d)* onto the carrier *(e)*, and the carrier is swung up into the loading position. When the fore-end is pushed forward, the bolt assembly moves forward and pushes the shell into the chamber. In the final part of the forward movement, a locking block *(f)* engages a lip *(g)* in the action housing to hold the shell firmly in the chamber, and the action cocks, ready for firing.

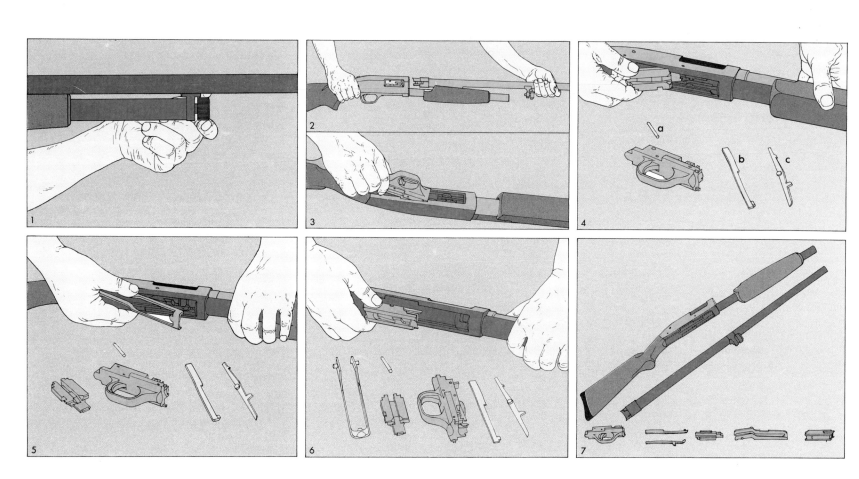

(Above) How to take the Mossberg 500 slide-action shotgun apart. *(1)* Push the fore-end forward about an inch (2.5 cm). Unscrew the takedown screw. *(2)* Remove the barrel. *(3)* Remove the trigger-housing pin and lift out the trigger housing. *(4)* Remove the bolt slide *(a)*, the cartridge stop *(b)*, and the cartridge interrupter *(c)*. *(5)* Compress and remove the carrier. *(6)* Remove the bolt assembly. *(7)* To reassemble, replace the parts in the reverse order.

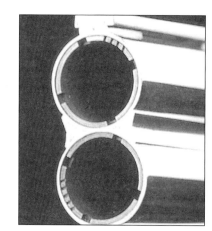

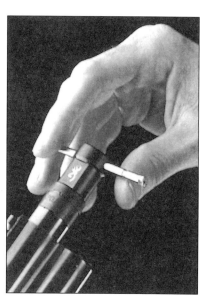

(Right) The choke of a shotgun controls the spread of the shot after it is fired from the barrel. A constriction near the end of the barrel causes the shot to spread with a certain intensity. Mechanical chokes that can be fitted to a gun barrel are available now, and this means that a shotgun's choke can quickly be adapted to the game being shot at. Three different chokes: *(1)* improved cylinder choke, for shooting grouse, dove, and quail at 20 to 30 yards (17 to 27 m); *(2)* modified choke, for pheasant, rabbit, and squirrel at ranges of 25 to 56 yards (23 to 41 m); *(3)* full choke, for duck and geese at 35 to 50 yards (32 to 46 m).

versatile field gun, as its interchangeable barrels require no special fitting and can be switched very easily. Today, the slide-action shotgun is probably the most popular shotgun in the United States and, perhaps, in Canada as well.

The Semiautomatic, or Autoloader, Gun

Originally, the semiautomatic shotgun, another design by John Browning, employed the long-recoil system. Guns with this system (the Browning Auto-5 type) are still popular, although during the last few decades, the gas-operated semiautomatic has largely superseded the recoil-operated. Gas operation has proved exceedingly reliable, as well as easier and cheaper to manufacture, but its greatest advantage is a significant reduction in felt recoil.

The average shooter does not realize how sensitive to recoil he is, although the experienced man will go to great lengths to reduce it. Light recoil reduces the tendency of a shooter to flinch after a shot. Thus, the gas-operated semiautomatic provides for very fast repeat shots without significantly reducing accuracy.

Some semiautomatics tend to be a little heavier than slide-action and double-barreled field guns. This extra weight helps to absorb recoil, but it can make a gun burdensome in the field. The lightest semiautomatic currently produced is the Franchi 48/AL—a recoil-operated gun. It is a 12-gauge and weighs only 6 lb (2.7 kg) with a 24-inch (61 cm) barrel. Remington is now making a lightweight 20-gauge version of its gas-operated, mild-recoiling Model 1100.

Semiautomatics are noted for breaking down in the field. However, the reason can usually be traced to the shooter, not the action. Gas-operated guns will simply not work well if they are not clean—the action, the slide, the gas ports, and the all-important chamber. In this respect, they can never be as reliable as slide-action or double-barreled guns. However, a good gas-operated semiautomatic will function reliably to almost one hundred percent of the time if the owner makes gun maintenance a priority.

This means taking down the gun after every shooting day. To do this, one must remove the fore-end, the action bar, the rings, and the bolt. All surfaces should be sprayed with a powder solvent and then wiped off after a couple of minutes. While the barrel is off, it should be cleaned with a patch and then with a wire brush; finally, it should be swabbed dry. Plastic shotshells leave a great deal of residue in the chamber area, so it should be scrubbed with steel wool wrapped round a brass brush. If the residue is not removed, fired shells will be too difficult to pull out of the chamber. As there is only a certain amount of gas available to work the action on each occasion, there is little chance that there will be enough left to perform the other functions, if the first function (pulling the spent shell out of the chamber) requires too much energy.

Semiautomatics are generally a little more expensive to produce than slide-action guns, but somewhat less expensive than double-barreled guns. They are popular in the field only in North America, but they are made in Europe and the Orient as well as in the United States, and some Europeans are beginning to use them for clay-target shooting, because of their low recoil.

The Side-by-side Double

This is the classic game gun. For years, famous gunmakers in England have produced very limited numbers of best guns, but their prices have been so high that their market has always been an exclusive one. Excellent side-by-sides are now being made in Italy, and a few in Spain. In the United States, only the special-order Winchester Model 21 approaches the standards of a best British gun. Less expensive models are reliable but lack the careful fit, smoothness, and fine appearance of costly doubles.

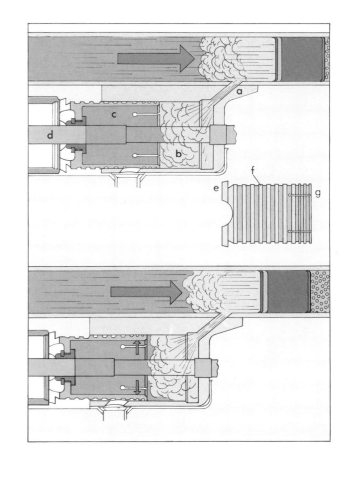

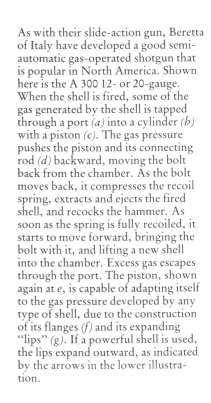

As with their slide-action gun, Beretta of Italy have developed a good semiautomatic gas-operated shotgun that is popular in North America. Shown here is the A 300 12- or 20-gauge. When the shell is fired, some of the gas generated by the shell is tapped through a port *(a)* into a cylinder *(b)* with a piston *(c)*. The gas pressure pushes the piston and its connecting rod *(d)* backward, moving the bolt back from the chamber. As the bolt moves back, it compresses the recoil spring, extracts and ejects the fired shell, and recocks the hammer. As soon as the spring is fully recoiled, it starts to move forward, bringing the bolt with it, and lifting a new shell into the chamber. Excess gas escapes through the port. The piston, shown again at *e*, is capable of adapting itself to the gas pressure developed by any type of shell, due to the construction of its flanges *(f)* and its expanding "lips" *(g)*. If a powerful shell is used, the lips expand outward, as indicated by the arrows in the lower illustration.

Gas-operated shotguns are popular on the North American continent but are frowned upon—and in some countries even forbidden—in Europe, although several European gunmakers produce such guns for export and for trap and skeet shooting.

A The Remington Model 1100.

B The Ithaca Model XL 300 Standard.

C The Weatherby Deluxe Model Centurion.

D The inside diameter of a shotgun's bore is designated by the number of perfect spheres fitting the bore that may be obtained from 1 lb of lead, e.g., a lead sphere that would fit the bore of a 12-gauge gun would weigh $\frac{1}{12}$ lb. A shotgun's gauge, or bore (as it is known in Britain), is usually marked on the barrel, and the shell's gauge is always marked on the shell. This Fiocchi shell *(1)*, for instance, is a 12-gauge shell. The Remington shell *(2)* and the Winchester *(3)* can be loaded with shot of different size, depending on the game hunted, the range, and the pattern required. *(a)* Metal head. *(b)* Primer. *(c)* Powder. *(d)* Wad. *(e)* Shot. *(f)* Plastic collar, to protect the shot as it goes through the barrel and to provide evenly distributed patterns. *(g)* Plastic hull.

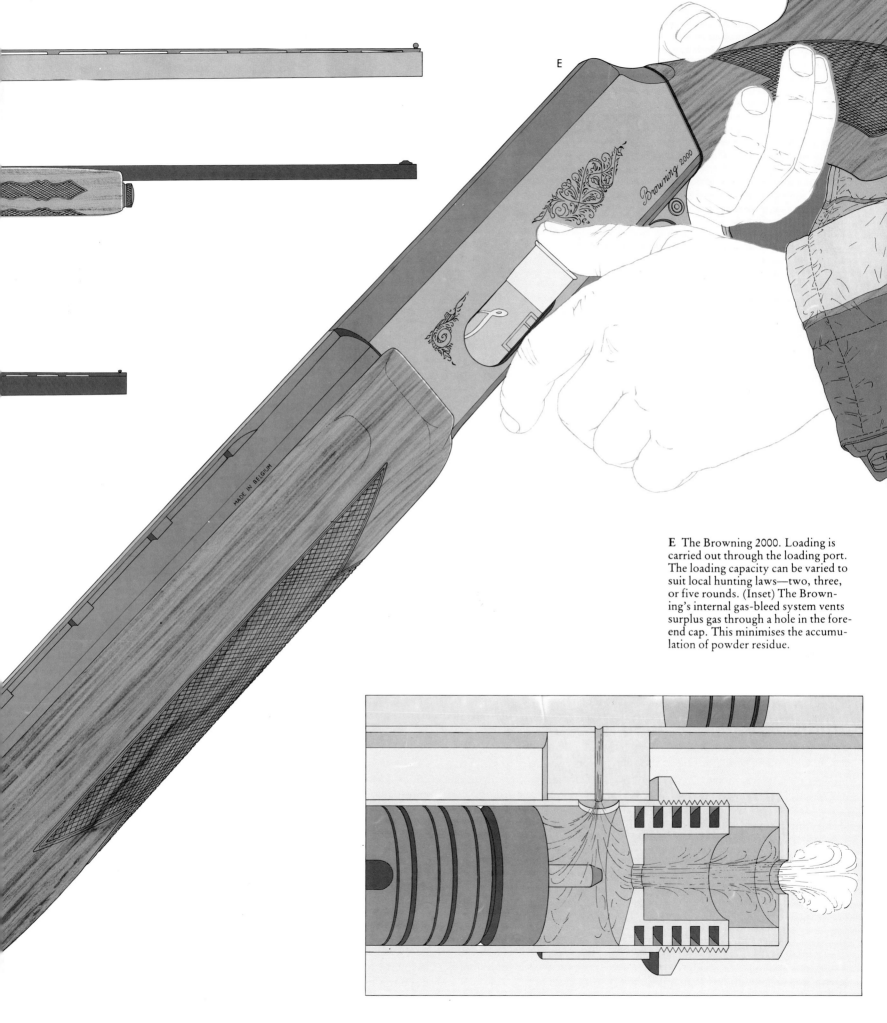

E The Browning 2000. Loading is carried out through the loading port. The loading capacity can be varied to suit local hunting laws—two, three, or five rounds. (Inset) The Browning's internal gas-bleed system vents surplus gas through a hole in the fore-end cap. This minimises the accumulation of powder residue.

MADE IN BELGIUM

Browning 2000

19

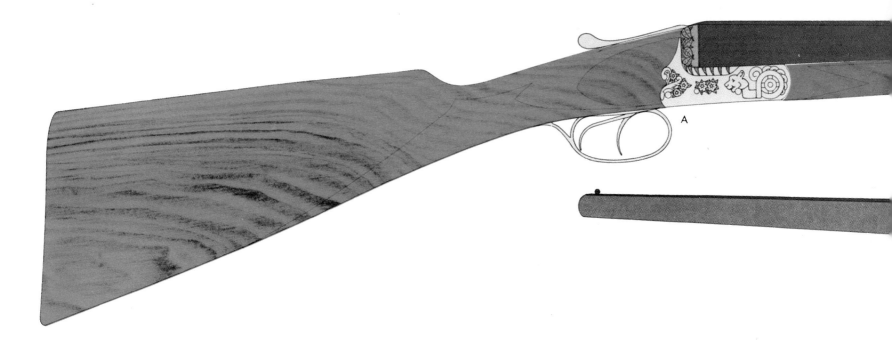

A double gun has a number of advantages compared with a pump or autoloader. It can be built with different chokes. It is more compact. Compared with an over-and-under or any single-barreled gun, its sighting plane is wider. These are objective differences rather than aesthetic ones.

Field doubles may have chokes of different sorts, depending on the type of shooting to be done. Chokes may be either improved cylinder and modified, or modified and full. When hunting upland game, the first shot is taken usually at closer range, the second at longer range; the shooter uses the more open choke for the first shot, then follows it up with the tighter choke. Conversely, when shooting driven game, the shooter often fires the more tightly choked barrel as the birds come into range, then uses the second, more open barrel as they are overhead or nearly so. This tactic is used by experienced dove hunters and, sometimes, by wildfowlers in appropriate situations.

A double is more compact than a pump or autoloader, either of which has a long receiver to feed in the next cartridge; a double is thus some 3 inches (8 cm) shorter. This enhances its balance, putting the greatest weight between the shooter's hands and making the gun more responsive, especially when handled by an experienced shooter.

The wide plane of the double is thought by some shooters to stand out far better in thick cover against a brushy, dark background than the narrower plane of the single barrel of a pump or an over-and-under.

By far the commonest action in side-by-sides is the box lock. With steady improvements in the steels used for actions, breakdowns, which were relatively frequent, have become rare. Since the box lock is less expensive to produce than the side lock, and does not weaken the stock of the gun as the side lock does, it has forged to the front in popularity. When ordering a fine side-by-side double, one should choose a gun that is suitable for a particular type of shooting. A duck hunter might want a fairly heavy, long-barreled, tightly choked gun, while a hunter who generally shoots upland birds might well prefer something different. A truly classic double might have barrels only 24 inches (61 cm) long; one might be bored a true cylinder, and the other an improved-cylinder bore. Such a gun can weigh less than 6 lb (2.8 kg).

There has recently been a trend toward heavier, blockier over-and-unders, pumps, and autoloaders, especially in North America, where heavier loads are being used more. These call for blockier actions and more solid stocking to absorb some of the recoil before it reaches the shooter's shoulder. At the same time, some shooters, particularly in 12-gauge, seem to be going back to lighter loads. In Europe, including the British Isles, 1-ounce and 1 1/16 ounce loads have long been popular; the 1-ounce load is beginning to attract many shooters in North America, for it is adequate for some types of game, notably in the uplands. In time, this might encourage the marketing of lighter shotguns of all types. At present, however, the top-grade side-by-side remains the ideal of hunters who prefer light loads.

Most American gunmakers ceased production of the side-by-side after World War II. The exceptions are Savage and Winchester. However, it is worth mentioning the now long-gone makes, as they have increased greatly in value over the past ten years or so. Leading the list is Parker, closely followed by L.C. Smith, Fox Sterlingworth, Lefever, Ithaca, and Baker.

The Over-and-under Double

Like the side-by-side, the over-and-under provides a choice of two chokes and is a shorter, better-balanced firearm than the pump or the autoloader. Its main weight rests between the hands, making it more responsive than a gun with a long receiver. Unlike the side-by-side, this type of double gun has a single sighting plane.

The over-and-under also differs from the side-by-side in how it recoils. The under barrel of the over-and-under is usually fired first, and its recoil tends to force the gun back into the shoulder, rather than up and into the cheek. In this way, the shooter is often able to get back on the target or to another target faster, since there is less muzzle jump.

The gun that made the over-and-under configuration so popular all over the world was the Browning Superposed. This extremely reliable gun was patented by John Browning in 1923 and was made first in Liège, Belgium; it has been in production ever since. The Grade 1, which was discontinued in 1976, was the model most produced; other models

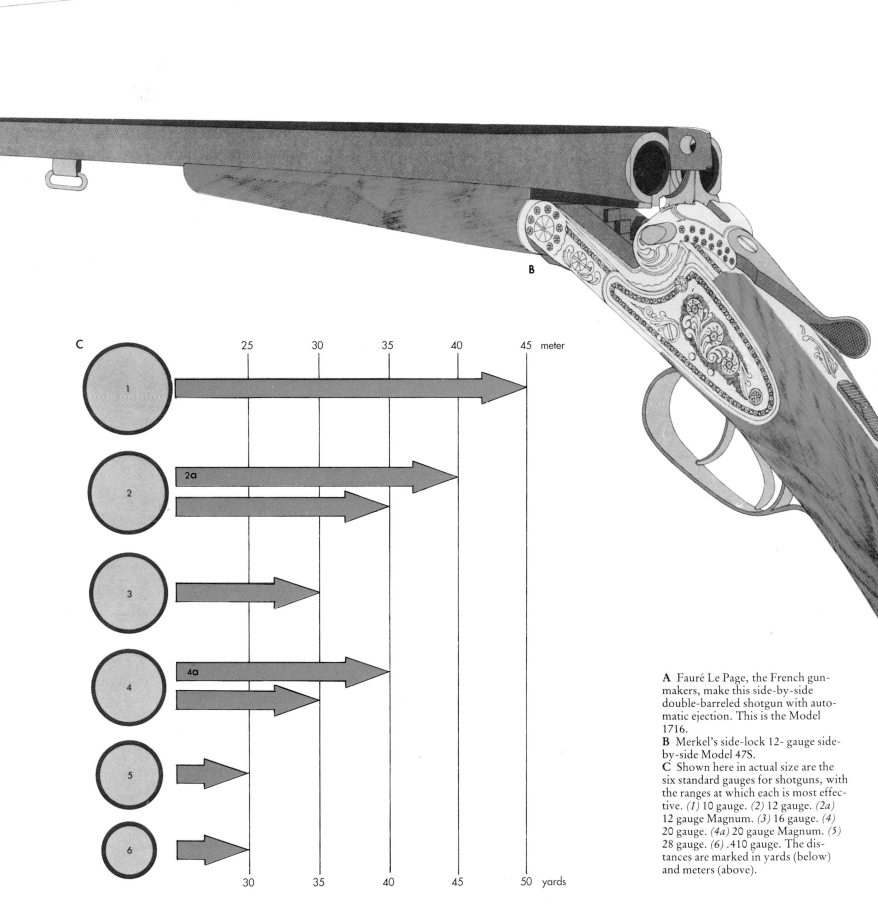

A Fauré Le Page, the French gun-makers, make this side-by-side double-barreled shotgun with automatic ejection. This is the Model 1716.
B Merkel's side-lock 12- gauge side-by-side Model 47S.
C Shown here in actual size are the six standard gauges for shotguns, with the ranges at which each is most effective. *(1)* 10 gauge. *(2)* 12 gauge. *(2a)* 12 gauge Magnum. *(3)* 16 gauge. *(4)* 20 gauge. *(4a)* 20 gauge Magnum. *(5)* 28 gauge. *(6)* .410 gauge. The distances are marked in yards (below) and meters (above).

25　30　35　40　45　meter

30　35　40　45　50　yards

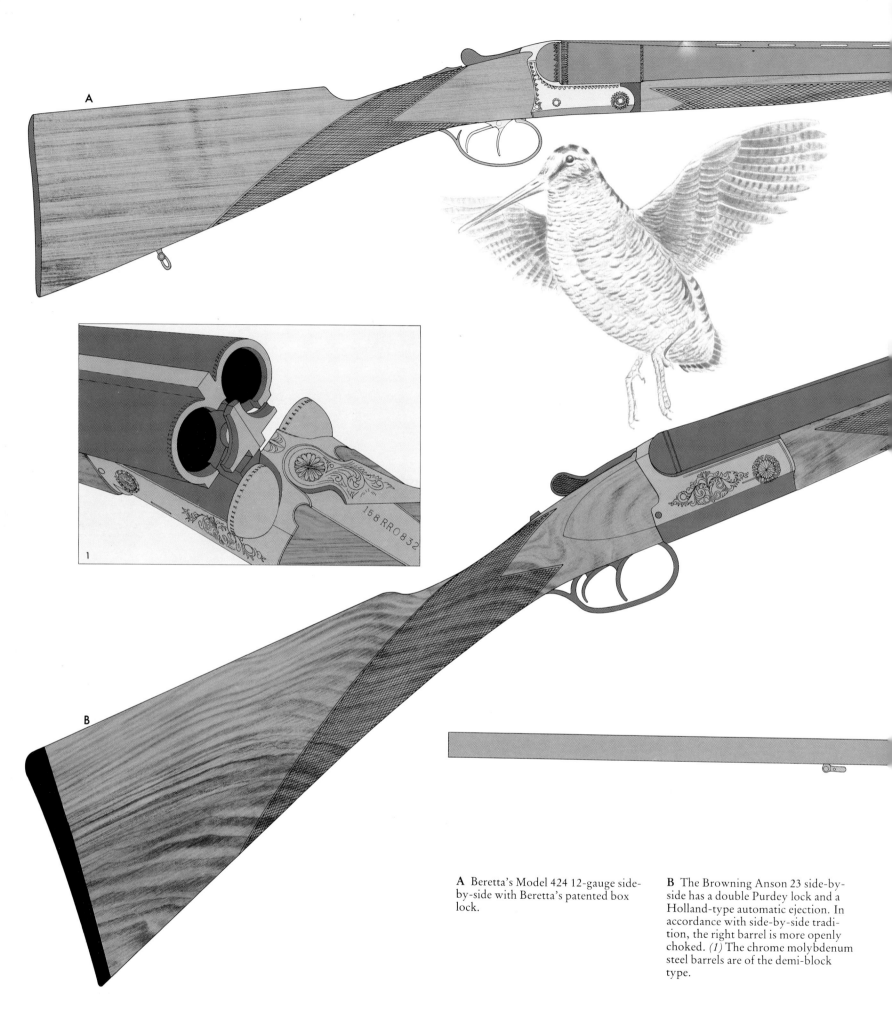

A Beretta's Model 424 12-gauge side-by-side with Beretta's patented box lock.

B The Browning Anson 23 side-by-side has a double Purdey lock and a Holland-type automatic ejection. In accordance with side-by-side tradition, the right barrel is more openly choked. *(1)* The chrome molybdenum steel barrels are of the demi-block type.

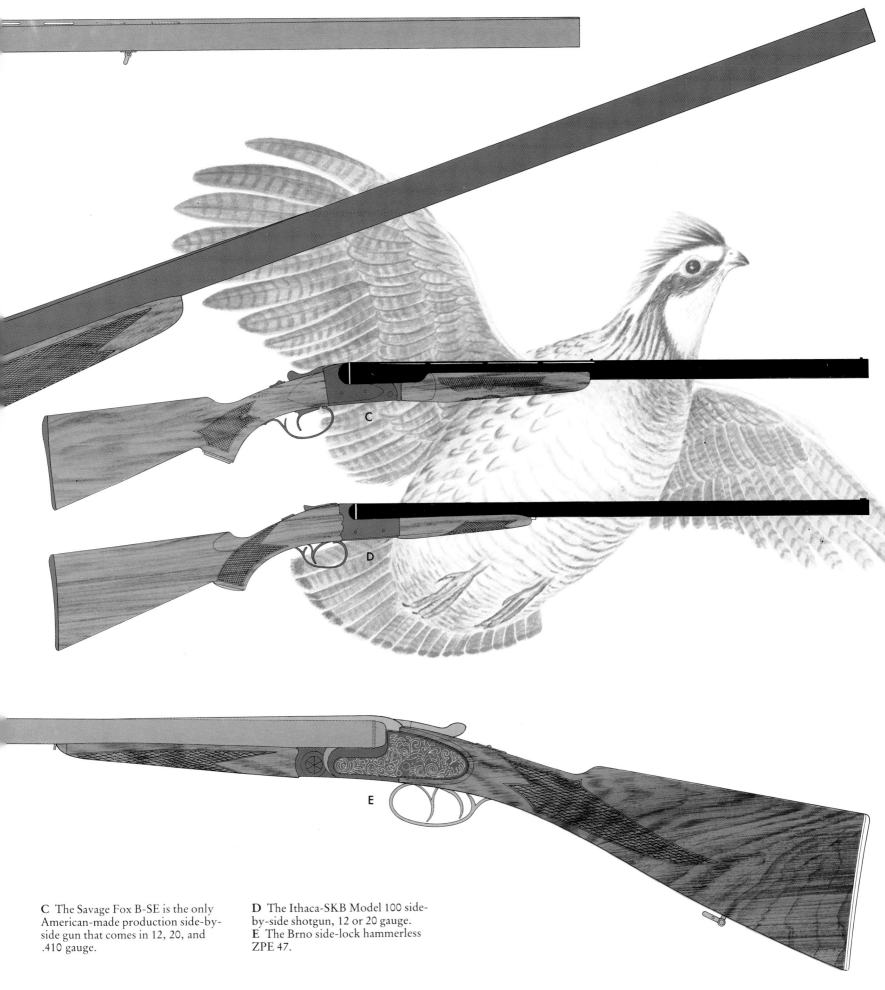

C The Savage Fox B-SE is the only American-made production side-by-side gun that comes in 12, 20, and .410 gauge.

D The Ithaca-SKB Model 100 side-by-side shotgun, 12 or 20 gauge.
E The Brno side-lock hammerless ZPE 47.

23

Some North American and Continental European side-by-side shotguns.
A The Winchester Model 21 is the only American-made custom-built shotgun.
B The Winchester Model 23 XTR is available in 12 and 20 gauge.
C Unlike British and American shotguns, this Suhler 127 double-barreled non-ejector gun is fitted for a sling. It is made in 12 and 16 gauge.

D The Bernardelli Premier Gamecock has the smooth lines of the straight grip.
E The Krieghoff 32 was made in 12 gauge only. It is a hammerless type, with a single, selective trigger, automatic ejectors, ventilated rib, top lock, and double bead sights. Illustrated is the Monte Carlo grade gun.

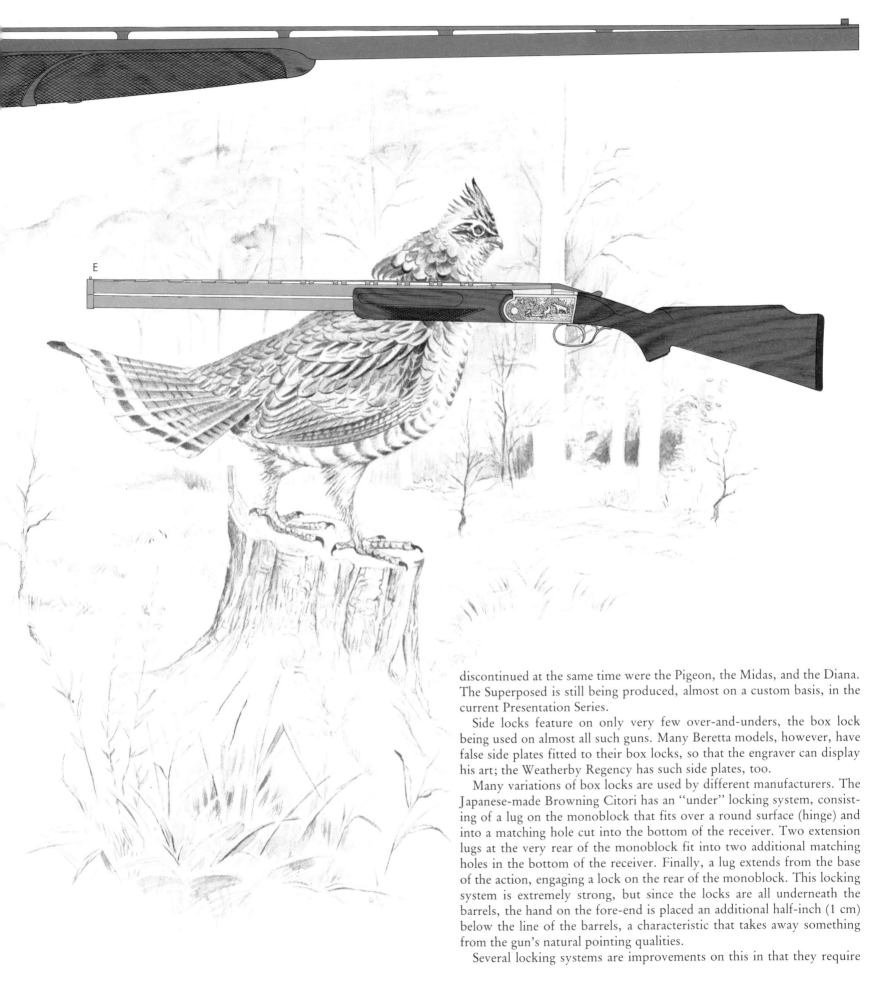

discontinued at the same time were the Pigeon, the Midas, and the Diana. The Superposed is still being produced, almost on a custom basis, in the current Presentation Series.

Side locks feature on only very few over-and-unders, the box lock being used on almost all such guns. Many Beretta models, however, have false side plates fitted to their box locks, so that the engraver can display his art; the Weatherby Regency has such side plates, too.

Many variations of box locks are used by different manufacturers. The Japanese-made Browning Citori has an "under" locking system, consisting of a lug on the monoblock that fits over a round surface (hinge) and into a matching hole cut into the bottom of the receiver. Two extension lugs at the very rear of the monoblock fit into two additional matching holes in the bottom of the receiver. Finally, a lug extends from the base of the action, engaging a lock on the rear of the monoblock. This locking system is extremely strong, but since the locks are all underneath the barrels, the hand on the fore-end is placed an additional half-inch (1 cm) below the line of the barrels, a characteristic that takes away something from the gun's natural pointing qualities.

Several locking systems are improvements on this in that they require

A

B

C

a

b

c

MADE IN JAPAN

receivers of lesser depth, putting the hand on the fore-end into a closer relationship with the barrels. Among guns with such systems are the Remington Model 3200, and its forerunners, the Remington 32 and the Krieghoff 32. Their actions have trunnions or hinge pins on the forward part of the inside of the receiver, which match up with radii on the monoblock. Additionally, this action type has a hood or top lock which slides over the top barrel when closing. Finally, the 3200 has two matching surfaces, or locks, which fit closely together—the rear of the monoblock and the rear of the receiver.

The new Ruger Red Label shotgun employs the trunnions in conjunction with two heat-treated lugs which extend out from the back of the receiver upon final closing and match up with recesses in the back of the monoblock, but between rather than below the barrels.

The SKB over-and-unders have trunnions in conjunction with a variation of the Greener cross bolt, called the Kersten cross bolt. Two extensions built into the top rear of the monoblock fit into recesses in the top of the receiver. Upon final closing, two bolts, or lugs, protrude through these extensions to provide a most positive lock-up. A number of other locking systems are used in over-and-under guns, but the types described are basic and representative.

Over-and-under shotguns for hunting, and skeet and trap shooting.
A The Miroku Model 3700HS is a 12-gauge shotgun. The hunting version weighs 6 ½ lb (3 kg).
B The Remington 3200 Competition Trap 12-gauge.
C A cutaway view of the action of the Winchester Model 101 Field Magnum over-and-under. *(a)* The combined safety and barrel selector is a thumb-operated slide-button on the upper tang. *(b)* Selective automatic ejectors for ejection of the fired shell only. *(c)* Full-length side ribs prevent foliage and other matter from getting between the barrels when hunting in thick cover.
D The Winchester Pigeon Grade shotgun, which is made in 12, 20, 28, and .410 gauge.

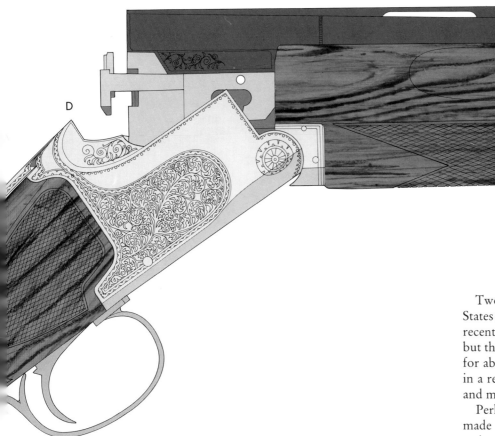

Two over-and-under guns are currently being made in the United States: the Remington Model 3200 and the Ruger Red Label. Both are recent introductions. The 3200 has become a popular trap and skeet gun, but the field grades have been discontinued. It is rather a heavy gun, great for absorbing recoil, but it is not quick-handling and is difficult to carry in a ready position for long periods in the field. The Red Label is lighter and more responsive.

Perhaps the most important good-quality over-and-under guns are made in Japan. These include such game guns as the SKB 500 and 600 series, the Browning Citori Sporter series, the Nikko, the Winchester 101, the Weatherby Regency, and the Weatherby Olympian. All are excellent but still cannot match the quality of those made by Fabbri or FAMARS in Italy.

Italian makers are doing a fine job with medium-priced over-and-under guns, too. The Perazzis are among the most respected trap guns of all time; Beretta makes many models, some of them for the most discriminating shooters, and the same can be said of Franchi. German manufacturers make equally fine guns, such as the Krieghoff and the Merkel.

A

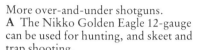

More over-and-under shotguns.
A The Nikko Golden Eagle 12-gauge can be used for hunting, and skeet and trap shooting.
B The Simson Bockhammerless 100 EJ 12-gauge ejector. This gun has twin triggers and is fitted with swivels for a sling.
C The Luigi Franchi 255 is a 12-gauge gun that weighs only 6 lb (2.8 kg). *(1)* The barrel selector and safety are combined. *(2)* The firing mechanism.
D The Beretta SO-4 is one of the most recent of a long line of Beretta guns.

B

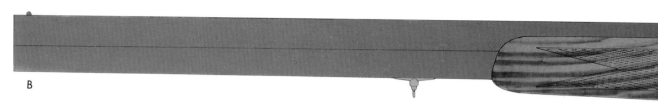

C

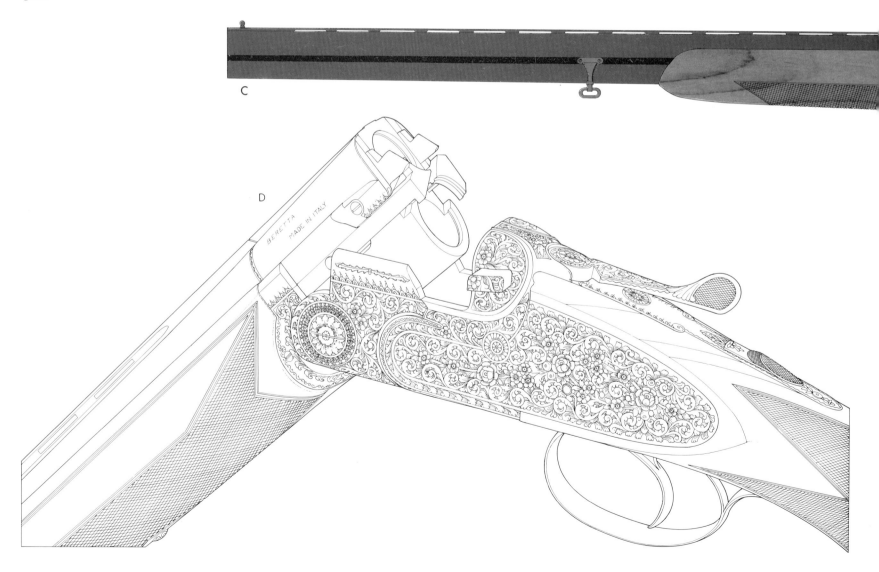

D

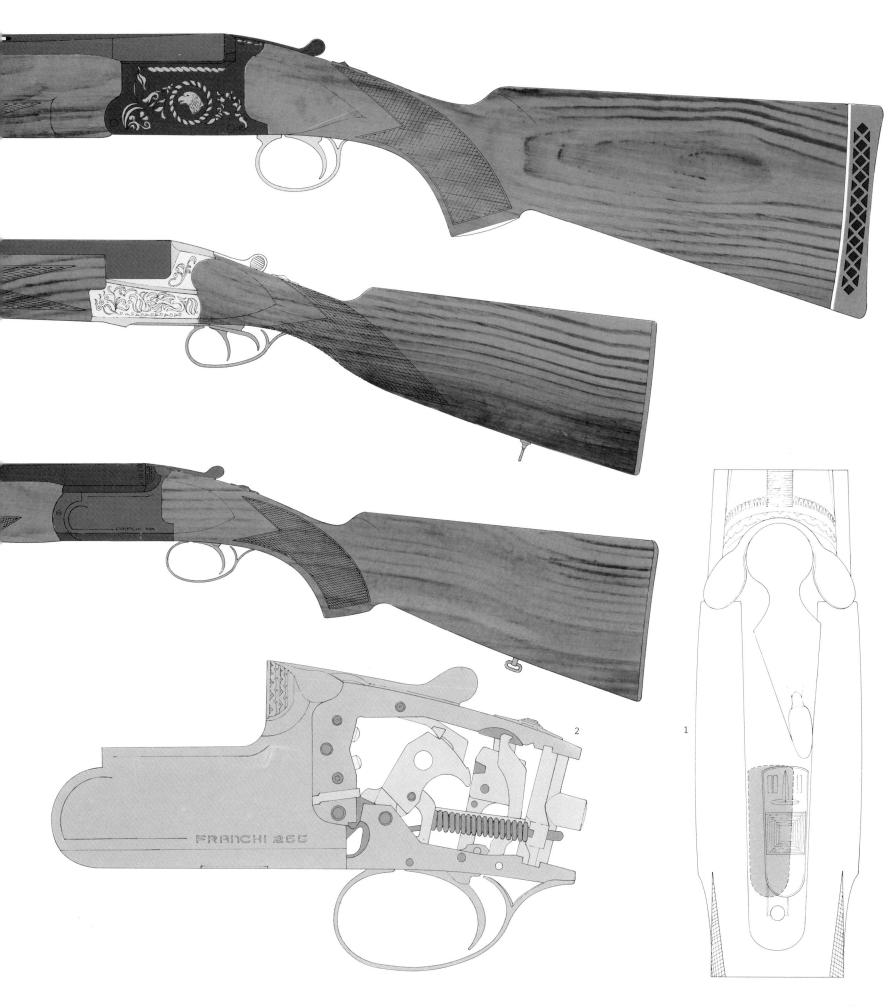

Chapter 2

European Arms

Tom Turpin

The type of gun most closely associated with hunting on the European continent is the combination rifle-shotgun, a weapon that was developed on the Continent and is the most commonly seen there today. There is, of course, an excellent reason for its continuing popularity, and that is the nature of the European drive hunt. Many such hunts do not limit the bag to either furred or feathered game, but include both. It is not uncommon, for example, for the participants in a drive hunt to get shots at hare, rabbit, partridge, pheasant, fox, wild boar, and—in some countries—even roe and red deer. In such a hunt, a combination gun is the ideal choice: it provides the hunter with a rifle for the furred game, excepting hares and rabbits, and a shotgun for the smaller game and the birds. Some years ago, combination guns were popular because the prevailing attitude was that a single gun, capable of taking any animal or bird that might occur on a hunt, was sufficient for a hunter. The gun fancier or collector who is interested in guns for their design or efficiency was then hardly known in Europe, but hunters who viewed firearms with aesthetic appreciation often had their combination guns engraved, carved, or embellished in some other way. Recently, however, it has become less uncommon to find a European hunter who owns several firearms.

Sporting firearms are made in most countries of Europe. Spain, Russia, East Germany, West Germany, Austria, France, Italy, Belgium, Czechoslovakia, Finland, Sweden, and Britain all export firearms for hunting. Production in some countries is rather limited or specialized; shotguns are produced primarily in Italy, Spain, and France, while both shotguns and rifles are made in Britain, Belgium, East Germany, West Germany, Austria, Czechoslovakia, and Russia. Combination guns are commonly produced in Austria and the two Germanies.

Combination guns are made in a variety of forms, varying from two to four barrels and, exceptionally, even five. The two most common are the over-and-under and the *Drilling*, which has three barrels. The usual *Drilling* arrangement has a rifle barrel beneath a side-by-side shotgun, while a much less common one has a shotgun barrel beneath a double rifle (*Doppelbüchsdrilling*). The major manufacturers of combination guns today are J.P. Sauer and Son, Krieghoff, and F.W. Heym, all of West Germany; Franz Sodia, and most members of the Ferlach Genossenschaft, in Austria; and Brno in Czechoslovakia. A few over-and-under guns, but not many, are made in Italy and Finland.

Although there are several technical variations in *Drilling* types, the guns most commonly produced are built on box-lock actions, with Greener cross bolt, Greener safety, and double underlugs. The selector for the rifle barrel is located where the safety would be on a double gun, and when it is pushed forward, a rear sight is raised on the rib and the front trigger is switched to fire the rifle; until this is done, the triggers fire the barrels of the shotgun. The hunter is thus assured of a means of rapidly changing from shotgun to rifle.

The other common type of combination gun is the over-and-under. German and Austrian guns usually have the rifle barrel beneath the

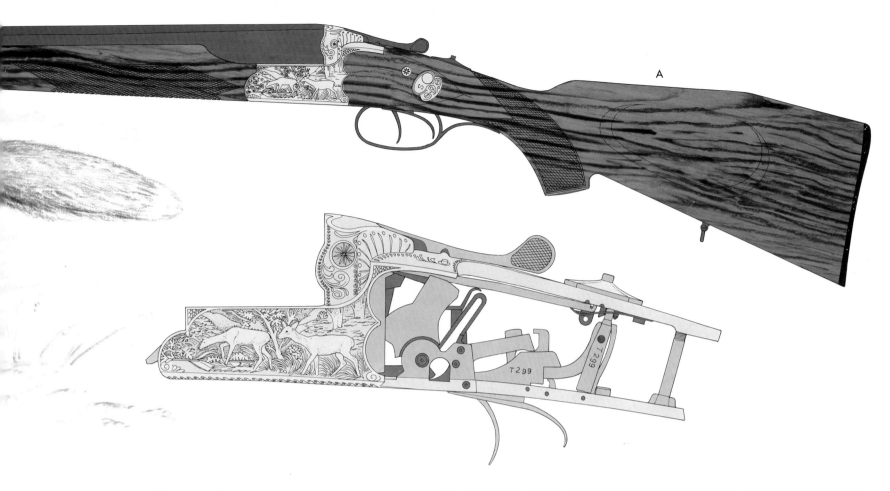

A The Carl Gustaf *Drilling* Standard: two side-by-side shotgun barrels over one of a range of rifle barrels. With 12-gauge, the range of calibers is from .222 Remington to 7×57. With 16-gauge, the range is 6.5×57 and 7×57. *(1)* The firing mechanism in close-up.
B The Merkel Model 32S is a *Drilling* that combines a side-by-side 12- or 16-gauge shotgun with a rifle of a caliber of between .222 and 7mm.

C The combinations favored by European hunters. *(1) Büchsflinte, (2)* rifle and shotgun, one above the other, *(3) Drilling, (4)* double rifle, *(5) Bockdrilling, (6)* single shotgun barrel under a double rifle, and *(7) Vierling.*
D A round-nose, soft-core expanding bullet and cartridge. *(a)* Primer. *(b)* Brass case. *(c)* Powder or propellant. *(d)* Thickening of jacket for added strength. *(e)* An expanding bullet after impact.

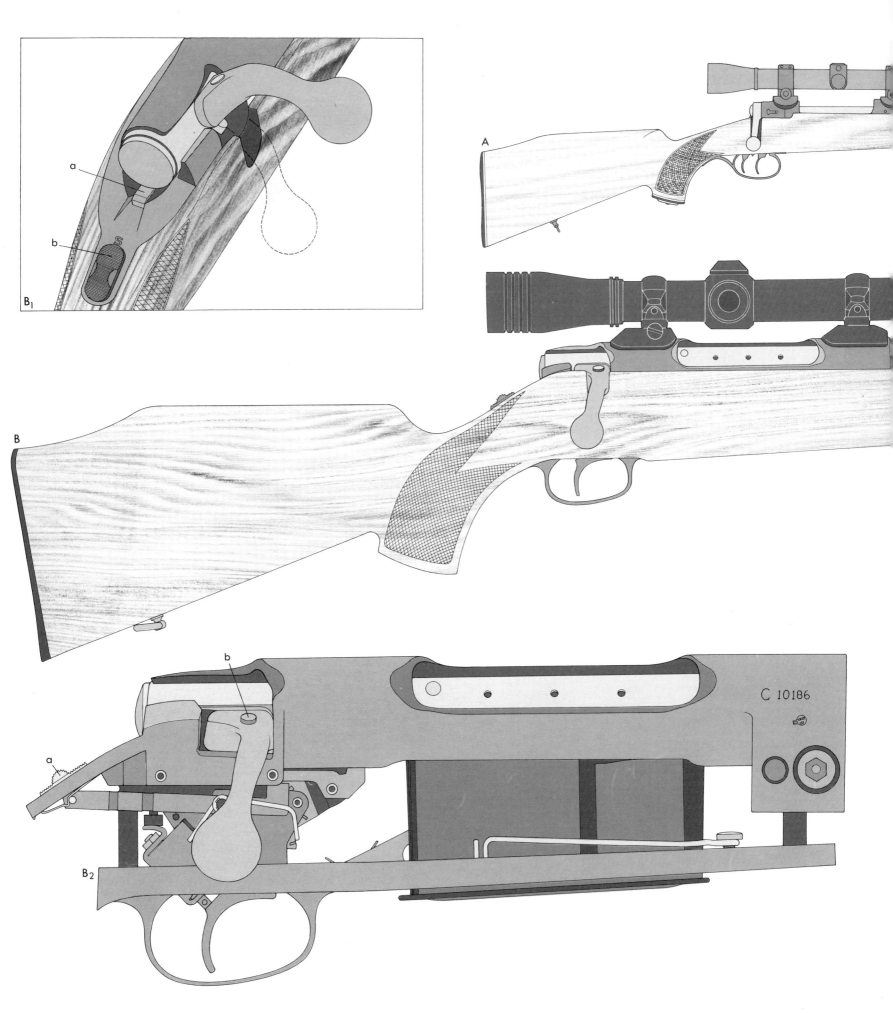

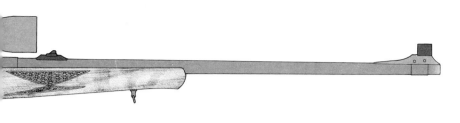

A The Anschütz Savage 7×57-caliber rifle fitted with a telescopic sight: a fine gun from the 1960s.
B The Carl Gustaf 3000 Standard is made with two mechanisms, one for 6.5×55, .30–06, and 9.3×62 calibers, the other—a shorter one—for .222 Remington and .308 Winchester. *(1)* The bolt action on the Carl Gustaf 3000 Standard from the rear. A red point *(a)* is masked only when the safety *(b)* is on. *(2)* When the safety catch *(a)* is engaged, a button *(b)* on the bolt springs up. When the button is pressed in, the bolt can be opened to withdraw the shell in the chamber without releasing the safety.
C The Husqvarna 1979 Monte Carlo rifle, available in 6.5×55, .30–06, .308 Winchester, and 9.3×62 calibers. *(1)* The engraving on the underside.
D The Sako Model 72, a modern Finnish bolt-action rifle.

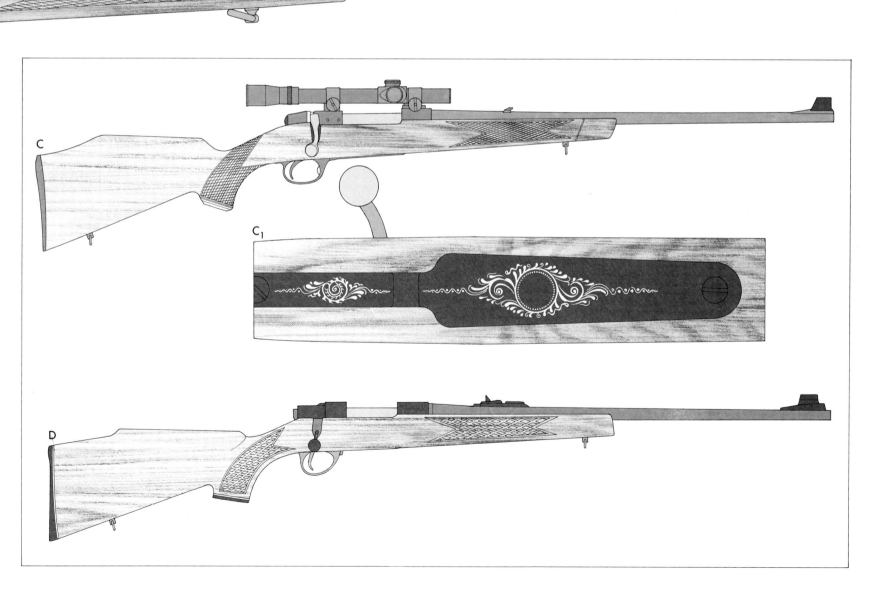

shotgun; on at least one Czechoslovakian model, and on some inexpensive guns made in the United States, the rifle barrel is the upper of the two. Some models feature a sliding barrel-selector button, others have two triggers. The latter arrangement, of course, gives the quickest choice between rifle and shotgun, being quicker even than the *Drilling*. It is sometimes a distinct disadvantage that the over-and-under contains one shot less than the *Drilling*.

Three further forms of combination guns are not produced in any significant quantities today. These are the Cape gun, or *Büchsflinte*, which is a rifle (usually the right barrel) side by side with a shotgun; the *Bockdrilling*, which is an over-and-under combination with a third barrel in the rib separating the other two barrels (the third barrel is normally chambered for a small, not too powerful cartridge, such as the .22 Hornet); and the most complicated of all, the *Vierling*, which combines no less than four barrels on one action. At a casual glance, a *Vierling* resembles a *Drilling*, but a closer inspection reveals the fourth barrel,

either in the heavy rib between the shotgun barrels and the rifle, or in the top rib. The fourth barrel is usually chambered for a small and relatively low-powered cartridge.

All the combination guns are somewhat more complicated than the standard double shotgun and are, consequently, rather more expensive. The over-and-under combination is less costly than the *Drilling*, for it has one barrel less and can be built on a strong over-and-under shotgun action. The over-and-under is often sold with two sets of barrels; the combination set and a set of shotgun barrels.

The *Drilling* is considerably more complicated, with a third lock for the rifle barrel and the barrel-selector system, in addition to its special action.

A telescope sight for the various types of combination gun is usually mounted on a claw mount, which presents several advantages. If properly mounted, it ensures that the scope, which can easily be detached from it, is always in exactly the same position. Once the scope has been

A The Merkel Model 220E double rifle has a caliber of 9.3×74.
B F.W. Heym have been making weapons since 1865. This is their repeating rifle Model SR 20L.
C The Ruger Model HR 38 de luxe.
D The HDF Standard rifle is made in 6.5×55, .30–06, .308 Winchester, and 9.3×62 calibers. It can put five shots into a circle of 1½ inches (3.5 cm) at 100 yards (90 m).
E The Krico Model 620L is available in .222 Remington and .308 Winchester calibers. It is unusual in that it is wooded throughout its length.

sighted-in, therefore, it may be taken off and replaced as often as this is necessary, without disturbing its aim or zero. The bases for the mount are not very noticeable and do not interfere with normal shotgun shooting. Claw mounts are expensive, however, for they require a great deal of hand work when being fitted.

For the shotgun fancier, Europe is a continent of double guns, both the side-by-side and the over-and-under models. There is also a large production of semiautomatic, or autoloading, guns, particularly in Italy and Belgium, but these are primarily for export. In some countries, autoloading guns are occasionally used for clay-target shooting, but it is relatively rare that anything but a double gun is seen in European hunting. A hunter who uses anything else might be regarded as a bit of an oddity.

The British best guns still enjoy a lofty reputation, but, in recent years, they have been challenged strongly by the Italian makes; there are many shooters today who say that the finest shotguns in the world are being made in Italy, and certainly, such firms as FAMARS, Fabbri, and Perazzi are turning out magnificent guns. But the debate will no doubt continue as to which is best.

Excellent shotguns are produced in Spain, too, for example by AYA, Victor Sarasqueta, Armas Garbi, and Ignacio Ugartechea, to name but a few. The great Belgian firm Fabrique Nationale has been making outstanding guns for years, and some French firms make limited numbers of excellent side-by-side shotguns. The German makers of combination guns, mentioned above, also make high-quality shotguns, primarily of the over-and-under type. Gebrüder Merkel, of Suhl in East Germany, has been recognized for years as a maker of top-quality shotguns. Austrian guns, particularly those from the Genossenschaft in Ferlach, are excellent, too, and so are those from the Czechoslovakian company Brno. Russian guns have also achieved a good reputation, and even the less expensive models are sturdily enough built to last the lifetimes of several careful hunters. The foregoing names should not be taken as an exhaustive list but as a representative sampling: a complete list would take too much space.

Rifles are made in Europe by a number of companies. The major producers are BSA (Britain), SAKO (Finland), Steyr (Austria), Mauser, Heym, and Sauer (West Germany), FN (Belgium), and Brno (Czechoslovakia). Some rifles are made in Yugoslavia, Spain, and Sweden.

The German rifle manufacturers are perhaps the most innovative, with Mauser taking the lead with a number of new technological developments. Their Model 66, introduced several years ago, has a multitude of new, efficient features, not the least interesting being interchangeable barrels. The recently introduced Model 77 also has many new features.

Voere, a smaller German company, has developed an excellent rifle which is an improvement on Paul Mauser's original design. This company is one of many that are not content simply to produce what are essentially copies of the venerable—but still excellent—Mauser design.

Among hunting accessories, not many are peculiar to Europe, but those that are have been developed to accommodate the style of hunting there: the use of high seats, for example, and the custom of hunting at dawn and dusk, for which special scopes and binoculars have been developed. Wild boar are hunted frequently at night, a fact that makes specialized optics all the more important. The 8×56 scope and binoculars were developed to provide maximum light-gathering qualities, as were the heavy, "picket fence" reticules so often seen on European scopes.

Many rifles and shotguns on the continent of Europe are equipped with slings, something that is seldom seen in North America. European hunters almost all carry hunting bags, made of strong leather, in which are carried ammunition, hunting knives, food, and other necessities. A game carrier is usually attached to the bag.

Hunting on the continent of Europe, and in the British Isles, is much

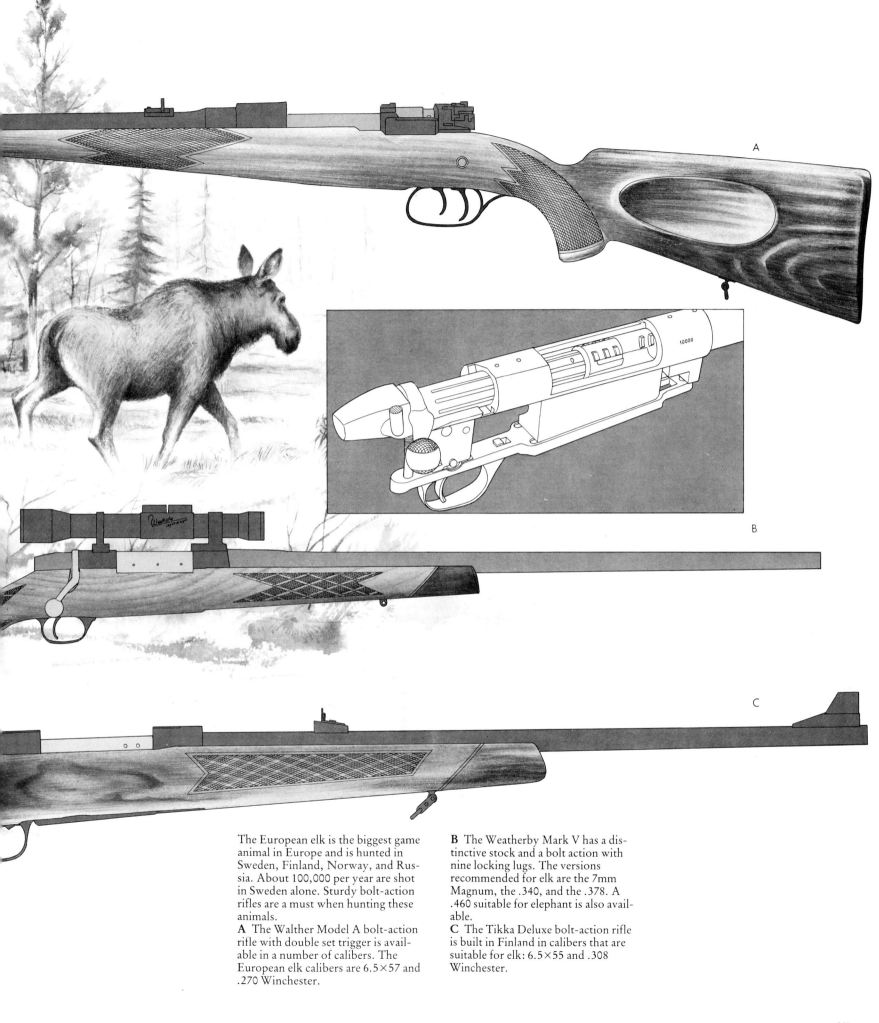

The European elk is the biggest game animal in Europe and is hunted in Sweden, Finland, Norway, and Russia. About 100,000 per year are shot in Sweden alone. Sturdy bolt-action rifles are a must when hunting these animals.

A The Walther Model A bolt-action rifle with double set trigger is available in a number of calibers. The European elk calibers are 6.5×57 and .270 Winchester.

B The Weatherby Mark V has a distinctive stock and a bolt action with nine locking lugs. The versions recommended for elk are the 7mm Magnum, the .340, and the .378. A .460 suitable for elephant is also available.

C The Tikka Deluxe bolt-action rifle is built in Finland in calibers that are suitable for elk: 6.5×55 and .308 Winchester.

more of a social event than it is in North America, and hunters in Europe are aware of aesthetic and social nuances, based on centuries of tradition, that continue to support a more complex, formal etiquette than is customary in other parts of the world. Dress, for example, is very formal compared with that normally worn in North America; it is predominantly green but can also be gray or brown. Hunters almost always wear ties. The hunting horn is used not only to control the hunt, but also to salute the animals killed in the course of it.

For many sportsmen, the formality of such traditions is extremely appealing, for it symbolizes the essential seriousness of the act of hunting, without detracting from its pleasures. Formality of dress, which may once have been an indication of aristocracy when game was exclusively the property of landowners, has come to stand for the aristocracy of the hunting spirit rather than a birthright. But, in fairness to the customs of others, it must also be said that formal dress of the sort worn in Europe would be impractical in many other parts of the world. The heat and humidity of Africa and Asia is hardly conducive to wearing a tie, while the hunting methods and extreme roughness of the terrain of North America would quickly shred a costly hunting jacket of the sort seen at continental European hunts.

Another European accessory that should be mentioned is the *Alpenstock*, sometimes called the *Bergstock*. It is a simple 6- to 8-ft (*c.* 2m) pole, usually of hazelwood and tipped with iron, which is used as a climbing and shooting aid when hunting in the high mountains, principally those of the Alps. The chamois guide would as soon go into the mountains, one might almost claim, without his shirt as without his *Alpenstock*.

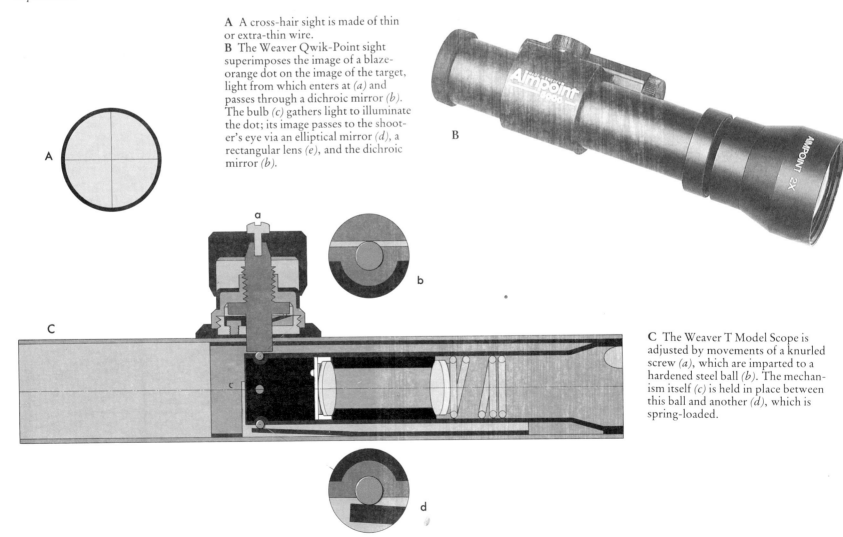

A A cross-hair sight is made of thin or extra-thin wire.
B The Weaver Qwik-Point sight superimposes the image of a blaze-orange dot on the image of the target, light from which enters at *(a)* and passes through a dichroic mirror *(b)*. The bulb *(c)* gathers light to illuminate the dot; its image passes to the shooter's eye via an elliptical mirror *(d)*, a rectangular lens *(e)*, and the dichroic mirror *(b)*.

C The Weaver T Model Scope is adjusted by movements of a knurled screw *(a)*, which are imparted to a hardened steel ball *(b)*. The mechanism itself *(c)* is held in place between this ball and another *(d)*, which is spring-loaded.

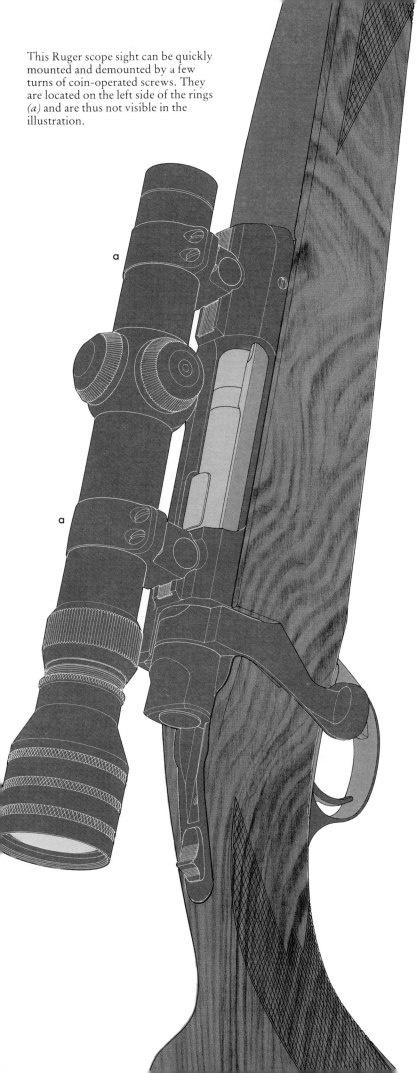

This Ruger scope sight can be quickly mounted and demounted by a few turns of coin-operated screws. They are located on the left side of the rings *(a)* and are thus not visible in the illustration.

Chapter 3

Rifles for American Hunting

Jim Carmichel

Bolt-action Rifles

The bolt-action rifle has recently come to dominate the North American hunting scene, especially among sportsmen who own, or intend to own, two or more centerfire rifles. One of the reasons is the modern emphasis on cartridge performance, most of all of Magnum cartridges. With the exception of the Browning BAR autoloader, the choice of a rifle firing a belted Magnum cartridge is limited to bolt-action guns.

Though most game in North America, as in all other parts of the world, is shot at ranges of under 100 yards (90 m), North American hunters like to be prepared for longer shots. This is most usual among hunters in the western states, where shots at pronghorn, elk, and mule deer may be at ranges as great as 300 yards (270 m) or more. This type of shot does not call for a high rate of fire, but it does require cartridges that deliver plenty of punch at long range, and a rifle capable of better-than-average accuracy. Thus, the appeal of bolt-action rifles is their combination of an excellent range of calibers and the inherent accuracy of the bolt mechanism. Added to that, some bolt-action rifles are extremely handsome and distinctive, and have a considerable appeal to today's shooters.

Though the basic bolt-action design has been updated and improved over the years, it has really not changed much since the days of Paul Mauser, who refined the turnbolt concept into a working reality a century ago. Its simplicity of design and operation, together with its high strength, makes it the safest and most reliable repeating action available.

Nothing quite matches the accuracy of a bolt-action gun. During the last hundred years, various falling-bolt, single-shot actions were considered the most accurate, but the bolt gun has ruled supreme for the past few decades. This is marked with current target rifles, both rimfire and centerfire, which are all based on bolt-action designs. The one exception, the British BSA rimfire match rifle, is notable just because it is the exception.

There are several reasons for this intrinsic accuracy. First among them is the inherent stiffness of the action. Any flexing or bending of a rifle action when it fires lessens accuracy, and the symmetrical locking arrangement of most bolt guns helps in resisting such flexing; so does the one-piece stock, which is (usually) rigidly attached to the action. The more modern bolt-actions are also capable of extremely fast lock times and have triggers that can be finely adjusted, two features which aid accuracy and performance.

Although the bolt-action is considered to be the slowest mechanism in operation of all repeating-rifle mechanisms, it can be fired at a surprisingly high rate. The American Match Course of Fire includes a 200-yard (183 m) phase which calls for ten shots to be aimed and fired within sixty seconds: the shooter begins in the standing position, must then get into the sitting position, fire five shots, reload the magazine, and fire five more shots. A good bolt-action rifle marksman can easily do this with seconds to spare and place all his shots into an area smaller than that of his hand.

Americans were introduced to the bolt-action rifle in a big way only during World War I, when hundreds of thousands of Doughboys were issued with 1903 Springfield rifles. Up until then, experiments with bolt designs had met with only limited success. In 1879, for example, Winchester began manufacturing the Hotchkiss bolt gun, and some 85,000 were made during the next twenty years. Remington made the Lee-designed bolt-action rifle from 1886 until 1906. A more successful rifle was the Krag-Jorgensen bolt gun, built under license by Springfield Armory and chambered for the 30/40 Krag round. This was the standard United States Service rifle from 1894 until 1904, the Army's first bolt-action rifle, and its standard arm during the Spanish-American War.

Since then, dozens of American-made and -designed bolt-action rifles have come and gone, and dozens of European models have been used by North American hunters. Most popular of the European makes have been the Sakos and various Mausers. At present, the most popular American centerfire bolt guns are the Remington M-700, Winchester M-70, Ruger M 77, and Savage M-110. Another popular bolt gun is the Weatherby Mark-V; this is the produce of an American company whose guns have been built in West Germany and are now being built in Japan. There are, of course, other bolt-action guns, too numerous to mention here, but the target-type centerfire guns should not be forgotten; smaller makers, such as Shilen and Wichita, produce guns that are among the most accurate in the world and are truly remarkable pieces of design.

The Winchester Model 52 rifle had been North America's most respected rimfire bolt-action gun when it was discontinued in 1979; for many years, it had been the leading target rifle in the United States and the one that had established a number of national records. The sportier version of the M 52 is considered to be the best of its type ever built in the United States, and collectors now pay several hundred dollars for a good specimen. At present, the German-made Anschütz Rimfire, another bolt design, is the overwhelming favorite among North American target shooters.

One of the goals of every American rifle-lover is to acquire one of the beautiful custom-made rifles built by one of the top American stockmakers. The demand exceeds the supply, prices are several hundred dollars at least, and, with very few exceptions, these superb rifles are all bolt-action guns.

Lever-action Rifles

The lever-action rifle, more than any other, has come to symbolize American hunting and the traditional American concept of arms design. This is so thanks to the tremendous publicity or image-making of popular literature, motion pictures, and television epics that consistently link the lever-action rifle with the "taming" of the American West.

It is fascinating to note that attempts to improve, refine, or streamline the basic nineteenth-century lever-action rifle have almost universally

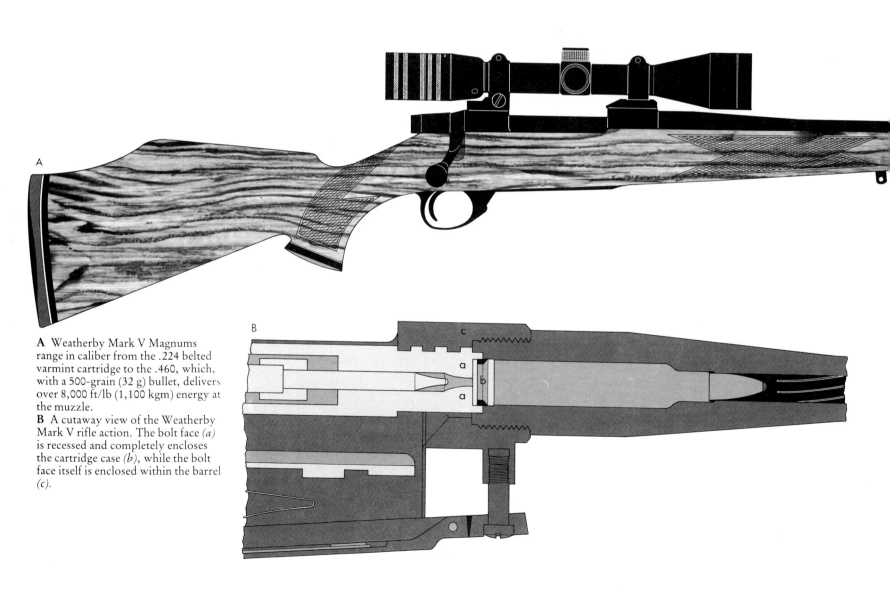

A Weatherby Mark V Magnums range in caliber from the .224 belted varmint cartridge to the .460, which, with a 500-grain (32 g) bullet, delivers over 8,000 ft/lb (1,100 kgm) energy at the muzzle.
B A cutaway view of the Weatherby Mark V rifle action. The bolt face (a) is recessed and completely encloses the cartridge case (b), while the bolt face itself is enclosed within the barrel (c).

failed. Examples of this are the modern-looking Winchester Model 88 centerfire (1955–1973) and Model 150 rimfire (1967–1973), Sako's Finn-wolfe (1963–1972) and Model 73 (1973–1975), Marlin's "Levermatic" rimfire Model 56 and Model 57, and centerfire Model 62 (1955–1965), and Remington's Model 76 (1962–1964). All were improved designs of the hammerless type, with short-throw mechanisms and greater strength and accuracy, but, despite their obvious improvements over lever-action designs dating from the nineteenth century, all were commercial failures within only a few years.

The most modern mechanical lever-action currently being produced, Browning's BLR, is carefully wrapped up in 1890s trappings to give it a distinctively "Western" flair. The only exception to the rule of Western appearance is the Savage Model 99, which, though dating back to 1899, has a hammerless profile. It has been constantly updated since its introduction; even so, Savage recently "reintroduced" the old Model 99A in an effort to lure shooters captivated by its "Gay 90s" configuration.

Historians of firearms seldom note that the lever-action was an early commercial disappointment, despite its place in American history. Oliver Winchester saw it as a military arm and promoted it as such in the war ministries of Europe, Asia, and South America. "Where," he asked, "is the military genius who will grasp the significance of this machine of war and thereby rule the capitals of the world?" The world's military genii remained skeptical and, except for sporadic orders for lever-action muskets, Winchester had to make do with a relatively small but steady civilian demand for his wares. Nevertheless, his Model 94 carbine has become the symbol of all lever-action guns and exemplifies them in discussions of their uses, virtues, and faults.

The lever-action gun in North America is most commonly classified as a "brush gun;" its use is in brushy or wooded areas where most shots are fired at less than 80 yards (75 m), and shots of over 100 yards (90 m) are an exception. For these conditions, a short, light, easily carried carbine capable of a relatively high rate of fire is needed.

Lever-action rifles have never been considered to be especially accurate, and certainly not when compared with bolt-action rifles and some types of single-shot rifle. This relative lack of accuracy is due to the two-piece stock design, the light barrel, and the comparatively non-rigid action (receiver) which flexes considerably on firing. Nor have lever-action rifles been chambered, until recently, for notably accurate cartridges.

Fine accuracy has, however, never been essential to the purposes of the lever-action rifle, although some models are capable of surprising accuracy. With selected ammunition, some guns can group five shots inside a circle of 2 inches (5 cm) diameter at 110 yards (100 m); even if this is an exception, virtually any modern lever-action rifle can group its shots within a circle of twice that diameter.

The first lever-action rifles were chambered for the early self-contained cartridges, which were also used in pistols. The Winchester Model 73 (1873–1919) fired .44/40 and similar pistol-type cartridges, which were barely adequate for deer and not adequate at all for bear, elk, and bison. Bigger, more powerful cartridges called for bigger, more massive rifles; a succession of lever-action rifles was designed for the .45/70 and larger cartridges. Winchester and Marlin made rifles to fire these bison-class cartridges, a development that culminated with the Winchester Model 1895 (1895–1931), which fired such high-powered cartridges as the .30/06 and the giant .405 Winchester round, which had a muzzle energy of 3,220 ft/lbs (444 kgm).

Lever-action guns might have been designed for bigger and bigger cartridges but for the advent of the bolt-action rifle; the surviving lever-action rifles are the light, fast-handling carbines used for hunting deer and black bear. An exception is the lever-action rifles made by Marlin,

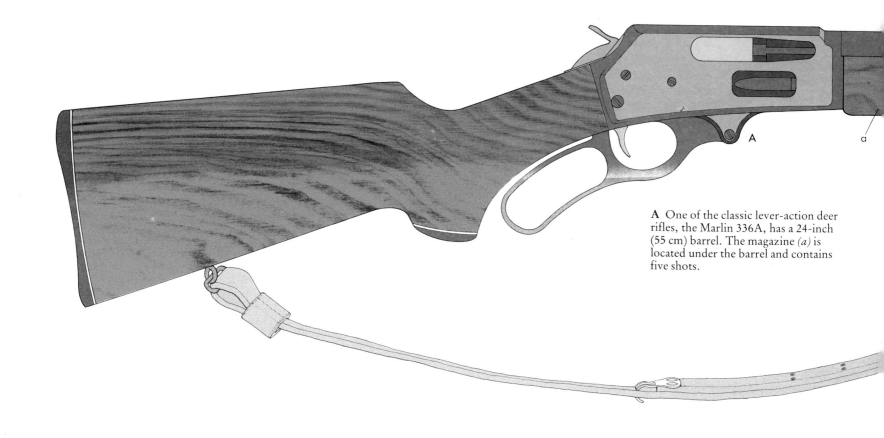

A One of the classic lever-action deer rifles, the Marlin 336A, has a 24-inch (55 cm) barrel. The magazine *(a)* is located under the barrel and contains five shots.

the .45/70 and the .444, which take Marlin cartridges made to a nineteenth-century pattern; these cartridges do not expand the practical use of the lever-action gun, and the combination appeals almost entirely to shooters who have a sentimental attachment to such old-fashioned styles.

The leading feature of lever-action rifles has been said to be their speed of action, but, in practice, this is seldom realized: to maintain a high rate of fire, the butt must remain against the shoulder and the sights be kept steadily on the target while the lever is operated and the trigger pulled. The typical hunter, however, is more likely than not to remove the rifle from his shoulder while he deliberately operates the mechanism between shots; this gives an operational speed about the same as that of a bolt-action.

The external hammer of most lever-actions has long been considered an important safety feature, but, in practice, this is not quite what it seems. To lower the hammer to the "safe" position, the trigger must be pulled; occasionally, the hammer slips from under the thumb and fires the rifle. To obviate this, Mossberg has recently introduced a modification to the Model 479 lever-action rifle; this takes the form of a manually operated cross bolt which blocks the hammer even if it falls by accident.

Lever-action rifles are usually sighted by means of open "V-sights" fitted in the factory; up until recently, this sighting arrangement could be refined by an adjustable "peep" sight fitted to the receiver or tang. While such peep (or aperture) sights are still manufactured by a few sight makers and are available for all current makes of lever-action rifle, today's buyer is most likely to choose a telescopic sight. However, this can lead to problems.

The popular Winchester 94 ejects its fired cases out of the top of the receiver, on which there is no solid place to mount a scope sight. Even if a scope sight can be mounted over the receiver, the ejected shells may strike it, fall back into the mechanism, and cause a stoppage. This problem is usually got round by attaching the scope mounting to the left of the receiver and positioning the scope off-center to the left, so that ejected cases do not strike it. Another solution, developed by the Leupold Optical Company, is to attach the scope to the barrel forward of the receiver; this calls for a scope with unusually long eye relief, such as Leupold's specially designed eye-relief scopes. They have 2× or 4× magnification and offer 10- to 24- inch (25 to 60 cm) eye relief. Some other lever-action models, for example those by Browning, Marlin, and Mossberg, feature side ejection and solid receiver tops, which permit conventional scope mountings.

The cartridge that is almost synonymous with the lever-action rifle is the .30/30 WCF and, indeed, the .30/30 caliber is one of the favorites for the lever-action rifles made by Winchester, Marlin, Mossberg, and Savage. While certainly adequate for deer and smaller bear, in terms of performance it is overshadowed by almost all other calibers for which lever-action rifles are currently chambered.

The Savage Model 99, for example, is currently available in .22/250 Remington, .250 Savage, .243 Winchester, .300 Savage, .308 Winchester, .358 Winchester, and .375 Winchester. The .22/250, a purely varmint cartridge, is not suitable for big game, but any one of the other cartridges is good for deer. The Browning BLR is available in .243, .308, and .358, all calibers of modern, high-intensity cartridges suitable for deer-sized game.

The Marlin rifles have not been adapted to high-intensity cartridges. They take medium-to-low pressure cartridges such as the .357 and the .44 Magnum pistol, the .30/30, the .35 Remington, and the .45/70. The Mossberg rifles are similar to the Marlin guns and take either the .30/30 or the .35 Remington.

It seems safe to say that lever-action centerfire rifles will remain popular for many years to come and that they will not vary very much from their present conventional configurations. The same can be said of

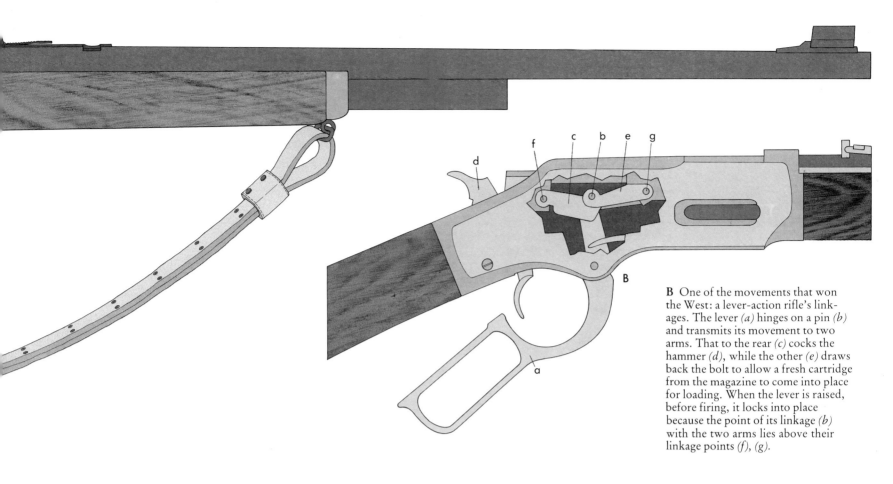

B One of the movements that won the West: a lever-action rifle's linkages. The lever *(a)* hinges on a pin *(b)* and transmits its movement to two arms. That to the rear *(c)* cocks the hammer *(d)*, while the other *(e)* draws back the bolt to allow a fresh cartridge from the magazine to come into place for loading. When the lever is raised, before firing, it locks into place because the point of its linkage *(b)* with the two arms lies above their linkage points *(f)*, *(g)*.

the lever-action rimfires in the .22 caliber; their appeal is based on their "Old West" styling, for their accuracy is about the same as most other rimfire rifles. In speed and ease of operation, they rank ahead of bolt-action rimfires. In one respect, they may be slightly superior to most other American rimfire hunting rifles, and that is that they are of an unusually high quality. The rimfire, lever-action rifles by Browning, Marlin, and Winchester are all markedly better made than most other rimfires, and if they are among the most expensive rimfires made in the United States, this is partly because they are made of the best materials.

Pump and Autoloading Rifles

No less a manufacturer than Colt made a pump-action rifle way back in 1885: the "Lightning." It was not especially successful and was discontinued after the turn of the century, even though it was well made. While the pump action is very popular in North American shotguns, it has never been really favored for rifles. The appeal of the pump-action rifle is mainly to those hunters who use pump- (or slide-) action shotguns and have become accustomed to ejecting shells by pumping the forestock.

Current centerfire pump-action rifles are pretty well summed up by Remington's Model 760 Gamemaster (in .243, 6mm Remington, .270, .308, and .30/06 calibers) and Savage's Model 170 (in either the .30/30 or .35 Remington calibers). In skilled hands, the pump-action rifle is second only to the autoloader in operating speed.

After firing, the forestock is pulled fully to the rear by the forward hand, then moved forward again until the action locks into battery position. This back-and-forth motion extracts and ejects the fired case, cocks the firing mechanism, and feeds a fresh cartridge into the chamber. It is a smooth, natural movement and offers the advantage of allowing the shooter's hands to remain in their firing positions. The main disadvantage in operation is the small mechanical leverage exerted during the extraction phase: if spent cases tend to stick in the chamber, extraction

may become difficult and may even cause a temporary stoppage.

Accuracy of pump-action centerfire rifles is on a par with that of lever-action and autoloading rifles. There can be considerable variation of accuracy, however, among rifles of the same make, model, and caliber, and even if blanket condemnations of the accuracy of pump-action rifles are sometimes heard, they are not necessarily justified.

Pump-action rimfires are somewhat more popular than the larger bores. Models are made by Browning and Remington, while the Brazilian firm of Rossi currently produces a replica of the discontinued Winchester Model 62, which was in production from 1932 to 1959.

No development of pump-action rifles seems to have occurred recently, if one excepts that incorporated in Browning's BPR rimfire, a pump rifle made possible simply because it has so many parts in common with the similar Browning rimfire BAR-22 autoloader.

Autoloaders, or semiautomatics, in centerfire and rimfire forms, are much more popular in the United States than pump-action rifles. At this writing, half-a-dozen or so American-made or -designed sporting-type centerfire autoloaders are on the market, together with another dozen or more copies of military-type rifles that should be classed as "junk guns." Browning, Harrington & Richardson, Ruger, and Remington all have centerfire sporting rifles available in many calibers, ranging from the .223 Remington and the .44 Magnum, up to the .300 Winchester Magnum. Experimental autoloaders have been made in the .458 Winchester Magnum caliber.

The obvious advantage of an autoloading rifle is its speed and ease of fire. The shooter needs only to pull the trigger and the extraction, ejection, and feeding operations are performed automatically. It is wrong to call these guns automatics, for an automatic is, correctly speaking, a machine gun which continues to fire as long as the trigger is depressed. "Semiautomatic" is more correct. On an autoloader, the trigger must be pulled for each shot. In the United States, private ownership of full automatics, or machine guns, is prohibited except under special license, and nowhere in the United States or Canada are automatics permitted for sport hunting. Autoloaders, by contrast, may be legally used for hunting, subject to the restrictions in force in some states, which limit magazine capacity to only a few rounds.

The objection to autoloaders that is most often heard is their alleged tendency to jam. The usual cause of stoppages is hand-loaded ammunition that has been improperly prepared, but apart from this, autoloaders are surprisingly trouble-free and reliable.

The mechanisms in current production are either the gas-operated or the straight-blowback. The latter is extremely simple: the rearward thrust of the fired cartridge pushes the bolt backward and thereby begins the new cycle of operation. The combination of simplicity and ease of manufacture has made this mechanism the logical choice for rimfire rifles, but it does not adapt well to use with higher-powered cartridges, which require an increasingly heavy breechblock to balance the rearward thrust. At one time, Winchester, for example, made centerfire sporting autoloaders that had simple blowback mechanisms—the Models 07 and 10—but they weighed up to 8½ lb (4 kg) with their massive breechblocks; they fired relatively low-energy rounds, the .351 and the .401 Winchester.

With rifles firing high-intensity cartridges, a more practical method is to use some of the gases from the fired cartridge to actuate the mechanism, the same system as that used for semiautomatic shotguns. This system is used, for instance, in the Browning BAR Sporter, the Remington 742, and the Ruger Mini-14.

Remington once built some autoloading rifles using the Browning long-recoil system, but they have long since been discontinued; this type of action is complicated to make and less efficient than the gas system, and it will probably not be used again for rifles.

Though the accuracy of autoloading rifles is often belittled, there is no reason to expect them to be less accurate than pump-action or lever-action guns, or, for that matter, many bolt-action rifles. Highly refined National Match versions of two United States Service autoloading rifles, the M-1 Garand and the M-14, are capable of astonishingly fine accuracy, sometimes grouping ten shots inside a 3-inch (7.5 cm) circle at 200 yards (190 m). However, many autoloaders suffer from hard, creepy trigger pulls and thoughtless stock designs, and these faults make for a lack of accuracy that has nothing to do with the actual firing mechanism.

Though autoloading big-game rifles are most common in the northeast of the United States, where close-range fast-firing is more desirable than long-range precision, they are widely used all over North America for every type of big game, while the rimfire versions are popular among those who shoot small game such as squirrels and rabbits.

A The Browning BAR 22 is a semi-automatic, and its magazine holds fifteen LR (Long Rifle) .22 shells. *(1)* A detail of the trigger *(a)* and safety *(b)* on the Browning BAR 22. The safety button has a vivid red color.
B The Remington "Nylon 66" Black Diamond has its stock and fore-end made of structural nylon. One of its advantages is its low weight: overall, the gun weighs only 4 lb (1.8 kg).
C The Harrington & Richardson Model 865 is a .22-caliber bolt-action gun. It has a detachable magazine holding five LR shells.

Chapter 4
Handguns

Jim Carmichel

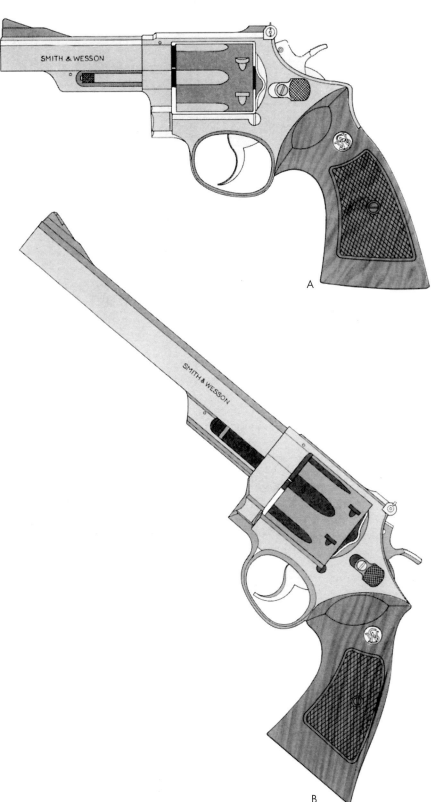

Handguns—pistols or revolvers—are used extensively for hunting only in North America and, for the most, only in the United States. Most governments severely restrict the possession, ownership, and use of handguns, and that of the United States is no exception. There are federal and state restrictions affecting handguns (and rifled weapons in general), while some administrative units within states impose further, local restrictions. Some restrictions are in the interests of general safety, while others limit the use of small-caliber handguns to shooting only small game and vermin; others again prohibit the use of handguns with poor sights or very short barrels. Despite all these discouragements, a large and increasing number of North American sportsmen hunt with handguns wherever it is legal.

During the 1970s, the use of handguns to hunt small and large game in North America increased significantly. The reasons for this have been the growing availability of more powerfully calibered guns, improved ammunition loaded with hunting-type bullets, the development of scopes and mounts, and an emphasis on handgun hunting in a number of sporting journals.

The handguns that are used include revolvers and semiautomatics (or autoloading pistols, which are often mistakenly called automatics although they are not capable of fully automatic fire). Both single- and double-action revolvers are used. The hammer of a single-action must be cocked manually after every shot, while a double-action revolver is cocked and fired by the trigger pull alone, a mechanical action that gives so long and heavy a trigger pull that the gun wavers, spoiling the aim. For hunting purposes, such a gun is almost always cocked manually before firing. With a good double-action gun, this gives a light, very short trigger pull, a fast lock time, and good accuracy.

There are autoloading pistols with single and double actions, but the single-action models outnumber the others. With an "auto," single-action means that only the first shot requires the gun to be cocked manually, for, upon firing, the mechanism automatically extracts and ejects the empty cartridge, feeds in a new one from the magazine to the chamber, and cocks and locks the action for the next shot.

It would be presumptuous to say that one type of handgun is superior to the others for hunting: all are popular in North America, and each has advantages and disadvantages. Choice is guided by individual preferences and experience as well as by the type of hunting most often done with the gun in question.

While the types of handgun so far described are the most common, there has been an enormous revival in the popularity of single-shot pistols. In large measure, this has been due to improvements in cartridges and in telescopic sights, specifically those with long eye relief (which enables the hunter to hold his pistol in the normal manner, without bringing it too close to his face). The most accurate, comfortable, and safe firing method is the straight-armed, two-handed hold; it is all the more accurate when the shooter's hands or forearms—never the gun itself—are resting on or against a solid support.

A The Smith & Wesson Model No. 19 .357 Combat Magnum is shown here with a 4-inch (10 cm) barrel; other barrel sizes available are 2½ inches (6 cm) and 6 inches (15 cm). The revolver is fitted with an S & W Micrometer Click sight, adjustable for windage and elevation.

B Smith & Wesson's Model 29 .44 Magnum is a six-shot revolver. Depending on its barrel length, it weighs from 43 oz (1.2 kg) to 51 oz (1.4 kg).

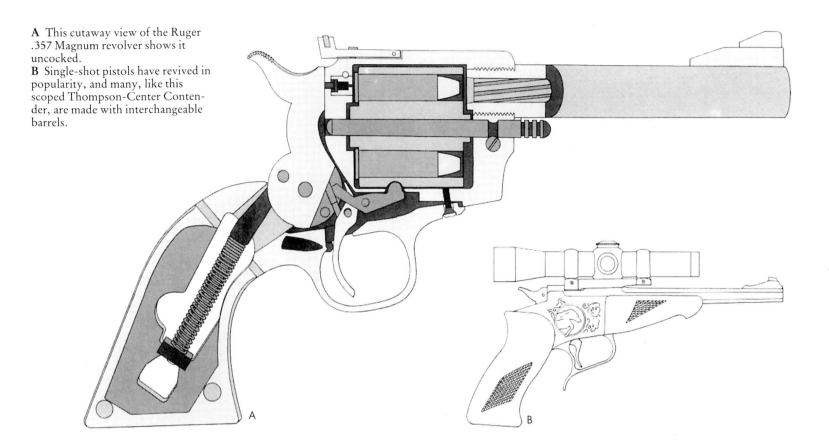

A This cutaway view of the Ruger .357 Magnum revolver shows it uncocked.
B Single-shot pistols have revived in popularity, and many, like this scoped Thompson-Center Contender, are made with interchangeable barrels.

Fitting a scope sight to a handgun will, if the gun is chambered for an appropriate cartridge, significantly increase the range at which it is possible to hit game. For long-range hunting in open terrain, fast repeat shots are—or should be—unnecessary, if the first shot is carefully aimed and a number of factors, apart from the shooter's skill, are assumed: the gun's mechanical accuracy, the accuracy of the sighting equipment, and the proper velocity, trajectory, and energy of the bullet. Because the single-shot pistol has been chambered for a wide variety of relatively long-range cartridges, it has acquired in recent years a significant place, together with the repeating handgun, in North American hunting usage.

Every species of North American four-footed game has been hunted with handguns. The writer has used them for small game such as rabbits, squirrels, and raccoons, and for big game, too: wild boar, deer, bear, elk, and moose. Some of these animals were killed with a handgun because they appeared at close range and could more easily be shot with a pistol than with a rifle. Most of the larger species were shot with a .44 Magnum Ruger Blackhawk revolver and one, a wild boar, with a .41 Magnum revolver. A variety of guns were used with deer: a .357 Magnum revolver, a .30 Herrett single-shot, and even the .45 ACP auto. The last-named is not often used for hunting. In fact, no single caliber can be said to be representative of North American handgun hunting of big game. The available choice is too wide.

For hunting whitetail deer, the .357 Magnum is very popular, and deservedly so. Most hunters who are out after bigger game use one of the .44 Magnum revolvers, usually a Smith & Wesson Model 29 double-action, or a Ruger Blackhawk single-action. A smaller number use the powerful but scarce .44 AMP Automag semiautomatic pistol, or the Thompson-Center Contender single-shot break-action pistol. The latter is available in rifle calibers such as .30/30 WCF and .35 Remington, in addition to the traditional handgun calibers.

There are several relatively inexpensive .22 rimfire autoloading pistols and revolvers which serve quite well for hunting small game such as squirrels and rabbits, but most serious shooters prefer a top-quality revolver such as the Smith & Wesson K-22 or one of the top-quality target-type autoloaders which, in addition to good accuracy, have adjustable sights and a crisp trigger.

One category of hunting in the United States is called "varmint" hunting because the animals that are shot were at one time classified as vermin. Although none of them is a candidate for a listing of the world's major game species, hunting them affords very popular sport in parts of the United States. Woodchucks, prairie dogs, and coyotes are the most hunted, although several additional species are, or have been, classified in the varmint group. When a hunter speaks of varmint rifles or pistols, he means arms designed for precise, long-range shooting, mostly at woodchucks or prairie dogs, but sometimes at coyotes and, on snow-blanketed open fields, red foxes.

Some varmint hunters use the same Magnum revolvers or rifles that they use for hunting big game, and it is typical that such hunters consider varmint hunting an enjoyable way to practice their marksmanship in preparation for hunting big game. There are, however, many devoted varmint hunters who use specialized arms for long-range shooting at these small animals, and they regard such hunting as a challenging sport in itself. A typical rifle for this sport is chambered for high-velocity .22 centerfire cartridges and is heavy-barreled and cumbersome; it may be equipped with very high-powered scopes. Some varmint rifles look rather like a cross between what is usually called a sporter and a target rifle. Stranger still in appearance are some of the handguns designed especially for varmint hunting; they are chambered for special varmint cartridges.

The best and most accurate of these is the Remington XP-100 which is, in effect, a short-barreled bolt-action rifle set in a plastic pistol stock. It fires the .221 Remington cartridge, a short, bottlenecked .22 centerfire cartridge best described as a shortened version of the .222 Remington rifle cartridge, as the rim and head diameters are identical. Fired from the

10¼-inch (27 cm) barrel of the XP-100, the .221 has a muzzle velocity with a 50-grain (3.25 g) bullet of 2,650 feet (800 m) per second. This combination of pistol and cartridge provides an accuracy good even by rifle standards. Fired from a bench rest with a high-magnification (10×) scope and well-developed handloads, the XP-100 is capable of 110-yard (100 m) five-shot groups which measure less than one inch (2.5 cm) between the most widely-spaced shots. This standard of accuracy, combined with the relatively high velocity and flat trajectory, makes it not only possible to hit woodchucks or other similarly small animals or targets at 110 yards (100 m), but also increases chances of success to probability.

A shooter using a more traditional handgun with open sights needs a high degree of skill—and luck—to hit so small an animal as a woodchuck at even 100 yards (90 m). Even so, shooting at such targets with a handgun, especially one of the powerful Magnum revolvers, possesses a charm of its own and attracts many shooters.

Until quite recently, target shooting with handguns in the United States fell into one of three major categories, none of which has any truly close connection with hunting: bull's-eye shooting according to the rules and procedures of the National Rifle Association; Police Combat Tournament shooting or that of the Practical Police Course; and the shooting done at the World Shooting Championships, the Olympic Games, and other major international competitions which are governed by the rules of the International Shooting Union, or the Union Internationale de Tir (UIT).

A fourth, still quite new, category has interesting similarities to hunting and has quickly become enormously popular. This is known as metallic silhouette, or metallic game silhouette, shooting; it originated in Mexico and quickly spread to the United States. Since 1975, it has attracted legions of shooters who were previously uninterested in target competition. At first, it included only offhand rifle shooting at ranges of 200, 300, 385, and 500 meters (220, 330, 420, and 550 yards) at full-size steel profiles of chickens, pigs, turkeys, and sheep, respectively. The rules are simple: five shots are fired in 2½ minutes, and a point is scored by knocking a silhouette off its stand. This is harder to do than might be thought, for the silhouettes are heavy, and the bullet must strike the right part of the target with enough energy to topple it. A hit just anywhere will not do.

This form of competition proved so popular that it was quickly adopted by pistol shooters, who retained the targets but lessened the distances to 50, 100, 150, and 200 meters (55, 110, 165, and 220 yards). A variety of equipment and shooting positions may be used, depending on the particular match. Both single-shot and repeating pistols have been chambered for the cartridges used for this sort of shooting.

The first competitors using pistols immediately found that those available, and the ammunition, were neither accurate nor powerful enough to topple the heavy steel targets. As a result, more handgun research and development has taken place in the past five years than in the previous fifty. It is likely that, in the near future, some of the results will be applied to arms and ammunition for hunting. In addition, since silhouette shooting resembles live-game shooting, it has encouraged thousands of American sportsmen to hunt big game with handguns for the first time.

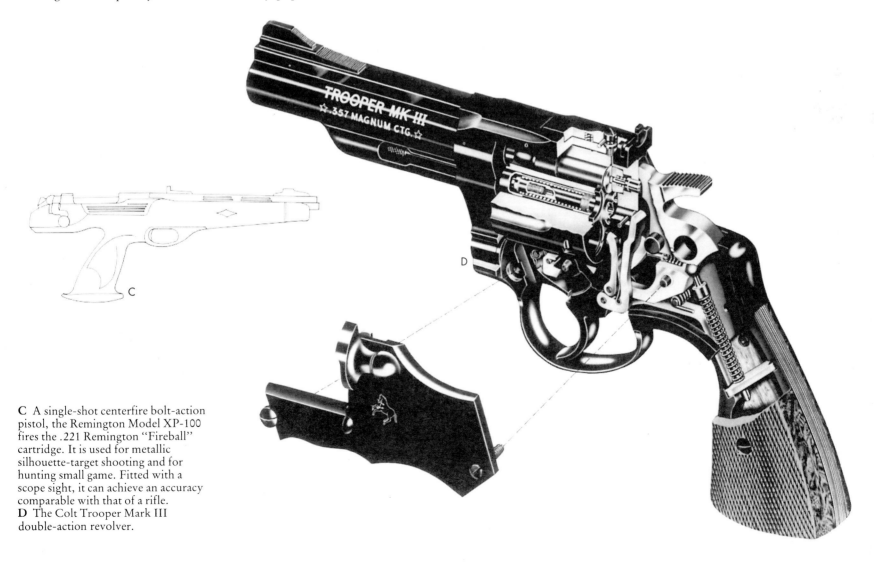

C A single-shot centerfire bolt-action pistol, the Remington Model XP-100 fires the .221 Remington "Fireball" cartridge. It is used for metallic silhouette-target shooting and for hunting small game. Fitted with a scope sight, it can achieve an accuracy comparable with that of a rifle.
D The Colt Trooper Mark III double-action revolver.

Chapter 5

Arms for Hunting in Africa and Asia

Robert Elman

Before undertaking a first safari in Africa or Asia, European and North American sportsmen tend to buy whole arsenals of new arms. This is wasteful for two reasons: a single rifle is fine for several kinds of game, and some of the arms commonly used in Europe and North America are appropriate for much of the game in Africa and Asia. Over and above this, one shoots best with a familiar rifle—a trusty old weapon that has taken game before and in which the shooter has confidence. In the following part, on hunting methods, there are suggestions for adequate calibers for African and Asian game and, valuable as these certainly are, they should not be taken as an encouragement to buy new weapons, if the shooter already has something suitable.

During the past decade or so, some unusual arms have been brought to Africa and Asia, expecially the former. Semiautomatic rifles have been used quite a bit, although their use is illegal in some countries, and even pump- and lever-action rifles have been seen. For that matter, a number of hunters brought their muzzle-loaders, which have been enjoying a great revival in North America because of the challenge, nostalgia, and romance of their use. In skilled hands, such a gun may be adequate for non-dangerous game.

But the rule, to which the foregoing examples are exceptions, is that modern bolt-action rifles are best for Africa and Asia. Some governments have restricted the use of certain types of arms and inadequate cartridges, but there will be no trouble about using a bolt-action of adequate power; there is no more versatile firearm for use in Africa or Asia.

Many professional hunters—that is, hunters who are outfitters and guides—treasure their traditional big-bore rifles with folding-leaf sights. Like the double shotgun, these classic rifles for Africa and Asia were perfected in Britain for the primary purpose of stopping big, dangerous game at short range. Though many have a series of three or more folding-leaf sights, these rifles have the "pointability" of a shotgun and can be aimed very fast; most of them are chambered for extremely large, powerful cartridges. They are sometimes called back-up guns, to be used by a professional hunter in the emergency caused by a client having fired unsuccessfully at some consequently enraged or wounded animal.

Cartridges for these doubles are not very accurate at long range, and their recoil in most instances is terrific. Although they can be lifesavers in particular circumstances and in the appropriate hands, they cannot be recommended to an average sportsman who has not practiced with big-bores. One must become accustomed to such a rifle, learn to handle it quickly and effectively, and become used to its recoil before it can be used effectively. Once it can be so used, the double rifle is a formidable weapon that has long since earned its reputation, although, at one time, doubles were even larger than they are now. Writing in the late nineteenth century, W.W. Greener noted that a double 8-bore of his manufacture, loaded with a spherical ball and backed with 10 drams (605 grains, or 39 g) of black powder, had put 8 shots into a rectangular target measuring about 1½ by 2½ inches (4 by 6 cm) at 50 yards (45 m)—impressive accuracy for such a cannon! He added that "the late Mr. A.

Henry, of Saigon, with a Greener double 8-bore rifle weighing only 13 lb., charge 10 drams, and spherical ball," had placed 147 out of 163 shots inside a 12-inch (30 cm) circle at 110 yards (100 m).

In 1906, Henry Sharp's book *Modern Sporting Gunnery* listed black-powder double rifles as large as 4-bore and the more modern Nitro Express models as small as .256 (a caliber more appropriate to gazelle than to elephant) but ranging up to .600. For the largest African game, Sharp recommended the .600 or .577. He noted that, in a test of accuracy, the .577 had placed ten shots (five from each barrel) into a 3¼-inch (8 cm) space from a distance of 100 yards (90 m). Loads were 750-grain (48 g) nickel-plated bullets propelled by the then modern charge of 100 grains (6.5 g) of cordite.

When the .577 had been introduced in the early 1880s, it was actually considered small, but it was an African favorite for many years and is still occasionally seen. Arthur H. Neumann, who has been called the most daring of all the ivory hunters, usually relied on a .577 double-barreled Gibbs rifle for elephant and rhino. "I always was an advocate of small bores," he explained. But many hunters preferred the .600 Nitro Express, introduced about 1910 and used in the very famous Jeffery double elephant rifles. For many years, it was the world's most powerful game cartridge: it fired a 900-grain (58 g) bullet with a muzzle velocity as high as 1,950 feet (600 m) per second and an energy as great as 7,600 foot-pounds (1,050 kgm). Since then, of course, many more modern chamberings have been popular, ranging from the .375 to quite a few in the .450 or .500 class. The most renowned of the latter-day elephant hunters, D.W.M. "Karamojo" Bell, has helped to popularize relatively small-bore bolt-actions, and the fact is that today's even more efficient bolt-action rifles are capable of handling any game in Africa or Asia.

In his book *African Hunter*, the well-known scientist and sportsman James Mellon recommends the following calibers for big African game such as elephant, rhino, buffalo, and hippo: .375 Holland & Holland Magnum, .378 Weatherby Magnum, .458 Winchester Magnum, and .460 Weatherby Magnum. (American and British calibers are most often recommended for African game.) He notes that the older British cartridges— .416, .450, .465, .470, .475, .500, .577, and .600—are also fine, although it has become difficult to find either rifles or ammunition in these calibers; very few double rifles, for example, are now being made.

For lion and eland, Mellon recommends cartridges ranging from the .378 Weatherby and the .375 Holland & Holland down to the .300 Magnums, versions of which are made by Holland & Holland, Weatherby, and Winchester. For zebra and the larger antelopes, he recommends the same cartridges plus the .30–06, the .308 Norma Magnum, the 7.62mm NATO (.308 Winchester), and the 7mm Remington and Weatherby Magnums. Other powerful European and American 7mm cartridges are also adequate for such game.

For gazelle and the smaller antelopes up to about 250 lb (100 kg), Mellon lists cartridges ranging from the .300 Magnums, the .30–06, and the 7.62mm down to the 6mm group. He classifies really small game as

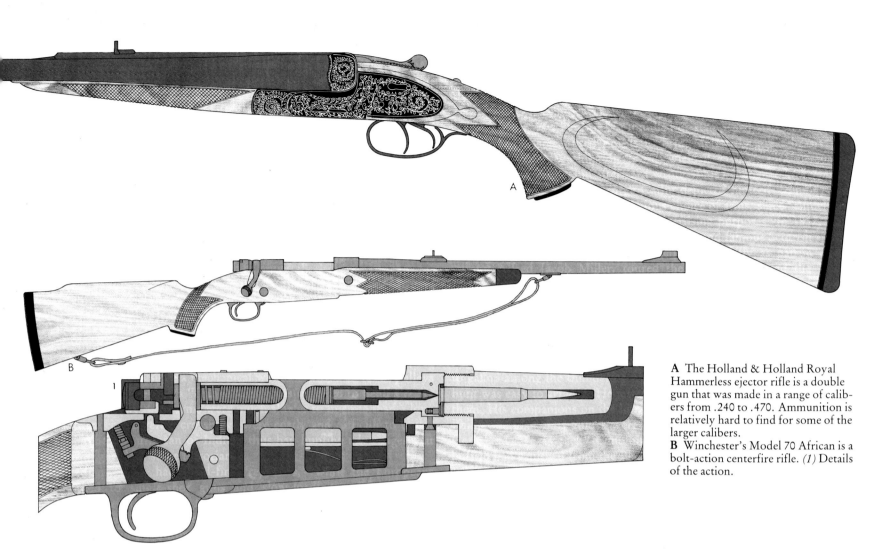

A The Holland & Holland Royal Hammerless ejector rifle is a double gun that was made in a range of calibers from .240 to .470. Ammunition is relatively hard to find for some of the larger calibers.
B Winchester's Model 70 African is a bolt-action centerfire rifle. *(1)* Details of the action.

including rabbit, birds, and dik-dik, all species weighing not more than 15 lb (6 kg), for any of which the smallest of the aforementioned cartridges is enough; so are, in the present writer's opinion, the .22 centerfire high-velocity cartridges known in North America as varmint loads. However, Mellon recommends rimfires—the .22 Magnum rimfire or the .22 Long Rifle cartridge. A great many sportsmen from many parts of the world own rifles chambered for one of these rimfires or for the slightly more powerful 5mm cartridge.

Asian game can be classified in pretty much the same way as the African, with the Asian wild cattle being comparable to the African buffalo and other large African game, while the antelopes are equivalent, too. The tiger can be compared to the lion, Asian deer to European and African deer, and Asian boar, goats, and sheep to those of Europe and North America.

Game birds, both upland species and waterfowl, are most often bagged with a shotgun, as in Europe and the Americas. While there are perhaps relatively few renowned as "major" game species, there is a variety that seems infinite to some visitors, who, after all, come to Africa and Asia for the most part to shoot big-game trophies. Many of the birds are fairly large—guineafowl, some francolins, and some waterfowl, for example—and shots are taken at rather short to quite long ranges; not more than one shotgun is needed, but its bore must be adequate for whatever presents itself, and that means a 12-bore.

In recent years, North American sportsmen have demonstrated the versatility of repeating shotguns equipped with variable-choke devices, which can be almost instantly changed from tight to open choke and vice versa, but, although much can be said for such devices, the conventional double-barreled shotgun remains an excellent choice for either Africa or Asia; it is versatile, and malfunctions are less likely than with the complex mechanisms of some repeaters. Whether the shotgun is an over-and-under or a side-by-side is a matter of personal preference, but the important thing is that it has two barrels, not necessarily of the same bore constriction. It may, indeed, have interchangeable sets of barrels, so as to provide at least two combinations of choke. A shotgun of which the barrels provide one tight bore and one rather open bore can offer enough of a choice to match the birds and conditions that present themselves at any time and, in Africa or Asia, one can hardly be better equipped for wingshooting.

Chapter 6

Maintenance, Sighting-in, and Ammunition

Wilf E. Pyle

The committed hunter will not be satisfied with just taking his shotgun or rifle out on the day of a hunt and putting it back afterwards. He will spend much of his leisure time doing the many chores related to being a hunter, and these form part of the lore of hunting. Weapon care, sighting-in, and reloading your own ammunition are just some of these chores, but they are among the most worthwhile.

Cleaning, Care, and Storage of Guns

Years ago, it was essential for a shooter to clean his gun rigorously after every few shots, because corrosive primer compounds and soft barrel steels rendered barrel life very short unless guns were cleaned without delay after use. Humidity combined rapidly with powder and primer residues to cause rust, which soon spelled the end for many a fine bore. The use of black powder in many of the old cartridges was often blamed for the severe damage, but it was not until smokeless powder began to be used that it was found that the primer compound, in fact, was responsible for much of the trouble.

Propellants and noncorrosive primers of modern cartridges are far less destructive for, unlike the old black powder, they leave a protective coating in the bore, so that it does not require scrubbing after each shooting session. If a firearm is to be stored for any length of time, on the other hand, it should first be cleaned and protected.

A good cleaning kit must contain a well-fitting cleaning rod; it can be made of aluminum, steel, brass, wood, plastic-coated steel, or twisted wire. Many rods comprise two or more segments that can be joined together in one way or another, but one-piece rods are best. Most rods are provided with a screw-on tip, which allows the shooter to choose the type he should use; there are three basic types—slotted, button, or jagged—and each works well in normal cleaning procedures.

The next important item in the cleaning kit is a good supply of patches made of flannel or cotton, and, while they can be made at home from old clothes, it is probably wisest to buy ready-made patches; the shooter is assured then that they will be of the correct size for the caliber and will be less likely to stick in the bore.

A good brand of powder solvent and a supply of oil are also needed, together with a tube of gun grease, to be used if the rifle is to be stored for any length of time. Many kits include a fine wire brush.

Cleaning procedures are simple: after making sure that the gun is unloaded, remove the bolt, or open the action completely, as may be appropriate. Place a patch on the tip of the rod, push it into the breech, and move it back and forth a few times while keeping the muzzle pointed downward; this is to avoid causing the powder residues to drop into the action. This method works well with a bolt-action rifle, or a pump-, lever-, or autoloader gun. It also works well with most shotguns. It is unwise to disassemble other types of rifle just for a simple cleaning. In such cases, it is better to clean the weapon from the muzzle; this calls for some caution, for the rod can damage the muzzle, and so it should be guided carefully into the muzzle between protective fingers. An alterna-

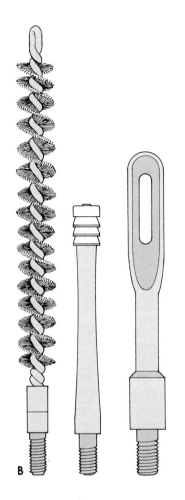

A A pull-through works well on rifles that cannot take a cleaning rod from the breech. Drop the weighted end through the bore and place the cleaning patch in the breech. *(1)* A quick tug and the patch is pulled through. *(2)* A dirty patch.

B A brush and two kinds of tips commonly available in cleaning kits.
C Cleaning the face of the bolt is necessary, as this area picks up a surprising amount of primer compound, grease, dirt, and even brass shavings. Use a toothbrush for this.

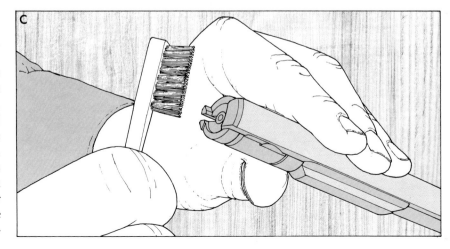

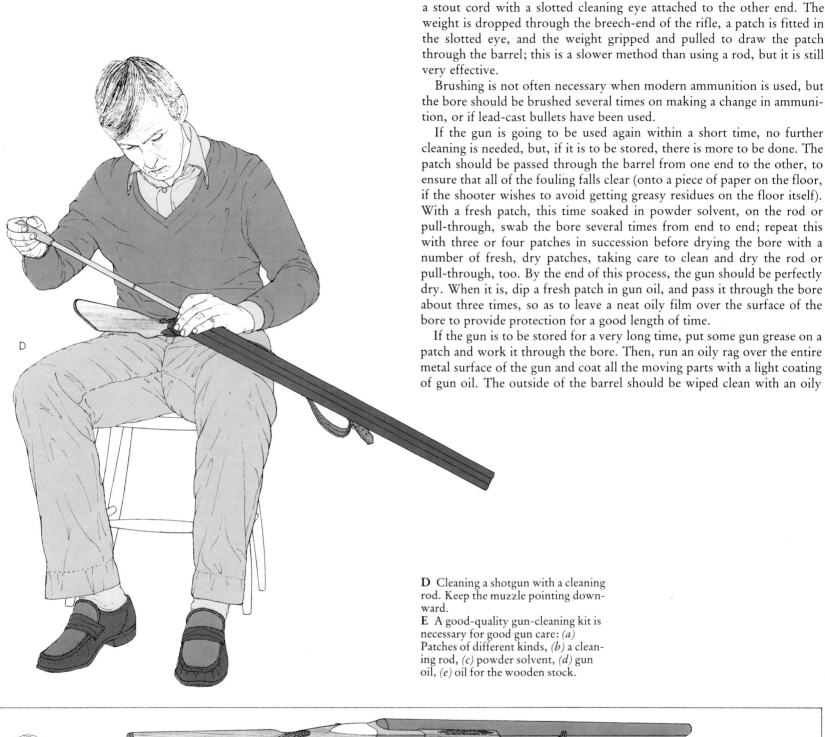

tive method is to use a pull-through: this consists of a weight fastened to a stout cord with a slotted cleaning eye attached to the other end. The weight is dropped through the breech-end of the rifle, a patch is fitted in the slotted eye, and the weight gripped and pulled to draw the patch through the barrel; this is a slower method than using a rod, but it is still very effective.

Brushing is not often necessary when modern ammunition is used, but the bore should be brushed several times on making a change in ammunition, or if lead-cast bullets have been used.

If the gun is going to be used again within a short time, no further cleaning is needed, but, if it is to be stored, there is more to be done. The patch should be passed through the barrel from one end to the other, to ensure that all of the fouling falls clear (onto a piece of paper on the floor, if the shooter wishes to avoid getting greasy residues on the floor itself). With a fresh patch, this time soaked in powder solvent, on the rod or pull-through, swab the bore several times from end to end; repeat this with three or four patches in succession before drying the bore with a number of fresh, dry patches, taking care to clean and dry the rod or pull-through, too. By the end of this process, the gun should be perfectly dry. When it is, dip a fresh patch in gun oil, and pass it through the bore about three times, so as to leave a neat oily film over the surface of the bore to provide protection for a good length of time.

If the gun is to be stored for a very long time, put some gun grease on a patch and work it through the bore. Then, run an oily rag over the entire metal surface of the gun and coat all the moving parts with a light coating of gun oil. The outside of the barrel should be wiped clean with an oily

D Cleaning a shotgun with a cleaning rod. Keep the muzzle pointing downward.
E A good-quality gun-cleaning kit is necessary for good gun care: *(a)* Patches of different kinds, *(b)* a cleaning rod, *(c)* powder solvent, *(d)* gun oil, *(e)* oil for the wooden stock.

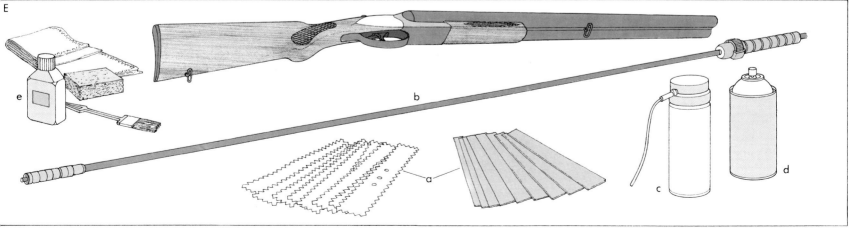

rag; fingerprints should be wiped off without delay, for they are often harbingers of rust. The bolt of a bolt-action gun should be lightly oiled and the face cleaned with a small brush; a toothbrush is ideal.

When the gun is to be used again, it is vital to remove the grease from the bore and the working parts: a bulged barrel can be caused by firing a shot when there is an appreciable amount of grease in the bore. An oily bore will not shoot accurately on the first shot, while an oily chamber can cause a marked rise in chamber pressure upon firing, followed by blown primers or extraction problems or·worse—a blown action.

Remember to store a gun muzzle-down if it is to be kept in store for a considerable period: this will prevent oil and grease from making their way into the action. Another caution is to use oil sparingly, for too much in the mainspring will impede the firing pin and cause unreliable firing; if in doubt, wash the bolt in gasoline.

Some shooters claim that they never clean their guns—and those guns show the consequences. Again, there are those who clean their pet guns so often that they do more damage to the bore than a year's shooting might do. The modern hunter must realize that many of the old ways can now be forgotten, even if good gun care, while not so crucial as in the past, is still important in maintaining a serviceable arm over a lifetime of use.

Sighting-in Rifles

Firearms and their related accessories are probably better made today than they have ever been, but, if a rifle is poorly sighted, the shooter who uses it will certainly miss shots.

Most hunting rifles come from the factory with some form of iron sights, and many hunters wrongly believe these sights to be correctly sighted-in for their purposes. The rifle may leave the factory capable of firing minute-of-angle groups, but its actual performance in the hands of the hunter depends on his or her physical build and how well the rifle fits it, and on the hunter's own style of shooting. Factory sighting does not meet the individual's needs of carefully tailored sighting-in.

There are three basic types of sights available: factory-installed front and rear sights, often called sporting sights; receiver, or peep, sights; and scope sights, which are the commonest type today.

The so-called sporting sights may come in many different styles and configurations, but, generally, they consist of a V or square-notched rear sight and a fixed-post front sight. Sometimes, the rear sight can be adjusted for windage, but, most often, it cannot. There is almost always an adjustment for elevation, often comprising a notched slide elevator or a sight with a screw holding the arrangement. Often, target-style or varmint rifles do not come equipped with these sights.

The second sort, the receiver or peep sight, in which the rear sight is some form of hole or aperture, is at present not as popular as it once was. When properly mounted and adjusted, such sights are very rugged and dependable; they are nearly always adjustable for windage and elevation, while older styles were adjustable only for height. Most modern receiver sights are graduated in half-minutes of angle ($\frac{1}{2}$ inch/1 cm at 100 yards/90 m); some front sights are adjustable, too.

The rifle scope common today is a tough, accurate, and reliable optical instrument, but it requires careful sighting-in. This is now very easy, for adjustments on most modern scopes are internal; they are made by means of elevation and windage screws placed on top of and to the right of the scope, respectively. The screws can be turned with a screwdriver or the edge of a coin; an arrow indicates movement up or to the left (or right), respectively, for elevation or windage. Many scopes are set in increments of one minute of angle, and lesser divisions are scribed between the full minutes: a minute of angle means, in practice, 1 inch (2.5 cm) at 100 yards (90 m), and proportionate differences at greater or lesser ranges.

Having acquired the sight you want, it is possible to sight-in the rifle, provided you have access to a target range or to some location that may be used for firing. For deer hunting, which may be taken as a norm, the rifle needs to be sighted so as to fire a group that prints 3 inches (7.5 cm) high at 100 yards (90 m); this allows for shots of up to 275 yards (250 m) without further adjustment, for the vitals of a deer form a target about 18 inches (45 cm) square, and a shot that is 3 inches high at 100 yards will still be within this target area at the greater distance. You will need ammunition of the same brand and bullet weight as you intend to use when hunting—the performances of different brands differ sometimes significantly—and a supply of targets; these can be either purchased sighting-in targets, which are usually marked off in squares of about an inch, or home-made—a 2-inch (5 cm) circle inscribed on a piece of paper will do.

If you do not have access to a target range, any fairly level piece of ground will do, if it has a good back stop; make sure that it is safe and legal to shoot there, getting the permission of the landowner if necessary. Take a rest along with you: a small table or a mat that can be folded over, or the hood of a vehicle, suitably padded, will all provide ample support.

Illustrated here are the steps you should take when sighting-in a rifle. A typical .30-caliber rifle so sighted should give most hunters the capactiy of shooting out to about 275 yards (250 m) without having to hold over the target.

When carried out with the right equipment and an understanding of what needs to be done, most sighting-in jobs are easy. The shooter who is to use the rifle in the field should do the actual sighting-in. Never believe that a rifle straight from the factory and put directly into the hunting field will deliver accurate shots.

The Basics of Reloading

The reloading of rifle and shotgun cartridges is not only a fascinating hobby but also one that can save the hunter between half and two-thirds of the price of factory-made ammunition. The wide assortment of components available allows the hunter to prepare ammunition for a particular gun or purpose without any loss of quality, for the bullets, primers, and powder sold for this purpose are subject to rigorous quality control. Furthermore, a variety of loads gives greater versatility to a rifle, shotgun, or handgun.

The most expensive part of the cartridge is the brass case, which is often thrown away, although cases can be used several times, the eventual number depending on the design of the particular case and the kind of load it is used to fire. The first step in reloading is to inspect the case, which must be cleaned and then checked for cracks. These often occur in the neck and the lower part known as the head; any cracked cases should be discarded. So should any with a ring or bulge, for such cartridges can develop head separation, which can be very dangerous for the shooter. Once the cases are selected, there follow five basic steps.

1. Depriming, or the removal of the spent primer.
2. Resizing, or returning the used case to its original size.
3. Repriming, which is inserting a new primer.
4. Charging the case with powder.
5. Seating the new bullet.

There is a variety of loading tools on sale from a number of manufacturers. Apart from the actual reloading tool, which is often called a reloading press, one needs a set of reloading dies for the caliber in question, a shell loader, a powder scale, and any of the many available reloading manuals. Many of these outline the necessary steps and describe the common problems. New editions come out from time to time, and the hunter who does his own reloading should keep himself up-to-date by buying them.

From this source one can obtain information about the many manufacturers of shell holders, the interchangeability of different makes, the

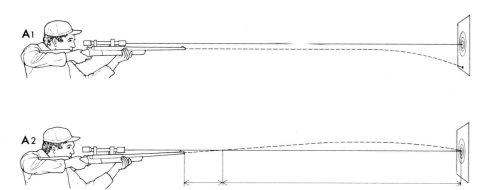

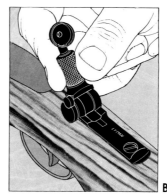

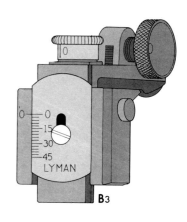

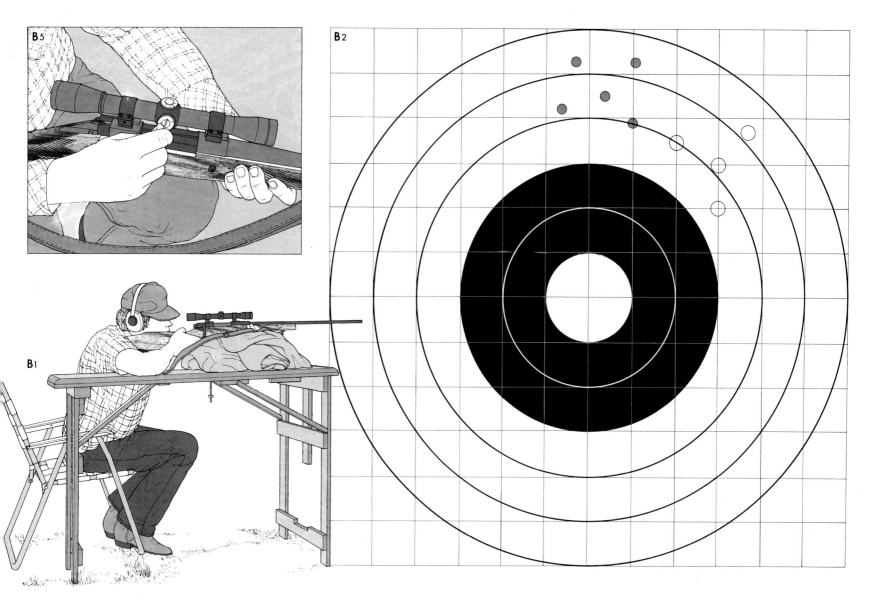

A *(1)* In the rifle that is not sighted-in, the line of sight and the line of bore are parallel, and the force of gravity will make the bullet fall low. *(2)* The trajectory of a bullet from a properly sighted-in rifle will cross the line of sight twice, once a short distance from the muzzle and once at the point of impact.

B To sight in a rifle, fire a group of shots at a target at 25 yards (23 m)

with the forepart of the rifle resting on a padded support, such as this table *(1)*. Commercially available targets *(2)* that are marked off in square inches can be used. Locate the center of the group on your target and measure its distance above or below and to the left or right of the bull's-eye. Work out how many minutes of angle these distances represent. Adjust the calibration on the sights

accordingly. When adjusting the rear sight, remember to move it in the direction in which you want the group to be moved. *(3)* A micrometer-adjustable peep sight with quarter-minute adjustments for elevation and windage. *(4)* The old-style peep sight is adjustable only for elevation. When you have made the necessary adjustments, fire another group, and if everything has gone well, the group

will print out at the point of aim. With the close-range alignment now accomplished, fire a group at a range of 100 yards (90 m). The center of this group should be about 3 inches (7.5 cm) above the bull's-eye. *(5)* The modern telescopic sight can be adjusted easily with a coin. The elevation adjustment is usually on the top, and the windage adjustment on the right side.

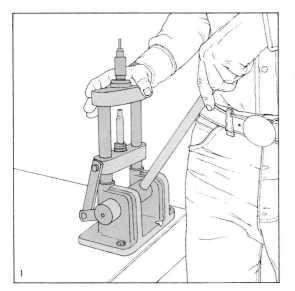

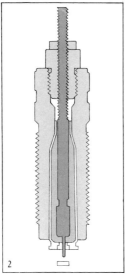

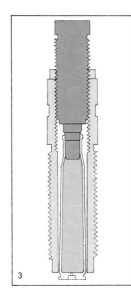

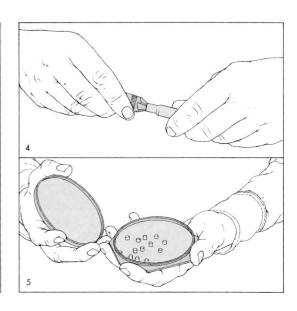

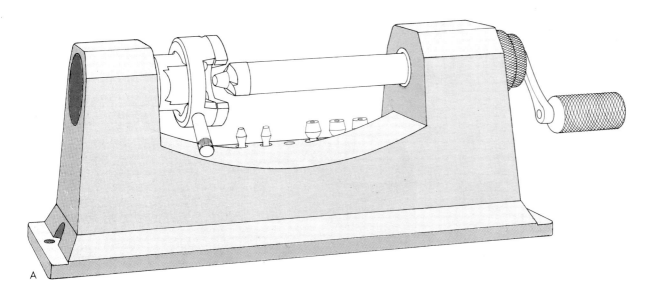

Reloading a rifle bullet. *(1)* The cartridge case in the reloading press, moving upward to engage with the appropriate die part. *(2)* A decapping rod. *(3)* An expanding plug. *(4)* Deburring and chamfering by hand. *(5)* Sorting primers. Try to handle them as little as possible. *(6)* Charging a case with powder from a powder measure. *(7)* Seating the bullet in the cartridge. *(8)* A cross-section showing the bullet in the bullet-seating screw.
A Lyman's Universal Trimmer for trimming and chamfering cases.
B Other necessary tools: *(1)* a weighing scale; *(2)* a deburring tool; *(3)* a powder funnel.

beginning and maximum loads for different cartridges, and new powders and bullets. Maximum loads should never be exceeded, while increases in loads should be made gradually, by not more than a grain or two of powder at a time.

Once the cases have been selected, they should be lubricated before running them through the full-length sizing die. Some reloaders dislike getting lubricant on the inside of the case, but if the lubricant is powdered graphite, there is not likely to be enough of it to damage the powder charge. Oil or lubricant that comes into contact with the primer can cause trouble, too, by breaking down the primer compound and rendering it inert or severely weakening it.

Depriming, full-length resizing, and expanding the mouth of the case to the correct size are all performed with a single stroke of the modern reloading press. The decapping is done by a shaft that runs through the center of the die to push out the fired primer by means of a pin. Screwed onto the shaft, or incorporated with it, is an expander ball or button that passes through the neck of the cartridge; as it passes, it leaves the neck with the correct diameter to accept a bullet of the correct caliber. The inside of the cartridge neck needs to be lubricated to facilitate this step.

When home-cast lead bullets are used, the expander button will not open the neck of the cartridge sufficiently, so it will be necessary either to use a larger size of expander, or to open the neck by hand with a pair of needle-nose pliers.

There has been much argument over the merits of full-length as against neck-sizing, which means resizing only the neck area of the case, a method that worked well enough until case shapes changed to the bottle-neck form, and chamber pressures increased. Full-length sizing is now recommended, because the actions of many autoloaders, lever-, and pump-action guns will not close properly unless cartridges have been full-length sized. The argument will continue among reloaders, but it is clear that neck-sizing will work if the cases are to be fired from the same gun.

The reloaded cartridge must fit what is called the head space: the distance from the face of the bolt, when closed, to the point in the chamber at which the cartridge is stopped from going any further into the chamber. The rim of rimmed cases stops them, while rimless cases are stopped by the shoulder resting against the chamber wall. Safety and accuracy depend upon correct head space; knowing what it means and how it relates to different cartridges is vital for successful reloading. The sizing die must, therefore, be set in the loading tool in accordance with the instructions for the particular set of dies in use, for incorrect placing of the die can give the wrong head space.

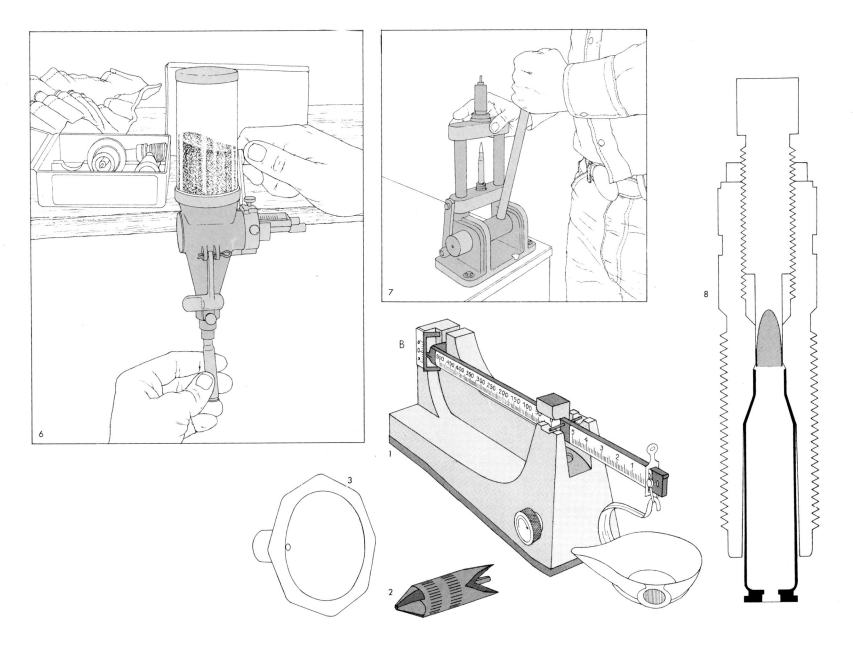

Priming the resized case is the next step, a simple operation, but still one requiring precautions. The primer must be placed anvil-side up on the priming punch or arm; most reloading presses are designed so that priming can be done when the case is extracted from the sizing die. Before the new primer can be neatly fitted in the priming pocket, all the old priming mixture must be scraped away or removed; a deburring tool can be used for this.

A primer is set in place with a gentle, steady push on the press handle. The primer must be seated firmly against the bottom of the pocket, and failure to achieve this could result in a hang-fire, since the force of the firing pin would be softened by the forward movement of the incorrectly seated primer. A caution: never seat a primer into a case that has been charged with powder. Once a case has been fitted with a primer, however, it may be charged with powder, and selecting a powder charge that meets the hunter's needs is what reloading is all about. As there are many powders, it is essential to consult a reloading manual. This will give a beginning load and, to begin with, this is what is best used.

The charge values for powders are expressed in grains, a standard unit of measurement for powder and bullets, and all reloading scales are marked in grains. There are 7,000 grains in 1 lb (16 oz); in metric, 1 grain is .065 gram. A pound (450 g) smokeless powder will load more cartridges than most hunters shoot in a year. Just which powder to use can be difficult to decide, for there are several types, and brands can be confusing; the best course is to read several manuals, see which powders are recommended for your needs, and experiment with loads and powder brands until you get the accuracy you can accept.

Once a load has been determined, weigh it out on a reloading scale and set the powder measure. Some writers recommend that each charge be weighed, but the excellent modern powder measures make this unnecessary. The scale is needed to set the powder measure and to check the charge periodically after that. Using the measure is, above all else, a matter of working systematically and consistently. Some powders, such as ball powder, pass through the measure more readily than other, more conventional powders; this will influence the accuracy of the charge given, and it is, therefore, wise to check every fifth charge on the scales.

The final stage is the seating and crimping of the bullet. Once again, set the die in accordance with the instructions. A couple of factors determine the seating depth; the rule of thumb for jacketed bullets is to seat the bullet to the bottom of the case neck, and this works well for most bullets. Another factor is the total length of the case and bullet: if the bullet is seated too far out, the cartridge will not work through the magazine of some clip-model rifles. Crimping is largely unnecessary, unless lead bullets are being used or a tubular magazine is on the rifle; jacketed bullets generally grip the neck sufficiently well for no crimp to be required. An exception may be when particularly hot loads are used in heavy Magnum cartridges. Bullets generally used in tubular magazines come with a factory-prepared crimping groove. Once seating has been completed, the cartridge is ready for a final inspection; wipe any grease or lubricant from the case.

Loading shot shells follows the same general procedure; there are six steps.

1. Deprime and size.
2. Reprime.
3. Place the powder charge.
4. Insert and seat the wad on the powder charge.
5. Drop the shot charge.
6. Crimp.

The plastic one-piece shot-protector wads have greatly simplified reloading and, in many instances, have enabled the powder charge to be reduced, as a consequence of the improved sealing of the plastic components. As with rifle-cartridge reloading, it is wise to choose a shell brand that is common in your area; the same applies to all the components. The combination of components is very important in shellshot reloading, and therefore, use only those that are recommended for the particular load you want.

Loading tools for shotgun shells are usually designed for an output of a large volume; many fine models exist. Although many older tools are still to be found, they were designed for paper cases using wads of card and felt, and are usually not effective in reloading modern plastic compounds.

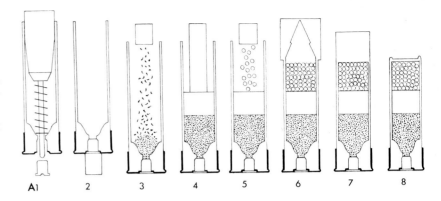

A1 2 3 4 5 6 7 8

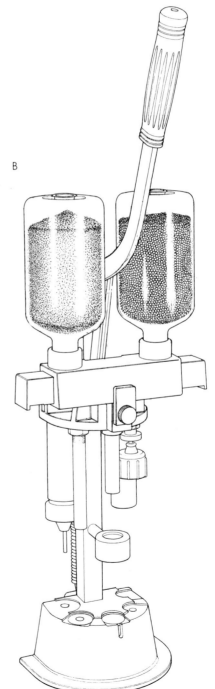

B

A Procedures for reloading can vary slightly, depending, for example, on the stage at which the cartridge is resized, and how crimping is carried out. In the illustration, sizing is the final operation. *(1)* Decapping; *(2)* priming; *(3)* charging with powder; *(4)* seating the wad; *(5)* charging with shot; *(6)* crimp starting; as some cases require different numbers of creases in the crimp, make sure you have the right head for the cases you are reloading; *(7)* crimping; and *(8)* sizing.

B This Pacific 105 Shellshot Reloader has five stations: resize and deprime; prime; load powder, seat wad, and load shot; start crimp; and finish crimp.

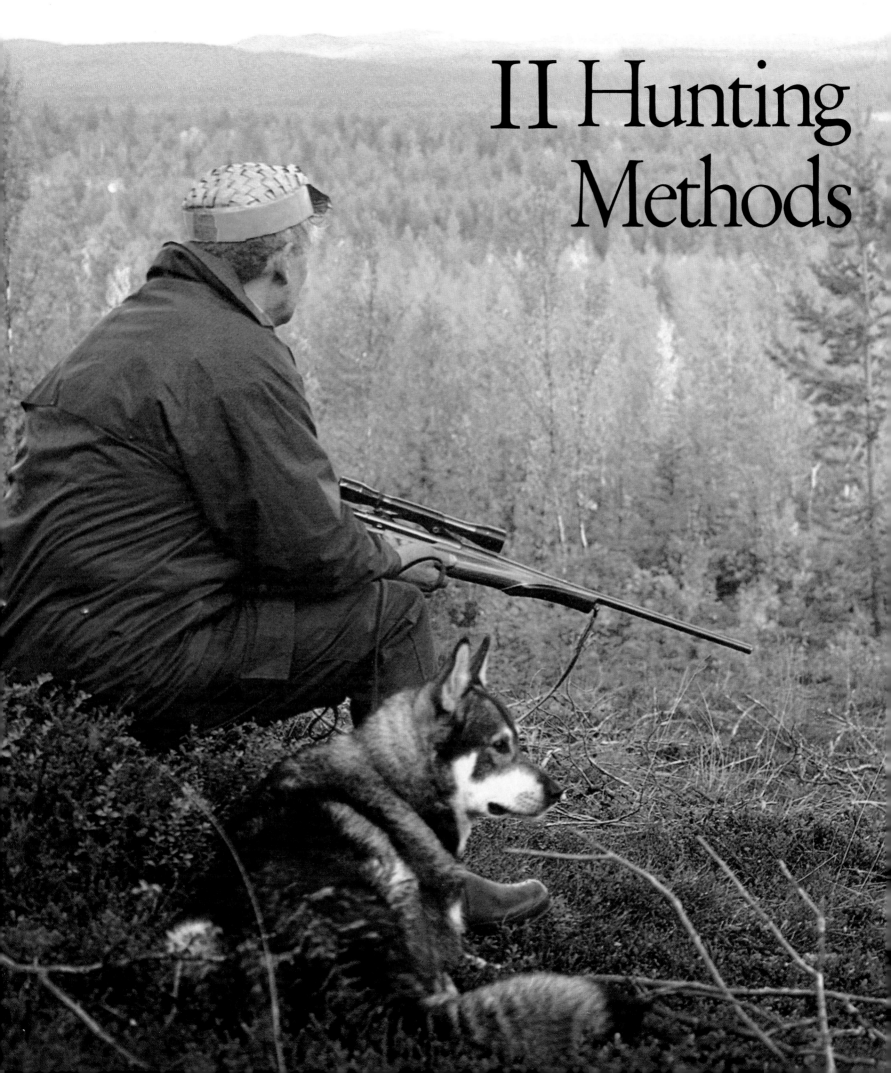

II Hunting
Methods

Chapter 1

Hunting in Europe and North America

Shooting humanely means shooting to kill, and a bullet that hits a deer's central nervous system, the heart, or the lungs will kill. The target area is small (10×12 inches; 25×30 cm) and centered (1) above the foreleg or (2) between the forelegs. When shooting from the rear (3), a shot to the back of the head breaks the neck; one to the pelvis cripples the animal. (Below) A typical permanent high seat, well situated at the edge of a glade.

Red Deer in Europe

The red deer is native to Europe and western Asia, and has been successfully introduced into Argentina and New Zealand, in both of which countries there are no native species for it to compete with. In North America, however, where its introduction on a small scale has been, perhaps, regrettable, it competes for food and habitat with whitetail, mule deer, and wapiti. Except for in Scotland and some moorland areas of England, such as Dartmoor in the West Country, red deer inhabit wooded or forested areas, which call for hunting methods rather different from the bare-ground stalking practiced in the deer "forests" of Scotland.

On the Continent, where the red deer become larger the further east they are found, the sportsman ambushes the stags from a well-placed high seat, stalks them through the thick forests, or, during the mating season, lures them by imitating their calls.

In a high seat, the hunter may be unable to avoid his scent being carried on the wind to a stag, which will flee at the first such sign of man. In addition, movements made while on the high seat are easily detected by a red deer stag and will cause him to vanish; roe deer, by contrast, are less sensitive to such movement. Still, if the seat is placed with care in an area of the forest known to contain red deer stags, the method can be quite productive. High seats are also used for other deer than the red.

Stalking is a widely used method, but, to be successful, it requires that the hunter is able to move quite noiselessly through the forest without giving his scent to the beast. This calls for woodcraft of a high order, in addition to a thorough understanding of where in the forest the deer are most likely to be found.

Luring stags in the mating season is a matter of calling to them in challenge, in the manner of another stag—and red deer stags roar like lions. The hunter or his guide issues a "challenge" and, if they are fortunate, a stag will reply; an experienced ear can distinguish the higher tone of a young stag from the deeper one of an older, more mature stag. Challenge and response alternate until the stag has been lured into a position where he can be seen, evaluated, and, if a good trophy, shot. This method is, however, used only from about mid-September until mid-October, just before and during the beginning of the mating season. The reason is that the flesh of stags is unfit for human consumption once the animals begin breeding. [TT]

Roe Deer and Fallow Deer

Roe deer and fallow deer are two European species, the latter having its origins in Asia Minor and Mesopotamia. While both species are hunted, the fallow deer has been semi-domesticated, especially in parks, and its instincts have become blunted. It presents nothing like the challenge of the roe deer, and although the methods described here can be applied when hunting either species, it is the elusive, wary roe deer that tests the skills of even the most experienced hunter.

A number of different methods can be used when hunting roe deer: stalking or still-hunting; ambush from a high seat; calling or luring, perhaps in combination with either of the two preceding methods; tracking in snow; driving with hounds or following with a dog.

The most demanding method is stalking; if the hunter makes only a slight mistake—a careless noise or movement—he will probably be detected and lose his chance of a shot. Even a small area affords good stalking, for the deer are strongly territorial and will not forsake their territory unless they have been much disturbed, for example, by human or canine intruders, during or outside the hunting season. A hunter who wants to stalk in an unfamiliar area can still follow the descriptions of someone who knows it well, rather than follow a guide, unless local requirements make the use of a guide obligatory. In any event, the hunter will need binoculars (and a telescopic sight) and should choose his clothes to match the colors of the season. Although rainy, blowy weather may be uncomfortable for the hunter, the resulting noise and movement of vegetation will help him approach the deer. Apart from the usual need to approach them from downwind, it helps to have the sun at one's back. A very early morning start is well worthwhile, for roe deer are then likely to be out feeding before seeking shelter for the day.

A high seat some 10 feet (3 m) or more above the ground will not only give the hunter a good field of view but will also be more likely to keep his scent off the ground and, therefore, away from the deer. Of course, any high seat affords an excellent way to observe birds and animals, so that the disadvantage of not being able to move through the hunting area is not that serious. Waiting in a primitive seat may be uncomfortable, but a seat can be a very elaborate structure, roofed and even equipped with a heater. The hunter or his guide will be able to keep a watch on the deer in the immediate neighborhood and determine if the animals in sight include any that should be shot. The question of shooting to cull is discussed below.

A good point about high seats of all sorts is that the trajectory of the bullet is most likely to end in the earth close to the shot animal. As a roe deer is relatively light, its body is often not enough to stop a bullet. For the owner of the hunting area, however, permanent high seats pose the problem of their use by poachers, and, for this reason, some are portable.

Roe deer bucks in rut can be called or lured quite easily, although the young bucks respond much more readily and obviously than the older ones. The sound that attracts them is made by blowing through the aperture formed by pressing the thumbs together, knuckles toward the face, with a blade of grass held between them: the noise to produce is a very faint mewing, the call of a doe trying to attract a buck. This is heard in summer, roe deer having an exceptionally early rut and, through the operation of the biological phenomenon known as delayed implantation, does enjoy the benefits of a summer's feeding before their reproductive cycle starts in earnest.

Where seasonal restrictions permit, roe deer can be tracked in snow by a hunter who takes advantage of their manner of moving off slowly when only slightly disturbed. They will usually stop and try to get a sight of the source of disturbance, a moment when a hunter who has managed to come up close to his quarry can get in a shot.

Dogs can be used to aid the hunter, but the sort of dog that does not frighten the deer away is essential. Some—dachshunds, for example—can exhibit traits that make the deer almost curious to find out what sort of beast is following them. An advantage of this method of hunting is that, as the scent of roe deer is very strong, the hunter does not need to make a start very early in the morning but should give the weaker scents of hares and foxes a chance to dissipate first.

The more usual form of drive, with beaters with or without dogs, works well with roe deer but, as with deer drives in North America, the deer should not be driven so fast that they present no chance of a reasonable shot. Roe deer are reluctant to leave their territory, however, and a drive without dogs may miss some deer, for they can hide themselves very capably. Even a concentrated line of beaters may not be enough to prevent a roe deer breaking back to its territory, while too much or too frequently repeated disturbance may cause roe deer to seek another territory altogether.

Roe deer are small and are best shot with light rifles, such as the .222 Remington, the .22–250, or the .243 Winchester. They present a small target area, too, not much more than the extent of a single hand, and situated just above and a little to the rear of the foreleg's joint with the body. Unless absolutely still, roe deer present a difficult if not impossible target; if a buck is moving only very slowly, a very slight intentional noise from the hunter may cause him to stop for a moment, which is when a shot should be taken. Shotguns are hardly suitable, except at very close range, and not always even then: the practice of driving deer toward hunters with shotguns was discontinued in Britain as recently as in the 1950s, when the method's brutality became obvious.

A consideration when hunting either roe or fallow deer is to cull the population rather than to shoot the most attractive trophy. Bucks that are past their prime, injured, or sick, or that are healthy and uninjured but undistinguished and likely to remain so, will all be shot. It would be a signal honor for a hunter to be allowed to shoot a buck in its prime: a fallow buck of about ten years of age, with fully developed palmations in his antlers, which would weigh about 5.5 lb (2.5 kg), or a roe of about six years, whose antlers look less impressive than those of a prime fallow buck but represent success in a finer test of hunting ability. [TT]

European Hunting Ceremony

Hunting in central Europe is more than a sport, it is practically a way of life. The would-be hunter cannot simply buy a hunting licence, as a hunter does in North America, for example; he must attend an approved course to learn not only hunting methods and law, but also the characteristics of the various game animals and birds, dog and hound care and training, shooting customs and traditions, and many other facets of the hunting life. In Sweden, elk-hunters are required to pass an annual test of their marksmanship. All this is evidence that hunting is something for which one must be capable and well informed.

The formalities required by law are matched, in some parts of Europe, by those exacted by custom. In this respect, central Europe is undivided, and a long tradition of how a day's shooting should be conducted continues unbroken. Naturally enough, these customs are most in evidence on occasions when many people participate and much game has fallen to their guns. As the light begins to fade, all the game shot during the day is arranged according to the rank each species enjoys. The numbers of each species can often be seen, almost at a glance, for every tenth bird or beast may be placed so as to show this—a tail is extended, for example. The whole display is sometimes framed with lines of fir branches. Huntsmen or gamekeepers who, during the day, have communicated with one another and the hunters by means of hunting horns, sound a tribute to each species of animal. The last hunt of the season may be marked by the firing of a salute by the assembled hunters.

A lighthearted moment comes when the hunting king is crowned, an honor accorded to the person who has shot most game during the day. Those who have been seen to have offended hunting custom and tradition are singled out for "punishment" before the whole party moves off, usually to meet in the evening for a hunting dinner. [TT]

Deer Stalking in Scotland

The antlers of red deer stags make magnificent trophies. With good feeding, stags from low ground in Europe can exceed the fourteen or, exceptionally, sixteen points that would be the limit for Scottish beasts, which live at high altitudes on the treeless hills and glens that are, nevertheless, called deer forests. Here, the deer are found together with grouse, ptarmigan, sheep, and other fauna, on ground subject to weather that, even in late summer and early fall, when the stags are stalked, can change from bright, warm sunshine to almost freezing mist in an hour or less.

Although roe, fallow, and sitka deer exist in Scotland, when "my heart's in the Highlands, a'chasing the deer," it was the red deer, *Cervus elaphus*, that the poet had in mind. This is the majestic, even self-satisfied animal painted by Landseer as "The Monarch of the Glen" and celebrated in many lesser-known works of art.

Deer stalking, in Scotland at least, is the term given to the sport of getting to within shooting range—80 yards (75 m)—of a red deer stag, and shooting it without its being aware of the presence of the sportsman and his accompanying stalker, who have approached it over open country for perhaps five hours or more. The stalker selects the approach routes and tactics; this may require the sportsman to walk knee-deep in the icy water of a burn for half an hour at a time, with his back bent double so as to keep out of sight of the deer or, perhaps, only of a single sheep that could alert the deer to the presence of intruders; to climb and descend a succession of hills; or to lie motionless in a stream or bog, while the deer, startled by a covey of grouse disturbed by the sportsman and the stalker, stare in the direction of the two men for ten or fifteen minutes continuously. The penalty of an unsuccessful shot that only wounds a stag at the end of such a stalk is not merely to see the animal vanish over the nearest hill. Deer stalking etiquette requires that the animal be followed and killed by the hunter, regardless of the time this takes.

Despite of, or perhaps because of, these difficulties, deer stalking in Scotland is in increasing demand, and many British devotees can no longer afford to compete against the many rich visitors from Europe, the Middle East, and North America. The costs of maintaining deer stalking are very high, and they are offset in part by the sale of venison. Although the British public have never acquired a general taste for it, there has been an increasing demand from the Continent, notably from Germany, and almost all carcasses find their way overseas, where the meat sells at high prices. The sportsman who shoots the stag is not thereby entitled to any more of it than the head, and, unless he has been stalking for about a week, in which case he may well be presented with a haunch, he will have to buy what he wants.

The legal season for shooting red deer in Scotland opens on 1 July and closes on 20 October; the season for hinds opens the next day, 21 October, and closes on 15 February. Different seasons are the rule in England and Wales (and there are different seasons, too, for other sorts of deer). In practice, very little stalking of stags is done in July and early August, when the beasts are still on the highest tops and consequently very difficult to find; also, their antlers are still in velvet then. Stalking proper begins at about the time of the opening of the grouse season (mid-August) and increases in popularity as the fall progresses, with the shortage of high-altitude grazing bringing the herds down to lower and more accessible ground. Hind shooting goes on throughout the legal season, often taking place in all but the most extreme of winter weather. This type of hunt is definitely not for the beginner, nor for the unfit, and invitations to stalk for the hinds are often extended only to hunters who have already shown themselves to be keen, agreeable, and expert stalkers of the stags.

Hind shooting is liable to take place in weather that varies between the miserable and the impossible, and there is no point in staying out longer than is necessary to complete the cull; half a dozen or more beasts may well be killed in a day's outing. When stalking stags, by contrast, it is very rare to take two in a day, unless there is absolutely no difficulty in getting both off the hill by night.

The laird and his stalker should have a good idea of how well stocked

Deer stalking in Scotland is a trial of a hunter's skill, patience, and endurance, and of the stalker's knowledge of the terrain and the animals on it. Even before the season opens, the stalker will have been out spying the herds (1) and the stags, still in velvet in July (2), that will be his quarry. The day's hunting starts early, with the approach march. Two or three hours' walking over the hills is often necessary before the stalker can begin to spy for herds and good stags; even at a half a mile's distance, he can tell if a stag is a good one. As the wind is blowing straight down to the herd, a long detour is necessary. This is the most demanding part of the stalk, as hunter and stalker must keep out of sight, sound, and smell of the ever-vigilant herd. The stalker, who is familiar with both the terrain and the herds on it, will, if need be, lead his "gentleman" over the rockiest ground and through the coldest water, in order to get him within range of a fine

stag. Often, a further detour is necessary if some sheep are in their way. When they have got to within 120 yards (110 m) of the herd, the stalker takes the rifle out of the case, loads it, and hands it to the hunter, signaling him to advance the last few yards on his own. (3) The hunter crawls forward until he is about 80 yards (75 m) from the stag, waits until he has a clear shot, and fires. "Reload!," the stalker orders, in case a second shot is necessary. At the sound of a shot, the pony-ghillie, who has been waiting in the far distance, comes up and helps with the gralloching (disemboweling) of the stag. (4) The carcass is loaded onto the pony for the long trek back.

the hill will be during the coming winter and early spring by reference to the calving successes of the previous spring, actual counts of deer during the summer and fall, and the number of stags shot during the season. This knowledge is the basis for their cull. First to be taken must be the barren—"yeld"—hinds, or those showing signs of not having calved that year; very old hinds are also likely to have given up calving and should be taken if recognized. A proportion of hinds will have natural injuries, causing limps and other ailments, and they should be shot; their calves are unlikely to thrive and should be taken, too. Occasionally, there will be a beast wounded by a careless sportsman (always, of course, from an adjoining forest), and that, too, should be added to the cull.

In many forests, no one applies to shoot hinds, and the job is left to the stalkers. For sportsmen who have the guts to go out in snow and gales, and, perhaps, lack the cash to pay for high-season stalking, a few evenings at hotel bars and a goodish outlay on drams of whisky might easily bring an invitation from a friendly stalker to join him for a day. But he will first have to be convinced that his prospective companion is an accurate shot with a rifle, and fit, into the bargain.

The rifle will be .240 bore or larger (anything smaller is illegal for red deer in Britain), and while a crack shot can consistently put a bullet into a 6-inch (15 cm) target at 200 yards (183 m) on the rifle range, the circumstances of shooting stags, to say nothing of hinds, are not those of the rifle range. When stalking stags, it is customary for the stalker to ask his gentleman to "test the rifle" before beginning the stalk. This may well be by shooting at a white-painted target, a sheet of tin, or a rock, visible 100 yards (90 m) away. The stalker will keenly inspect the results of one or two test shots and decide for himself what will be a safe range when a stag is to be killed. Many stalkers will not allow their gentlemen to take a shot at more than 80 yards (75 m), at least not until the individual has proved his skill and sang-froid at shorter shots. Running deer are never shot at. Wounding a deer is the worst thing a sportsman can do; he will certainly have to trail it for the rest of the day, and he will, perhaps, be obliged to devote the following day to finding and dispatching it.

Ammunition should be such as to give a more or less flat trajectory for a couple of hundred yards (or meters); performance over that range is of academic interest, for shots should never be fired at more than that distance from the target. Judging distances is often hard for those unused to the soft, changing, and uncertain light of the high hills. Many shots have to be taken downhill, and they are often missed. If the stag is below the gun at an angle of 45°, calculate the horizontal distance, and set the sights on that. At 80 yards (75 m) horizontal, the deer's eye is visible; at 150 yards (140 m), the ear is just visible; and at 200 yards (185 m), the ear is invisible. These indications do not apply, of course, to guns with telescopic sights, which are now widely used in deer stalking, having formerly been scorned by traditional stalkers. Most visitors would be given the option of shooting with one if, as is often so, the visitor does not have his own rifle with him, but borrows one from the estate. It should be noted, for visitors to the United Kingdom, that extremely strict regulations govern the ownership and possession of firearms—rifled weapons as distinct from shotguns—and it is not always possible to be granted a firearms certificate.

Dressing for deer stalking, as for grouse shooting, is not a matter of fashion but of camouflage. Heavy tweed is best, not only for its visual qualities, but because it generates no noise when moving against itself. Knickerbockers are preferable to trousers and should be worn with whatever leather shoes or laced boots will be the most comfortable, wet or dry.

A visitor to Scotland may recall, or hear references to, the feat known as doing a Macnab. This got its name from a novel called *John Macnab*, published by the Scottish writer John Buchan in 1925. In its essentials, the story concerns the poaching of deer and salmon from a private estate, after the owner has been given notice that "John Macnab" is going to attempt this feat. He does and succeeds. The name now applies to the considerable sporting—and organizational—achievement of killing, in the course of one day, a salmon, a stag, and a grouse. The day to choose will probably be in late September, when all three seasons coincide. It is more or less essential to try for the salmon before breakfast, shortly after dawn, when light, wind, and temperature all provide tremendous stimuli for the fish. With the fish landed, a rapid move to the stalking ground must be made, where a stalker must be on hand. It can happen that, with both salmon and stag killed, rain descends with such force and persistence as to make the grouse quite unapproachable. In the writer's experience, success was achieved when the sharp-eyed stalker spotted grouse feeding on stooks of oats in a stubble field, where they could be stalked, like deer. [JMG]

North American Deer and Antelope

North America, and particularly the United States, is rich in a wide variety of deer, which occur throughout the continent, and in the state of Hawaii. Deer afford an abundance of hunting, in which many different methods—some familiar from the Old World, others learned from one or other of the North American Indian tribes—are used to follow, drive, or attract the animals. They range in size from the 100 to 125 lb (45 to 55 kg) pronghorn, which can run at over 60 mph (100 km/h), to bull moose, which can weigh up to 1,800 lb (800 kg).

Probably the most challenging, elusive, and wary of North American big-game animals are whitetail deer. They are primarily nocturnal feeders, normally moving toward their bedding areas at daybreak; some go directly, others browse on the way. In hilly or mountainous areas, feeding grounds are often in the valleys, where wet soil supports good browse, or on hardwood flats at the foot of slopes. Once the hunter has located the feeding grounds and identified the routes the deer take to reach and leave them, he should watch quietly from dawn to about 8 or 9 o'clock in the morning; deer follow a routine, but, if disturbed, they are inclined to wander, and to feed more by day than at other times.

In wilderness areas, where little hunting takes place, the hunter must be prepared to hunt the deer in their resting areas, where they have bedded down for the day. High ground under a ridge line, preferably along the margin of a thicket, and in the sun, is a likely area to find them; by contrast, deer bedded down in thick swamp are difficult to locate if the hunter is alone and confined to narrow, winding game trails. Still-hunting—walking very slowly on ridges or game trails, stopping every few steps—is a good technique. Look and listen continuously. Move upwind, for deer have good noses. Keep both eyes open for signs of deer. The bucks leave marks called rubs and scrapes. In late summer and early fall, the bucks rub the velvet off their antlers, using—and frequently destroying—saplings in doing so, for they rub off the bark as they rub the velvet from their horns; trees are marked from about 12 to 36 inches (30 to 90 cm) off the ground. Later, throughout the rut, which may fall anytime between mid-October and early January, depending on the latitude, the bucks continue to rub and polish their antlers on tree trunks, saplings, and accessible branches. It may not always be possible to see if a rub is fresh or not, but scrapes—bare patches of ground, pawed out by a buck's front hooves—containing fresh prints are a sure sign that bucks are in the area. The scrapes mark out their mating territory.

Two hunters stalking together more than double their separate chances of taking a deer. One hunter should move along the side of the hill, just below the crest, taking care not to break cover; the other should precede him by some 50 to 100 yards (45 to 90 m), but some way down the hill on a parallel course. Deer started from a resting place but not so badly alarmed as to flee headlong downhill, often try to move uphill and around the cause of disturbance before doubling back around it. The

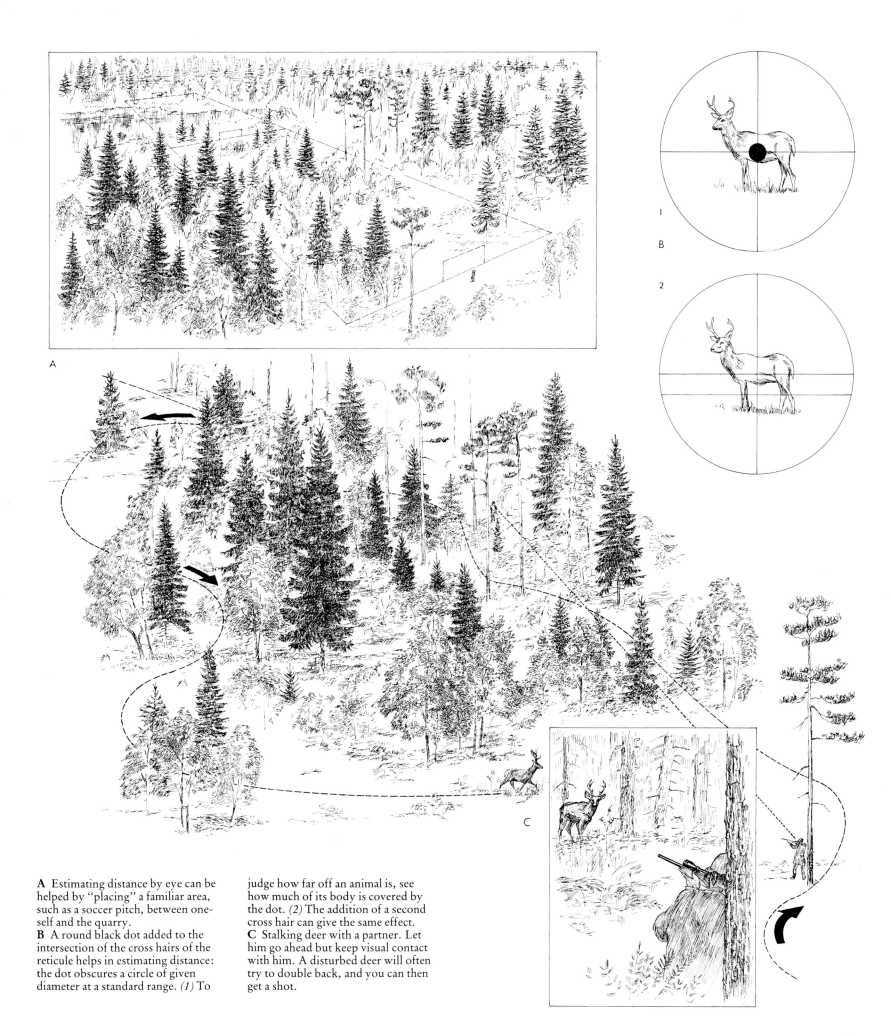

A Estimating distance by eye can be helped by "placing" a familiar area, such as a soccer pitch, between oneself and the quarry.

B A round black dot added to the intersection of the cross hairs of the reticule helps in estimating distance: the dot obscures a circle of given diameter at a standard range. *(1)* To judge how far off an animal is, see how much of its body is covered by the dot. *(2)* The addition of a second cross hair can give the same effect.

C Stalking deer with a partner. Let him go ahead but keep visual contact with him. A disturbed deer will often try to double back, and you can then get a shot.

(Far left) In recent years in the United States, handgunning has come into its own. When shooting with a handgun, forget all the cowboy movies you have seen. In the double-handed grip *(1)*, rest the gunbutt in the palm of your non-shooting hand. *(2)* Shooting from a sitting position, use your knee to steady your aim. *(3)* If you steady your gun on a rock or such-like, place the palm of your non-shooting hand between the butt and the rock.

(Left) Stances for rifle shooting. *(1)* When standing free. *(2)* When sitting. *(3)* When using a tree or suchlike for support, keep the fingers of your non-shooting hand between the tree

and the stock. (Below) Rattling up a whitetail buck is one of the most exciting of hunting methods. The guide rattles a pair of antlers, simulating the sound of bucks fighting over a doe. The quarry approaches to take part in the fight. It is essential that the hunters remain completely hidden until the buck is close enough for a shot. One hint of a trap and he will be gone in a flash.

upper of the two hunters will have a good chance of getting in a shot, even if his companion will not; for obvious reasons, each should have an exact knowledge of where the other is.

Something of an elaboration on this is the use of the high seat or tree stand, a method much used in Europe and popular also for whitetail in parts of Texas. Some high seats are very much more than mere rough platforms in trees; those in Europe may even be equipped with heaters. High seats keep the scent of the hunter well off the ground; they also place him above the usual level of observation of deer, with the exception of red deer. A further advantage of a high seat is that the trajectory of shots fired from it is generally downward, so that bullets that miss their targets are most likely to expend their energy in the earth.

Deer are also hunted by means of drives. A simple drive involves no more than a single gun and two or three drivers; an elaborate one, with many guns and drivers, properly requires almost military precision. The more drivers, the better the results, if care is taken to work the deer slowly and quietly, so that they break cover at hardly more than a slow walk. Does and yearlings usually show themselves first; the bucks hang back, sometimes trying to sneak past a stand. This sort of driving is much used in Europe for shooting wild boar.

One of the advantages of a drive is that the participants need not know the country intimately; they need a reasonable sense of direction, and a guide who knows the terrain well enough to ensure that areas are driven that actually contain deer. Short drives, of perhaps not more than about half a mile, or one kilometer, are more effective than longer ones.

Two or three hunters who are used to hunting together sometimes organize a still-hunt over country they all know well. Agreeing in advance to converge simultaneously on a given point, each of the hunters should be able to get a number of chances of shots at animals moving away from the disturbance.

In the southern United States and in Ontario in Canada, hounds are used to drive whitetail deer past hunters on stands; this is the only effective way to hunt them in thick swamps and forest. When shot at, the animals are nearly always moving at close range (30 to 40 paces); for this reason, shotguns loaded with buckshot are used in the United States; in Ontario, however, most hunters use rifles.

A particular method of luring whitetail bucks has been successfully developed in the southwestern United States, especially in Texas. It involves the use of a pair of whitetail deer antlers, which the hunter clashes together to simulate the noise made by two bucks fighting over a doe, so as to lure another buck to the scene. This method can be practiced with any chance of success only in the rut. The hunter should conceal himself well, usually on the edge of a thicket; some hunters mask their own scent in the odor of skunk glands, which can be purchased or prepared at home.

Whitetail deer have been introduced into Czechoslovakia and Finland. In the first of these countries, they are not too abundant but provide limited hunting; the usual method is to take up stands along game trails. In Finland, they are doing very well and have become second in number only to the moose (or European elk); the most popular, indeed virtually the only, method of hunting them is the drive, which is conducted very much as in the eastern United States.

A diminutive form of the whitetail, called Coues deer, occurs primarily in the southwest of the United States and just over the border in Mexico, in the state of Sonora. Another relatively small deer of the American west is the blacktail, a small subspecies of mule deer.

In the mule-deer country of the West, the mountains and hills have broken patches of pine, fir, and aspen, usually growing on the shadier sides of draws (shallow ravines); the patches of trees are interspersed with low grass, sagebrush, and isolated clumps of head-high chaparral and chokeberry bushes, which can be as extensive as a city block.

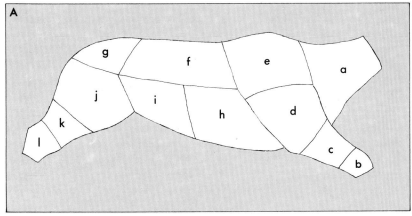

A

B

C

D

A Cuts for butchering. *(a)* Neck gives ground meat. *(b)* Knee: good only for your dog. *(c)* Shank: stews or ground meat. *(d)* Knuckle: roast. *(e)* Shoulder: roast or steaks. *(f)* Loin: chops or steaks. *(g)* Rump: roasts. *(h)* Ribs: roasts or stew. *(i)* Flank: steaks or stew. *(j)* Round: steaks. *(k)* Shank: stew. *(l)* Hock: throw it away or give it to your dog.

B, C Two ways to move a carcass. The first employs a hitch around the muzzle once the line has been secured to the horns. The other requires a stout canvas sheet secured to a pole.

The animal is placed on the sheet, and its head or antlers are secured to the pole.
D Once in camp, the deer should be gutted and hung up to cool.
The carcass should be held open—thin sticks can be cut to size—to speed up the cooling.
E When field-dressing a deer, some hunters remove the metatarsal glands *(a)*; others simply take care not to touch them. The first essential cut is between the genitals *(b)* and the base of the rib cage *(c)*: the cutting edge of the knife is held upward, so as to

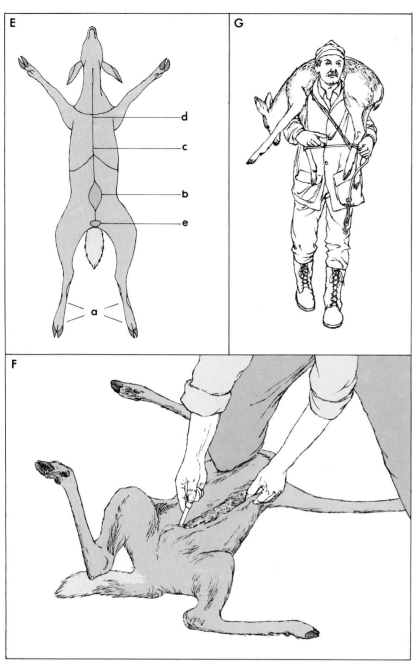

avoid puncturing the intestines. Once this cut is made, the intestines and stomach begin to bulge out. They can be gently removed, being attached to the walls of the stomach cavity only by delicate tissue which can easily be severed with a knife. It is not necessary to open the rib cage (although it can be done with a light ax).
The windpipe and the esophagus can be reached and severed as close to the animal's head as possible (d). Then all the viscera can easily be removed together. The genitals (b) and anus (e) are then detached by a series of rela-

tively deep cuts around them, care being necessary lest the bladder or anal canal be punctured.
F The latter part of gutting is done straddling the carcass, facing away from the animal's head.
G Relatively light deer can be carried on the hunter's shoulders. "Flag" the animal's horns, lest some unobservant hunter take a shot at the head.
H Even a relatively big and heavy animal can be hoisted up with a light block-and-tackle.

Just after daybreak, and in the evening when the hills begin to cool off, mule deer can be seen respectively going to and leaving cover. A hunter with binoculars can observe a wide area and can try either to stalk or intercept a deer, or mark where it has bedded down, and go there later, with the wind in his favor, to try to jump it. Particularly the old, wise bucks frequently bed down just below ridges of hillsides and canyons, whence they can keep watch for their traditional enemies—wolves and coyotes—which, like inexperienced hunters, approach from the valleys. An experienced hunter uses the high ground.

A single hunter or, better, a pair of hunters, should slowly and carefully work into every clump of cover, out of which a disturbed muley will usually try to escape uphill. A variation is for the hunters to stalk around each clump, and for the man uphill to throw stones into the cover; the deer will often try to get away downhill.

In some parts of the West, there are forests, and driving methods can be used there. Small wooded valleys and brushy canyons can be effectively driven by only three or four hunters. In larger expanses of woods, still-hunting, such as is used for whitetail, is a good method. Blacktail deer, being a forest form of the mule deer, can be hunted in this way. In the rain forests of the Pacific coast, which are usually too thick to permit clear shots, the hunter should remain near openings, such as meadows, fire-clearings, logged-over areas, and logging and access roads; these generally contain shrubs and small trees, and blacktail deer emerge to browse there early in the morning and late in the afternoon. Taking a stand by a game trail is effective, too.

Hounds may be legally used to drive deer in some western states, but not all; the methods are similar to those used in the southern states. The hunters take up their positions on forest roads, ridges, or game trails.

Pronghorn are very numerous in the western part of North America and can be stalked, once they have been observed, for example, through binoculars from a high ridge. They are not only very wary but very fleet of foot, too, being capable over short distances of speeds in the order of 60 mph (100 km/h). For these reasons, shots are usually taken at long range; rifles must be very accurately adjusted and equipped with a 4× or even 6× telescopic sight.

A good rifle for deer in the forests of eastern North America should be light and handy for quick shooting. The caliber is unimportant, but the larger calibers—.30 and up—are better when shooting through brush.

A good rifle for mule deer should be relatively flat-shooting, for shots can be long compared with those for whitetail deer. Any caliber from .243 to .30 is a good bet. Many hunters like the flat-shooting .25–06 and the .270. The 7×64 would be an excellent choice; so would the new 7mm Remington express.

Pronghorns are generally shot at long range, and a high-velocity cartridge with a flat trajectory is needed. Anything from .243 or 6mm to a .300 Magnum is a good choice. Calibers such as the .25–06, .270, and 7mm Remington are probably best. [JK]

Elk, Moose, and Caribou

Three more outstanding game animals in North America are the American elk, or wapiti; the moose, which is known as the elk in Scandinavia; and the caribou, which is also familiar as the reindeer. The elk and the moose are lovers of undisturbed country; the caribou is a sub-arctic species, occuring at high latitudes all round the northern hemisphere, where it roams the treeless or almost treeless tundra.

Hunting caribou is not technically difficult. Especially in remote areas, where hunting rarely takes place, the animals tend to be inquisitive and may even approach a hunter. The best method of spotting them is to use binoculars from the crest of a hill or ridge. In Newfoundland, hunters out after woodland caribou walk through the forest and glass the flat expanses of muskeg barrens. The forest animals are generally more wary

Hunting mule deer in the southwestern part of the United States. On typical terrain of the sort depicted, a simple drive can be organized by two or three hunters. One of the hunters moves slowly down a canyon. At the end, the other two have taken stands. If there are deer there, they will move toward the hunters. The young deer and does usually comes first, while the stag hangs back cautiously. It is important that the driver goes slowly, so that the deer are moving at not more than walking pace. Sometimes, the driver can get a shot at the stag, especially if it tries to double back.

than those living on more open ground. The method of getting within range of any sort of caribou is a stalk, using available cover, and working upwind toward the animal.

Any moderately powered rifle, from .270 up to .300, preferably with a scope sight of moderate power, is suitable for caribou. The woodland animals weigh up to 400 lb (180 kg), those of the arctic tundra less than half this, but caribou flesh is probably the best venison of all in North America. It is superior to that of the elk, but the hunting provided by elk more than compensates for that.

Elk are animals of the deep wilderness and readily move away from disturbing noise; when hunting elk, therefore, it is important to keep noise to a minimum. Despite their fondness for quiet, however, bull elk in rut emit loud, unmistakable bugling or high-pitched trumpeting calls, almost a cross between a squeal and a deep whistle; they start on a low note and go up by overtones through four steps, before descending the scale again. The volume increases with the pitch; the crescendo is a deafening screech. Bulls challenge each other by this means, much as red deer stags do by roaring; individual animals are attracted to the source of the noise, especially if it comes from some point downhill. These habits have given rise to the hunting art of elk calling.

The hunter calls either to locate bulls, from their responses to his imitation of their calls, or to attract them. In the first case, he positions himself on a ridge in a likely area, whence he can hope actually to see the answering animals, once he has a line on them. The best time is early on a frosty morning. Calling to attract bulls is best done from some relatively low-lying position, ideally at the edge of a small meadow or by an opening in trees, where the hunter can sit comfortably with his rifle ready, yet be reasonably well hidden. Then, he utters a call and waits for replies. It is important not to call too frequently, but to maintain a tempo—with the answering animal or animals—that keeps up the excitement. Some bulls, however, will approach quite silently, and the hunter must therefore have his eyes about him, for one may appear without warning.

Elk calls can be bought in many sporting-goods stores or can be made by the hunter; a ½-inch (1 cm) conduit pipe or bamboo of the same dimension is good. A piece about 12 inches (30 cm) is the right length. The call is really just a big whistle. Bamboo gives a more mellow note than metal or plastic, but elk are attracted by calls from instruments of any material.

Elk provide challenging hunting for those whose woodcraft enables them to move silently in heavy forest. Once an elk has been spotted through binoculars, the hunter must keep his scent away from the animal, for elk are keen-nosed as well as sharp-eared. When spooked, an elk clears out at once, unlike a whitetail deer, which may try to sneak round a hunter before returning to where it was.

As a bull elk is a big, tough animal, the hunter needs a rifle of at least .270 or 7mm caliber, but the more powerful .30 calibers, such as the .30–06 or the various .300 Magnums, are probably even better.

Moose are even bigger than elk and, as they have different habits, hunting them requires slightly different methods. In North America, especially in the remote regions, a moose that evades a hunter is very likely to get away. As moose are good swimmers, they can cross lakes and streams which the hunters cannot. Moose are stalked in North America, but they are even more wary than whitetail, and noises or scents that make them nervous cause them to move off at once. In the West, where their terrain is more open than in the East, they can be spotted at a distance and approached, perhaps at first on horseback, then in a stalk. In winter, when they are very much slowed down by deep snow, they can be hunted by those who can use snowshoes; even if moose tracks cannot be found, the noises made as moose break down saplings while feeding— the noises sound like pistol shots—indicate where the moose are, and an

In the early part of the rutting season, a wapiti bull can give away its position by the noise it makes when rubbing off the last of the velvet or when staging mock battles with saplings or bushes. The guide lures it into the open by issuing a challenging call with his wapiti whistle, cupping his palm over the end of the whistle to control volume and tone. The bull often reacts aggressively to the call and comes out into the open, looking for a fight. When the animal is within range, the hunter, who has been examining it through binoculars to establish if it is worth taking, can take a shot at it.

Bugling wapiti is an art that goes back to the early American Indians. A hunter should train at bugling before trying it out, as it must not be done too often or too low; this can scare the wapiti off. Normally, it is best to leave the bugling to the guide.

A typical drive for moose (European elk) in Sweden, where over 100,000 moose must be shot annually. The shooters are positioned at numbered stands. Before the hunt, the arc of fire for each stand is marked and cleared of hindering vegetation. When moose are disturbed, they make for swamps or heavily wooded cover, and they normally move downwind, to keep track of where their pursuers are. The drivers, positioned between 50 and

100 yards (45 and 90 m) apart, move the animals along slowly, for if the moose become scared, they can move at such a pace that there will be no chance of a killing shot. Here, the hunter on stand 12 has a clear shot at the cow (the team will have been allotted a certain quota of stags, cows, and calves). (Below) Wounded moose are tracked down by specially bred and trained hounds.

72

(Top right) Getting the carcass out of the woods is no easy job, and the team of drivers and hunters have often to lend a hand at getting the animal to where it can be butchered. Horse- or tractor-drawn sleds are sometimes used, too.

73

approach upwind is often successful. With these exceptions, the method that is most effective is the oldest. North American Indians long ago learned how to call moose, and the art is still very much alive today.

Two types of call are used, one to imitate a bull in rut, the other, a cow in heat. Many sportsmen have learned these from Cree and Ojibway Indians. While most guides still use birch bark and spruce-root thongs to make their calling megaphones, equally effective ones can be made from stiff paper. A prosaic way to learn to make the right noises is to buy and imitate a record or tape; these are sold in sporting-goods stores.

The functions of the two calls, in the field, are to challenge a bull (the bull call) or to entice him (the cow call). The latter works, naturally enough, only for a bull in rut without a cow; the former may induce any bull, even one with a cow, to set off to challenge the supposed intruder. After calling only a few times and only relatively softly—novices often call too frequently and too loudly—the hunter listens some ten or fifteen minutes before calling again. If a moose answers, a soft call is a much more effective response than a loud one. A wrong note at any time can ruin the effect. A moose will not approach even the most seductively calling hunter from downwind. Sometimes, moose content themselves with answering without moving out of cover, or begin to move and then stop or turn aside.

Many hunters believe that calling works only in the eastern parts of North America, but this is unjustified, for it works well with western moose, too. Even if there are some openings in the woods of eastern Canada—for example, in Ontario, Quebec, and northern Manitoba, there are cutovers, old forest-burns, and marshes—the country is generally too thick for stalking, and so calling is very much in favor. In the western part of Canada, the country is open enough to permit still-hunting or stalking, and guides seldom call moose. [JK]

European Elk in Scandinavia

Elk shooting in Scandinavia is carried out in the fall. In Sweden, a complicated system of licensing ensures that seasonal differences between the north and the south of the country are not overlooked, and that the rights of landowners and of the owners of hunting rights are balanced against the national policy of preserving the ecosystem of the elk. The season in both Norway and Sweden provides, in effect, a national cull. The numbers of animals—bulls, cows, and calves—that may be shot in each administrative area are calculated; hunters who exceed their permitted totals land in trouble.

In both countries, the visiting hunter is not exempt from a requirement that each hunter must demonstrate his or her abilities with a rifle suitable for the game to be hunted. The formalities are not great, and an experienced shot will have no trouble in passing this test.

The different methods of hunting relate to the size of the area being hunted: in areas that are relatively small, dogs are kept on the leash. In larger areas, the dogs are slipped. Whoever possesses a good elk dog is able to pick and choose his hunting, for finding and tracking elk with a single dog is the classic method of hunting in Sweden, and a good dog and his owner will always be welcome. Sometimes, two or more dogs are used in very much the same manner. A dog is virtually essential in tracking a wounded elk.

The method used in a large area is to slip the dog and let it range back and forth in front of the hunter or hunters until it picks up a scent. A well-trained dog will often sniff the wind from some high point, such as a rocky outcrop, whence it may also catch sight of its quarry. Some dogs are uncanny in their ability to detect the sounds made by an elk. A dog must be able to keep silent when it picks up the scent of an elk. If the quarry gets frightened or startled, it will run off, and the hunter, if not his dog, will have trouble keeping up. But a good dog can bring an elk to bay and, when this happens, the sound and tone of its barking informs the hunter of what is happening and where. A shot might be taken at up to 100 yards (90 m).

Some hunting is done without dogs, in the manner of North American still-hunting (stalking). This requires sound woodcraft and is a method that is effective at dawn and dusk. Sometimes, high seats are used, and care must be taken to make them inconspicuous.

Driving elk is popular and much practiced, especially in southern Sweden, where extensive areas can be driven. When shooting stands are determined in advance, it is prudent to cut vegetation that may obscure the hunter's sight in directions giving onto likely target areas, and to mark the arcs of fire that are forbidden, as a grouse shooter might do on first entering his butt before a drive begins.

Two problematical matters in Sweden, particularly for hunters in smaller areas, are wounded animals that cross boundaries into other, neighboring hunting areas, and the shooting of more animals than have been permitted by license. The second of these often troublesome events can be guarded against by the use of an unambiguous system of signaling between hunters, sometimes by means of multiple shots; walkie-talkie radios are perhaps more reliable. National regulations require hunters to track down and despatch any wounded animal. For this reason, prudent hunters cease shooting some time before sunset, the legal close of the day, for tracking can take a very long time. This is one reason why responsible hunters shoot only when confident of being able to kill the animal.

When an elk is hit in the central nervous system, it falls at once. A heart shot will drop it within ten or fifteen seconds and so will a lung shot, but this margin of time may be quite enough for the animal to vanish from the sight of the hunter and pose problems of tracking. A shot in some other relatively vital area—the liver, for example—may well kill the animal after some minutes, when it has sought and found shelter; if not immediately pursued, this is where instinct will take it. The problem for the hunter, and his companions if he is not alone, is to find it. Over and above the legal requirement to do so, the excellent meat the animal provides spoils unless it can be taken care of without delay; this is an urgent matter in warmish weather.

A wounded animal should be given time to find shelter because, once it has begun to rest, the effects of shock progressively weaken it, making it less and less able to get up and get away. An hour's delay is enough. The time must be spent examining the terrain where the animal was hit; the hunter must be able to ascertain what kind of wound it has and where it went afterwards. If the wound is only light, a trail may have been left on tree trunks, bushes, or on the ground. A tracking dog is of very great help, but it must be so well-trained that it will follow only the scent of the wounded beast, and not that of any other elk it may encounter. It should be kept leashed, lest it find the carcass of the shot beast, give no audible sign of its find, and then go on to look for something of greater interest.

Elk hunters in Sweden generally use medium-caliber rifles—6.5×55, for example—in part because it is customary to do a lot of practice shooting before the season begins, and ammunition of this caliber is relatively inexpensive. Hunters in North America might regard such a rifle as on the lighter side; most knowledgeable hunters would not recommed the .270, for example, except for a shooter who had problems with recoil. The 7mm Magnum, with a heavily constructed bullet of 175 grains (11 g), is a better bet than the old faithful .270. The .308 Magnum or, if the hunter can handle them, one of the .338s or .350 Magnums would be an excellent tool for elk hunting. Such rifles weigh about 10 lb (4.5 kg), or about twenty-five percent more than a .270, but they provide the power to get the job done. [RE]

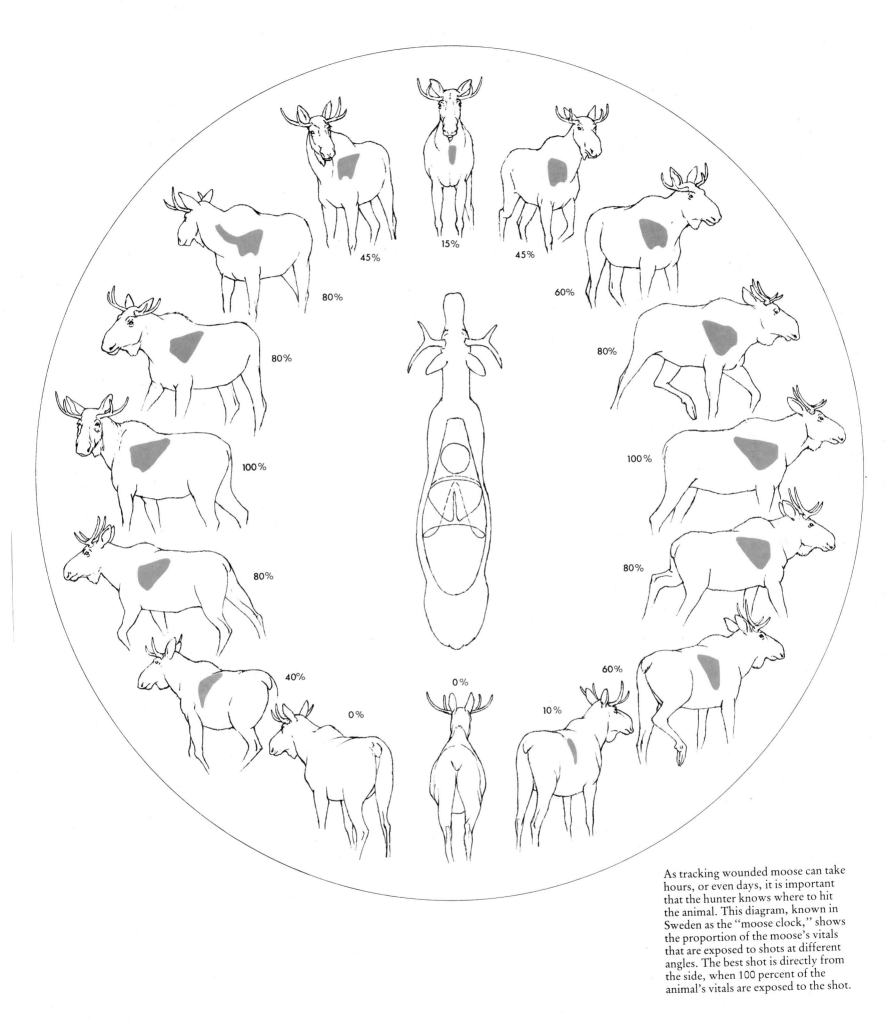

As tracking wounded moose can take hours, or even days, it is important that the hunter knows where to hit the animal. This diagram, known in Sweden as the "moose clock," shows the proportion of the moose's vitals that are exposed to shots at different angles. The best shot is directly from the side, when 100 percent of the animal's vitals are exposed to the shot.

Wild Sheep and Goats

The high mountain ranges of Europe and western North America afford hunting that is as demanding and, physically, perhaps even more rigorous than deer stalking in Scotland. The quarry are the wild sheep and goats of North America, the chamois, which is a relative of the mountain goat of British Columbia, southern Alaska, and the Yukon, and the rare mouflon, or wild sheep, that has been introduced from its native Corsica and Sardinia to the mainland of Europe, and thence to the Hawaiian island of Lanai.

The method of approaching to within range of any of these animals is the stalk, although some hunters use a four-wheel-drive vehicle for scouting, or as an aid in stalking; this is, however, unusual and, in some parts of the world, actually illegal. In North America, it is usual to get into the mountains on foot, with the necessary gear carried on pack horses (see Part VI: Hunting Allies). But whatever the means employed to get to the mountains, the hunter needs to be in good physical shape and prepared for a great deal of climbing and walking.

One of the best tactics is to climb to a high vantage point and to glass the surrounding country with binoculars. However, the animals often blend in well with their backgrounds. Brown bighorn sheep, gray Stone sheep, and, in winter, white Dall sheep may not be easy to spot; both chamois and mouflon are dark brown to black. A contrasting background, such as green vegetation, will help, but when the animals are set off against rocks or a stony terrain, particularly if irregularly shadowed, the hunter will need sharp eyes to locate his quarry. It is always possible to begin by glassing from below, before undertaking a climb, but all these animals are keen-sighted; the natural enemies of Dall and Stone sheep—wolves and cougar—usually approach from below, and the animals are sensitive to movement below them. Mouflon are particularly wary, but can be distracted from noticing a hunter and his guide if they inconspicuously leave a vehicle that is then driven off in full view. Chamois are sometimes just as wary, especially in areas where small populations have been subjected to heavy hunting. Where little hunting occurs, such as in the more inaccessible heights, chamois seem not to associate the sight of man with danger.

Once an animal is in sight, the hunter must decide, from a careful scrutiny through binoculars and telescopic sight, if it is a good trophy and, if it is, how he can approach within range of it. His approach route may require mountaineering techniques (with his rifle slung on his back to leave both hands free for climbing), and a scrupulous attention to the avoidance of noises likely to alarm the animal; mistakes can be fatal to the progress of the stalk, to say nothing of the life and limb of the hunter. It can happen that the animal is so placed as to be inaccessible to the hunter, or likely to fall and be lost or broken up when shot; in some parts of the world, it may be possible to induce the animal to move in a helpful direction, for example, by firing a shot so that the bullet strikes a rock to one side of the animal and so causes it to move to the other.

A rifle for sheep hunting should be chambered for a cartridge that drives a bullet at moderately high velocity to achieve a flat trajectory. Such calibers as .25–06, .270, 7mm, .30–06, and any of the Magnums, are good bets. Goats are harder to kill than sheep and nothing under .270 or 7mm is recommended. Rifles for either sheep or goats should be fitted with a scope sight of moderate power.

Excellent American calibers of rifle for the chamois are the .243, .257, .270, and .25–706; for the mouflon, the .270, .308, 7.62mm NATO, and .30–06 are adequate calibers. Fine European calibers for either animal are the 6.5×57, 7×57, 7×64, and 7×65; the 8×57 is satisfactory for the mouflon. Relatively long shots are sometimes called for, because it is not always possible to get as close as might be desirable, particularly to chamois, before taking the shot. [JK, TT]

The mouflon is the only European wild sheep. It is a wanderer by nature, and this and its extreme wariness make it a difficult and challenging animal to hunt. Perhaps the best method is to use a vehicle for scouting and as an aid in stalking. This method of hunting is illegal in some parts of the world but is often used in Europe for taking mouflon. Like many other animals, mouflon have little or no fear of a horse-drawn wagon but will immediately take to flight if they sense a human being. When the mouflon herd is spotted, the hunter and his guide determine if there is a shootable ram among them. If so, they sneak out of the vehicle, which is then driven away, keeping the attention of the animals. The hunter then gets into a shooting position and tries for the ram. The best ram is known as an A-class ram and is at least six years old. Its horns must be at least 24 inches (60 cm) and form a three-quarter curl.

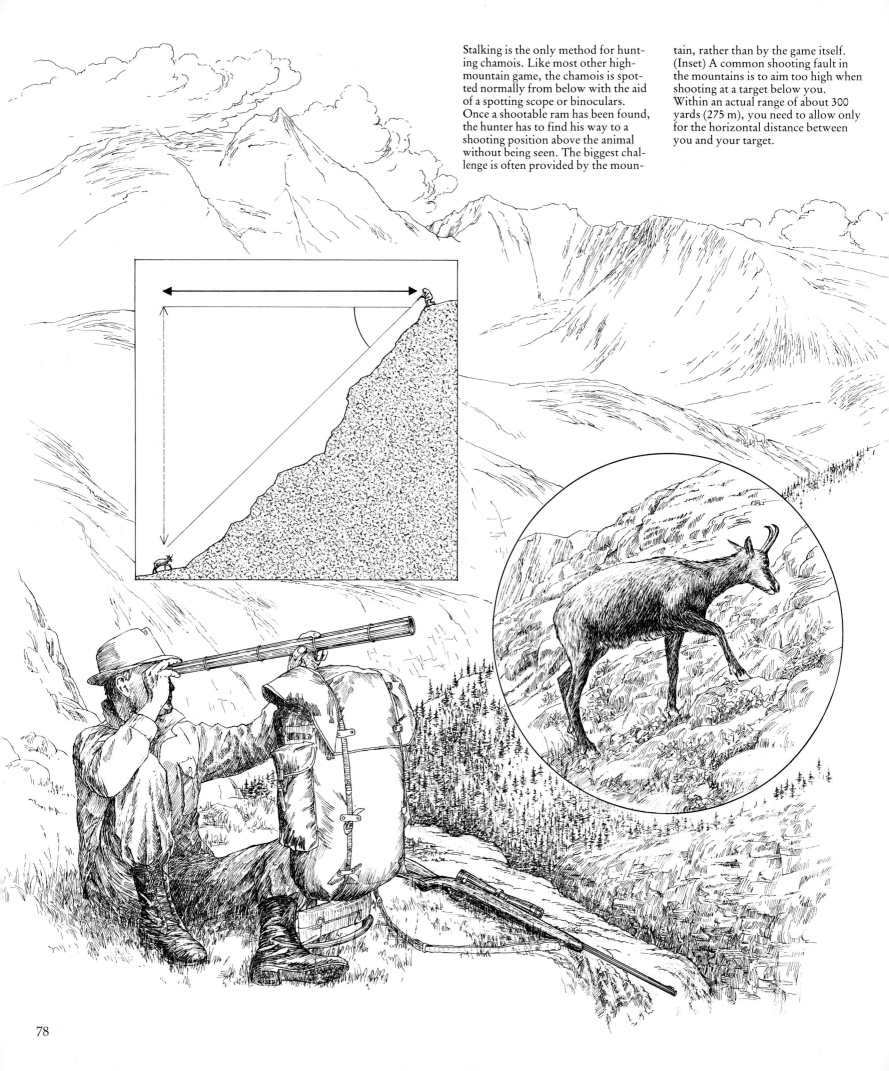

Stalking is the only method for hunting chamois. Like most other high-mountain game, the chamois is spotted normally from below with the aid of a spotting scope or binoculars. Once a shootable ram has been found, the hunter has to find his way to a shooting position above the animal without being seen. The biggest challenge is often provided by the mountain, rather than by the game itself. (Inset) A common shooting fault in the mountains is to aim too high when shooting at a target below you. Within an actual range of about 300 yards (275 m), you need to allow only for the horizontal distance between you and your target.

Bears

In North America, the ranges of the Dall and Stone sheep, and the mountain goat, overlap that of the black bear and, in the Northwest, that of the grizzly. For these bears, the .270 rifle is at the lighter end of the scale; for grizzlies, the .30–06, the 7mm Magnum, the various .300s, the 8mm Remington, and the .338 and .350 Remington are all good; the .358 Norma and the .375 Holland & Holland are even better, provided that the hunter can shoot them accurately, for they afford greater bullet diameter and heavier bullets; still, placing the shot is more important than its size.

Rifles and cartridges for black bears include the old .30–30, which is adequate in the hands of a good rifle shot. Others may prefer more modern cartridges, such as the .270, the .308, and the .30–06, particularly in the West, where ranges can be quite long. In the eastern woods, cartridges such as the .35 Remington and the .358 Winchester are excellent.

Both grizzlies and black bears may be observed by hunters glassing for sheep, goats, moose, or caribou. In the fall, grizzlies may be seen in meadows and on mountain slopes, or near streams, along which numbers of the bears gather to fish for salmon; lesser concentrations of grizzlies gather in berry patches in late summer and fall. Among their other vegetable foods are many different kinds of leaves, sprouts, twigs, roots, and tubers. Grizzlies eat carrion and animals they kill themselves; these include marmots and ground squirrels. On emerging in spring from their winter dormancy, grizzlies feed almost exclusively on green grass shoots and other vegetation.

Black bears love wild berries, fruits, honey (and bees), nuts, and a wide range of other, largely vegetable, foods. They catch and eat fish, too (but not on the same scale as grizzlies), and feed on carrion, such as the carcasses of winter-killed animals. In spring, black bears feed to a very large extent on fresh vegetable growth; later, toward the end of summer and in the fall, they may be expected to be seen on the blueberry barrens of the Midwest and in abandoned orchards anywhere in their range.

Once a bear has been seen and identified as a trophy animal, it must be stalked to within good rifle range. Bears have very keen noses and ears, even if their sight is relatively poor; it is essential for the hunter to work upwind toward the bear as quietly as possible. Open mountain country is ideal for this method; stalking in forests and forest meadows requires more patience. It is literally vital to get as close as possible to the bear, especially to a grizzly, to reduce the chances of merely wounding him; wounded bears have mauled or even killed many guides and hunters.

Both sorts of bear may be shot over bait in those parts of North America where this method is not illegal: baiting for grizzlies with meat or fish is illegal, but natural baits—winter-killed moose, elk, or caribou, or such animals drowned by breaking through river or lake ice—may be used. The trick is to find such carcasses, and to watch them, hoping to see the bear. Offal from animals shot by the hunter may also be used. Baiting for black bear is legal in eastern Canada, in some Rocky Mountains states, and in some northern Great Lakes states, but some hunters might consider the method unsporting, even if legal.

Most of the black bears taken over bait are shot at dusk. The bait is hung in a burlap bag or a metal pail on a tree, just a little too high for a bear to reach it comfortably; the tree should be one just on the edge of thick cover, for old boars—male bears—seldom cross open spaces during the day but will do so at night. The bait should be replenished daily if need be: pork fat or meat scraps are good; rotten meat may attract bears, but they seem to prefer to eat fresh meat; fish is not so good. Scent baits—vanilla extract, aniseed, or peppermint oils, for example—may be used if not illegal.

Hunting over bait requires enough persistence and patience to wait quietly for several hours a day, day after day, hoping to see a bear; a bear will itself watch a bait for half an hour or more before coming to it, frequently circling round, testing the wind, and will not approach more closely if its suspicions are aroused. However well placed the hunter may have been at first, a change in the wind, or movements by the bear, can put him upwind of the bait or the bear, rather than downwind, which is where he wants to be while he is keeping watch. A black bear against a background of dark woods can be difficult to see at twilight, and a scope sight will give the hunter a better chance of placing a killing shot.

The most exciting and sporting method of hunting black bears is with hounds, a tradition developed primarily in the hill country of the southern United States, where the hound tradition is still strong. There are now fine packs of bear hounds, some private, and some available for the clients of commercial outfitters, in many parts of the United States.

The classic method is simple: the hounds are taken to good bear country, and, when they find a fresh trail, they are let loose to chase the bear. The hunters follow. When the bear is brought to bay—usually against a fallen tree, in thick brush, or by an upturned stump or a rocky outcrop—he stands his ground and fights off the hounds, frequently mauling or killing some of them, until the hunters close in, from upwind, to take a shot. This is the method used in Finland and Russia. Winter hunting of bears in their dens is still practiced in Russia but is illegal in many areas of North America.

In the old days, all this was done on foot, over forest trails or even directly through the forests in bear country. This has given way to the use of a pick-up truck, driven on logging or forest access roads, sometimes with the keen-nosed strike hound riding on the hood and baying when it scents a bear. Another hound or two may be used to test the trail and, if it is fresh enough, the pack is released from the back of the truck, where they have been confined. Following the pack on foot, carrying a rifle, is not a sport for unfit hunters.

A modification of this method is used in areas where there are many roads through likely country. Hunters take up their positions at stands in a forest that is believed to contain bears; the stands are always placed at the ridgetops or ravines overgrown with brush, which bears would probably cross. Two or three hunters walk with the hounds and, if they put up a bear, their fellows who are waiting may get a chance for a fast shot at the moving bear.

Most black bears, however, are not shot in front of hounds but incidently, so to say: a bear disturbed by hunters may amble into sight of a perhaps surprised deer hunter waiting on a stand with a rifle loaded just for deer.

Polar bears, having been hunted to excess from aircraft off the coast of Alaska, are subject to the United States Marine Mammals Protection Act, which makes illegal in the United States the hunting of, or importation of trophies from, polar bears (and other marine animals). Very restricted hunting, with the help of the Eskimo of northern Canada and their sled dogs, is still available to sportsmen prepared to undergo the rigors and dangers of hunting polar bears on foot on the ice. Because of the restrictions in the United States, this is of greater interest to Canadian and European hunters. [JK]

Wild Boar

Another "international" game animal occuring in North America is the wild boar. The hound chase is the most exciting way to hunt boar and is similar to bear hunting with hounds. Hunters are posted at points where boar may cross ahead of the hounds; the hounds are used to find and follow a fresh track. Like bears, wild boar can be brought to bay by hounds, but a pursuit can last for several days. In Florida, hounds are used to bring hybrids—razorbacks, as they are called—to bay so that one hunter or more may actually catch the animal, which is then taken off to be penned and fattened before being slaughtered.

(Above) In Europe, wild boar are tracked and driven in winter, when there is snow. Tracks *(a)* are noted leading into an area surrounded by country roads. As no tracks emerge, the animals must be in there. Drivers *(b)* enter the area. Hunters *(c)* take up stands at intervals of about 100 yards (90 m) and the boar are shot as they emerge. The hunter must never shoot into the area being driven or before the boar has cleared the line of hunters.

(Above) Boar can very quickly destroy a field of vegetables, so they are not the most popular animals with farmers. When boar are feeding in cultivated areas, they are hunted by night from portable high seats. Here, a seat has been erected in a field of sugar beet.

(Left) Boar hounds are used to hunt in the United States. A typical situation is illustrated diagrammatically here. The hounds are released where the road crosses a stream *(a)*, which flows through a valley covered with brush and trees. The hounds track upstream, and hunters *(b)* wait at the foot of the ridges enclosing the valley or where streams meet *(c)*.

Still-hunting, however, has become the most common way of hunting wild boar in many areas. The animals are most active at dawn and dusk, when they feed out in the open. As when hunting deer, the hunter must walk slowly, working upwind, for wild boar have a very keen sense of smell and sharp hearing. He must stop frequently to look and listen. He must concentrate his efforts in areas where there are plenty of signs of wild boar, such as tracks and droppings, fresh mud wallows, and rootings in the earth for roots and tubers. It is a good idea to look for such indications before starting the actual hunt; waterholes and other places where the boar drink are rewarding places to look.

Two typically European methods of hunting boar are driving and using a high seat. The latter method is often employed at night, using a portable seat that can be moved to fields where wild boar have been observed. Further equipment, in addition to a rifle, includes binoculars suitable for night use—usually the heavy but effective 8×56—and a telescopic sight with good light-gathering qualities. Again, the 8×56 with a coarse reticule is most desirable, if not actually essential.

Driving is often employed in winter after snowfall, for it is then relatively easy to track boar to specific areas so as to drive them out. Because wild boar are nomadic, one must be certain that there are boar in an area before driving it. The success of a drive depends on having beaters who know their business and can be relied upon to beat through thickets where boar may be lying. The hunters, too, must understand the rules: for instance, never to shoot into the area being driven but to wait until a boar has run through the line of hunters before shooting.

Drives can take different forms. In the more elaborate, each hunter takes up his place by a numbered stand and stays there until the drive is over; especially in Germany, where hunting methods are highly developed, the hunter will need to be familiar with the system of signaling by hunting-horn when a hunt is to begin and end, when shots may be taken, and when they may not. Walkie-talkie radios may be used instead but lack the panache of the horn.

A circle drive, as its name suggests, entails encircling an area with a ring of hunters alternating with beaters at distances apart of perhaps 20 to 50 yards (or meters), depending upon the type of country being driven. The circle may have a diameter of up to 1 mile (1.6 km). In major hunts, with between seventy-five and a hundred hunters, each must clearly understand when shooting is permitted into the circle, and when not. In this form of drive, the hunter must be prepared for all sorts of game, both four-footed and feathered. In its final stages, only the beaters converge on the center of the circle. The hunters remain at some prearranged distance, and shots are taken only when animals have passed through the line of guns.

Wild boar are heavyset, muscular animals but do not require an exceptionally heavy rifle. The .270, the .30–06, and the .308 are all adequate; European cartridges include the 7×57, 7×65, 8×57, and any of the 9.3mm loadings. Some European hunters prefer a *Drilling*—a three-barreled gun, usually with side-by-side shotgun barrels over a rifle barrel—loaded with two shotgun slugs for close-range shots, and a rifle bullet for one at longer range. At short ranges, the shotgun slug is most effective for boar.

Wild boar are also hunted in Asia and Africa (where other sorts of wild pig are to be found), while the collared peccary, known as the javelina, occurs southward from the southwestern United States through Central America, and southward again into much of South America. [TT]

Collared Peccary (Javelina)

Javelina can be hunted by one or more of the methods used for wild boar. The wise hunter, intending to hunt over a particular area, will go out before the season begins and look for fresh signs such as tracks and droppings, or for a waterhole used by these little desert pigs. When hunting, he can wait by the waterhole, if he is patient, but still-hunting is perhaps more appealing and more productive. The hunter must move slowly along the edges of brush patches or scrub forests and surprise the pigs in the open. They congregate in herds, and one or two animals are always on the alert; getting close to a herd is not easy. Planning his stalk carefully, the hunter works upwind toward it, avoiding dry, noisy brush and undergrowth. Sometimes, one disturbs an entire herd in thick cover and suddenly the animals appear on all sides, racing away in different directions.

Javelinas can be hunted with dogs. Unlike wild boar proper, javelinas have no great endurance and are soon brought to bay by well-trained dogs. But javelinas have sharp tusks, and dogs can be injured. Hunting with dogs is not legal in all parts of the United States, however. Rifles for javelinas are of calibers suitable for wild boar; some American hunters have taken to using bows-and-arrows, others again use large-bore handguns, but both should be used only by hunters who are proficient in handling them. [JK]

Chapter 2
Fowling: Upland and Water

Capercaillie

This great grouse holds a position of lofty esteem in the eyes of hunters in central Europe, where it ranks high as a trophy. It is hunted during the spring, when advantage may be taken of its preoccupation with its mating display to approach it. In Scandinavia, however, it may not be shot during the spring, and other methods must be employed to get close enough to shoot it. The capercaillie occurs quite frequently in Scotland but does not excite the same interest as it does on the Continent.

During the mating season in April and May, the hunter must be up early, long before sunrise, if he is to stalk it successfully. Well before the season has begun, hunting guides have ranged the forests and mountains in the areas where capercaillie live. The birds use certain trees year after year for their mating displays and, if one bird is shot, another will take over its tree. About an hour-and-a-half before sunrise, the cock begins his morning serenade, a repeated four-verse call. Although it is normally a very wary bird, with excellent senses of sight and hearing, the capercaillie is vulnerable during the fourth verse of its song. This is a hissing, during which it is to all appearances deaf. The hunter listens for the start of the call: a snapping sound. This is followed by a warbling and then a popping. The hunter can move only when the hissing begins. It lasts for no more than a few seconds, time enough for three or four careful steps. The hunter then "freezes." The bird begins his song again, and the hunter moves again. While he waits, he plans his next move.

Even under the most favorable conditions and with the most well-planned stalk, it may not be possible to get within shotgun range. For this reason, the most suitable gun will be a *Drilling* or some other combination of rifle and shotgun. If a shotgun is used, it should be a 12-bore and loaded with heavy shot, for capercaillie have thick feathers that take a lot of piercing.

On warm, dry days, when the birds have already flown down and begun feeding on the ground, they can be hunted with the help of a pointing dog. If a covey is found, the hen birds are likely to fly up first, cackling as they do so, but the cocks may run before lifting. The dog needs to be a good and fearless retriever, for if a cock is only winged, it is large enough to present quite a challenge.

In the fall and winter, the hunter must use other methods. The birds inhabit woods, where they perch in trees and fly down to feed in stubble fields or on the edges of the woods. Dogs are used in Sweden and Finland; they are trained to find the birds in the woods and to scare them up into the trees; the dog barks and draws the bird's attention from the hunter, who must work himself into position downwind of the bird and take whatever chance offers itself. As when stalking in spring, distances may be so long that only a rifle is suitable. Later, when the ground is frozen, the birds can be stalked and shot. A light-caliber rifle with a telescopic sight is necessary, as the range may be as much as 150 yards (135 m). The birds can be driven, too, if the members of a small party of hunters take turns to drive and shoot. A good retrieving dog is essential. [TT, JMG]

Grouse Shooting in Scotland

The red grouse (*Lagopus lagopus scoticus*) is indigenous only to Britain. It is found largely in Scotland, especially on the drier east side; in Wales; in Derbyshire; occasionally in Devon; and extensively in Lancashire and Yorkshire, which probably provides the cream of the shooting. It has been introduced into the Ardennes in Belgium.

The red grouse does not seem able to survive without a partial diet of young heather shoots, and good moor management includes burning old heather so that the young growth can come up. Such "muirburn" is governed by ancient laws and customs; it is performed in late winter, on a ten- to fifteen-year cycle.

The terrain for grouse is wild, high, and often damp. Grouse share the land with sheep and cattle, and with red deer, blue hare, rabbit, fox, wild cat, and other game birds such as black grouse, ptarmigan, and snipe, but the grouse are the most numerous birds on an average stretch of country. Attempts to rear grouse artificially have always failed. Keepering is concentrated on good heather management and on a ruthless war on vermin, notably stoats, weasels, and foxes.

Grouse are found in coveys of a pair of old birds plus anything up to a dozen young. Late in the season, the coveys amalgamate into packs that can contain a hundred or more birds. Numbers of grouse are said to have increased tremendously since the introduction of driving, which was made possible by the invention of the breechloader and cartridges in the nineteenth century. When grouse are driven toward the butts, the old birds fly in front and get killed off, to the benefit of the younger stock, who are thus rid of quarrelsome and barren oldies.

Grouse shooting is very much of a social sport, with anything between 3 and 100 persons involved at a time. In Scotland and Yorkshire, huge parties assemble in country houses for "the Glorious Twelfth"—12 August, which (unless the day is a Sunday) is when the legal season opens. It closes on 10 December, but little shooting goes on after the end of October. Both sexes of grouse are shot, for it is virtually impossible to distinguish between them on the wing.

There are three principal methods of shooting grouse. Walking up is a gentle and undemanding form of sport normally practiced at the beginning of the season, when the grouse have not yet become afraid of man and will allow the Guns (as the shooters are called) to get within range before getting up. Shooting over dogs is a refined form, now increasing in popularity after some decades of neglect. It gives the additional pleasure of seeing well-trained dogs indicating the whereabouts of the game. Pointers and setters are used, as against labradors and spaniels when walking up.

The best-known method is, perhaps, driving. The Guns stand in wait in butts made of stone or peat or a mixture of the two, while a line of beaters drives great stretches of moorland toward them. There may be half-a-dozen or more drives in a day, and very large bags of grouse may be obtained, the record being 1,464½ brace by eight Guns in Lancashire in 1915. (As with partridges, grouse bags are counted by the brace, while pheasant and most other game go singly; snipe are counted by the couple.) There are no legal bag limits for game in Britain, but a prudent landowner and his gamekeepers would never allow dangerously large bags, lest the following season's population be diminished. This has always been a sporting consideration, but recent increases in the costs of estate management have forced most lairds to regard their shooting as a business. They now let their grouse shooting either to a season-long syndicate or by the week or even by the day to parties of overseas sportsmen. The demand is now for driven grouse, and on a big commercial moor, the gentlemanly few days of walking up are now sacrificed to the start of driving on the Twelfth—a practice simply Not Done before World War II.

The logistics of grouse driving make the same demands on the owner

Grouse shooting—at the butts. The grouse come in fast and low, and the Gun and his loader have their hands full, shooting, loading, and marking the fall of the birds. When he reached his allotted butt, the Gun took careful stock of the surrounding terrain, noting the positions of the other butts and marking a 45° safety angle covering the area within which he will shoot. Some Guns, knowing the tricks of light, especially in the Scottish highlands, pace out 50 yards (45 m) in front of the butt and mark the distance with a stone.

as taking a company of soldiers into battle, even to the extent that bad organization can lead to fatal casualties. The object in driving is to put the greatest possible number of fast-flying grouse over the waiting Guns as many times as possible during the day's sport. On a typical day, there would be eight Guns, and, on a very prolific moor, each would use two guns and be accompanied by a loader. There would be five or six drives, each lasting about an hour. The bag could be around 150 brace, and a Gun would expect to get through 150 cartridges or more. There would be half-a-dozen gamekeepers, and twenty or more beaters.

Before the first drive, the host produces a leather case the size of a playing card, from which protrude a number of ivory or plastic slips. Each Gun draws one and memorizes the number now visible, for it is the number of the first butt he will occupy. Butts are numbered from lowest to highest up the hill or, on level ground, from the right. After each drive, each Gun adds two to his number to identify his next butt: thus, number 3 at the first drive takes butt number 5 at the next; if there are eight Guns, number 7 takes butt number 1 on the next drive, and so on.

Grouse driving, of all forms of shooting in Britain, is the most likely to produce accidents. Once the coveys start arriving, the action is extremely exciting, the light is often poor, the terrain is unfamiliar to most Guns,

In the western United States, sage grouse fly down in the evenings to water holes, ponds, and other expanses of water from the dry hills and mesas. Hunters hide themselves behind haystacks and shoot at the passing birds.

and it may be hard to remember that one or two butts are in a gully out of sight, and that number seven is only 80 yards (75 m) away through that slight haze. The biggest danger is when an inexperienced Gun follows a covey "through the line" and fires when his gun is pointing toward neighboring butts: it is possible for him to bag several fellow-sportsmen, loaders, and spectators with one unforgettable shot—after which he will be required to unload and make his way home. Even swinging through the line, without firing, is considered totally taboo, and the wise Gun raises his barrels almost to the vertical, greatly exaggerating the normal 45° safety rule to show that he is ultra careful, before bringing it down again to take a shot at the departing covey. Guns must avoid the temptation to shoot even at high birds that are directly over the line, since pellets can ricochet and alarm, even if they do not harm, neighboring Guns.

The most skilled Guns make most of their bag in front of the butts, a practice much praised by their host, since a hit in front is nearly always a kill, while a miss is a miss, and leaves no bird wounded. By contrast, hosts look unkindly on Guns who fire one shot in front and another—easier—shot behind at the birds going away, since many pellets find their way into the unarmored rearparts of the birds, making them barren or wounding them, so that they die much later when they do not drop immediately. An expert shot with two guns and a really good loader can drop five or even six birds from a big pack, especially if the birds are flying against a stiff wind.

Near the end of a drive, care must be taken by Guns to see that they mark the distance remaining between the butts and the approaching beaters, and begin to anticipate the flight of the grouse and the likely positions of the coveys at which shots can safely be taken. When the beaters reach the line, the drive is over. All guns should be unloaded and put into their leather or canvas slips to avoid a dog knocking into them, for example, and damaging them. During the pickup, it is better that a wounded bird should get up and escape than that Guns should take urgent and unsafe steps to bring it down while keepers, beaters, Guns, and spectators are scattered everywhere.

In grouse driving, it is accepted practice to count your bag, not to boast of it, but to make sure that all birds are picked up. It would be appropriate to say to a keeper: "I have six still to find." To tell him, "I shot eighteen but have found only twelve," might sound like bragging. It often happens that two neighboring Guns shoot simultaneously at the same bird, which drops dead. There is no quicker way to friendship than to award it to your neighbor. If the drive was very successful, be quick to congratulate host and head keeper on the way the birds were presented.

The bag from your butt is laid out and collected by keepers for transfer to pony or Landrover, and the host usually tells the Guns the total for the drive before moving on to the next. At the end of the day, each Gun is often given a printed card with the totals of the types of game—Grouse, Blackgame, Snipe, Hares, Rabbits, and Various—filled in as a memento of the day.

A moor of the minimum size to provide a day's grouse driving—say 3,000 acres (1,200 hectares)—will need 3 to 6 lines of butts. A large commercial shooting estate, of 200,000 acres (80,000 hectares) or more, may have as many as 100 lines, each consisting of eight or more butts. A great deal of the time of keepers and other estate staff during the close season is spent on building and maintaining butts, especially on moors that are grazed by cattle, which seem to have a natural inclination to destroy butts.

According to the foremost grouse expert in Scotland, Richard Waddington, the ideal butt should be square or rectangular, rather than the normal round shape; a Gun may thus be more likely to keep his sense of direction, by reference to the recognizable corners, during an exciting drive when considerations of safety may be hard to keep in mind. The entrance should be at the side, which enables the butt to be used from either direction. The minimum inside width should be 48 inches (120 cm) and the height from the floor to the top of the wall from 48 to 54 inches (120 to 135 cm); the top turves should be movable to accommodate extra tall or short Guns. Butts can be sunk, semi-sunk, or built entirely above ground. The first type wins for concealment, but such butts are expensive to construct and hard to drain—an hour spent by a Gun in a butt

with water over his shoes spoils the pleasures of even the greatest drive. Butts above ground are cheap to construct but are easily seen by grouse and very easily damaged or even destroyed by cattle. The best compromise is the semi-sunk butt.

The best butts have a rough wooden floor mounted on stakes, a plank seat, and a shelf for cartridges. Peat butts are made from turves 24 by 12 inches (60 by 30 cm) and are about 6 feet (180 cm) deep; all the turves except the two top layers should be laid heather side down. Stone butts are sometimes essential on steep hill faces where the ground is lacking in heather but is covered, instead, with rocks and scree. They last for a long time compared with peat butts; their rims must be covered with earth or peat, however, so as to afford a soft surface on which to rest guns without damage.

The siting of butts is an art in itself. Even on moors where grouse have been driven for 50 or 100 years, perfect butt positions sometimes have to be altered after a farmer has reseeded some old grass or has erected a haystore on the hill. New or altered butt positions should be tried out for a season with a makeshift wall of peat or planks until the success of the new position has been tested. Part of the skill in siting butts lies in the point of view adopted by the constructor: think only of the grouse, do not think of the Guns. The grouse wish to make for a warm and secure resting place, such as a dry, well-heathered hillside. The butts should be sited so as to intercept their line of flight there, being best sited just below the skyline on the side from which the grouse are to be driven. It is apparently tempting to put butts along the bottom of a ravine or gully, but the result is often poor shooting, with the birds in sight and shot for only a second or two, and often so high as to be virtually out of range; this results in a lot of pricked birds with few killed. However, a line of butts across the V of a wide ravine can result in spectacular sport when the birds are driven downhill.

On many moors, particularly in the north of England, that lack the scenic hills of the Scottish highlands, the country is flat or bumpy, and different tactics are used. One highly prolific moor has only one line of butts, in which the Guns face alternately one way and the other, the birds being driven back and forth by two teams of beaters, who receive signals to start by means of a Very pistol.

In planning a day's driving, a good rule is to start with the best drive first, preferably downwind, and arrange to repeat it again as the last drive of the day. In theory, at least, a moor can be worked so as to accumulate the stock from all over the ground as the day goes on, with an increasing number of birds going over the Guns at each drive. It will be apparent, however, that at least one drive on such a day must be taken against the wind, the direction in which grouse are most reluctant to fly. If such a drive can be kept short, there is more of a chance that the birds will not turn back over the beaters' heads and be lost to the Guns. In working out the tactics, it should be borne in mind that grouse at the beginning of the season are unwilling to remain in the air for more than a minute, and not more than a minute and a half at the end of the season.

Beating is not a mechanical business, and Richard Waddington is emphatic that a drive cannot be successful unless the beaters act intelligently; for this reason, he chooses university students as beaters. One beater in a line may, for instance, round a bluff and find himself putting up covey after covey which escapes sideways, there being no other beater in sight. It is best, then, if he furls his flag and sits down until the line on either side has advanced, so as to help to push the grouse forward—where they are wanted. The flag is part of the normal equipment of each beater—a white one, some 2 feet (60 cm) or more across. The line of beaters, which may be nearly 1 mile (1.6 km) in some cases, should be controlled by the head keeper, who stations himself near the middle. On some moors, he is armed with red and green flags for signaling to the flanks; the extreme flanks should be manned by experienced keepers or others who can swiftly remedy mistakes by altering the rate of advance.

Flankers are really specialist beaters whose job is to funnel the birds along the required lines, and agile and intelligent flanking can do more to perfect a drive than any one other factor. When a line of beaters nearly 1 mile (1.6 km) long is trying to drive coveys of grouse toward a line of Guns only some 400 yards (360 m) long, many grouse are likely to pass on either side of the line of Guns, usually on the downwind end of the

When walking up, you form part of a line of anything from three to twelve Guns, with a Gun on each end and a spectator or gamekeeper between each pair of Guns. In warm weather near the start of the season, when the grouse are sitting tight, the people in the line may be only 10 yards (9 m) or so apart—and still be able to walk by a sitting covey crouching invisible in the heather. Later in the season, if walking up is done at all, the birds move out if the people are 50 yards (45 m) apart, and this can give a very long line. Whoever is in charge—host or gamekeeper—should be in the middle of the line and be able to communicate with the flanks either by shouting or whistling, or passing messages. Since grouse favor the face of a hill as a resting spot, the walking line customarily follows the contours of a slope, with the lowest Gun taking his mark from a burn (stream). Since the dogs used are for retrieving only, it is seldom that Guns get advance warning that a covey is about to get up, which may happen just under foot or at medium range. When the Guns are close together, three of them often get a chance to shoot at one covey.

When a bird or birds are shot, the line stops walking without further instructions and waits until the keepers and their dogs have accounted for all the bag. A straight line is essential for the safety of all present, and a host is within his rights to tell a Gun very firmly if he is constantly pushing too far forward or lagging behind. Experienced grouse shots have learned to expect a very large safe angle of fire and are much upset if this is cut down. Bags from walking up are not large—five to ten brace a day per Gun would be perfectly satisfactory.

(Above) When shooting over dogs, the party follows the animals' noses, the dogs being held on very long lines by their handlers. If two dogs make a point at the same covey (a) but from different angles, an exact fix on the birds' location should enable the Guns to be entirely ready for their appearance. Shooting over dogs is most likely to be successful when the approach is made upwind, but, unless the wind shifts during the day, some part of the day's walking will be downwind. Late in the season, or after wet weather, when grouse tend to be easily scared and rise too far out for shooting, it is possible to keep them sitting until the Guns are within range by use of a kite. Given enough wind, one of the keepers moves to the windward of the covey the dogs have pointed, raising a small kite as he walks. While it is hovering over them, the birds are reluctant to fly until the Guns have approached to within a dozen paces or so. Shooting over dogs is for the connoisseur who savors the way in which his quarry is taken, and is less interested in the grand total, which is likely to be smaller than that achieved by walking up.

line. So one stations four to six men there, to lie in the heather, flags furled, with orders to show themselves suddenly with waving flags when a covey would otherwise go wide of the Guns. On occasions, it may be necessary to station flankers directly in front of the line of Guns, particularly when known combinations of wind and terrain have in the past allowed covey after covey to escape without being shot at. Here, the Guns must be particularly careful and alert, making sure that they know where each flanker is, and that they do not shoot in their direction. Flankers are most useful when working at the foot of slopes rather than on the tops of hillocks, where they often ineffectually station themselves, as grouse do not fly over, but rather round, hills.

Dress for grouse shooting is largely a matter of camouflage, and, in the opinion of most Guns, there is nothing to beat tweed. The special color known as heather mixture is a little too dark, and a lighter color is normally better. The kilt is often worn by those entitled to it, but it can have its awkward moments. The writer's grandfather and his two brothers once had to cross a stone dyke topped by barbed wire and, as they jumped down, a sudden gust of wind swirled up their tartans so that all three caught up behind. Since all three men were dressed, so to say, as Scots traditionally are, the keeper who was required to unhitch them was greeted by a strange sight. Those whose everyday business is on the hill—the gamekeepers—universally wear knickerbockers, and there is no more practical garment for the job. The best approach to the feet is to assume that they will get wet in any form of grouse shooting and to wear stout shoes with tackets (studs) in the soles. Walking through the abrasive stems of heather is extremely tough on shoes or boots, and toecaps soon wear through. Some kind of waterproof coat is essential: in the Scottish highlands, even the bluest sky can turn to mist or rain within an hour. A hat is essential, too, for a head, especially a bald one, can spoil the sport for the rest of the party.

Normal side-by-side 12-bore ejector shotguns are almost universally used. An automatic would certainly be frowned on and, in any case, would get far too hot during a hectic drive. Over-and-under guns are thought to take longer to reload because of the greater distance that must be traversed to load the lower barrel. Bores smaller than 12 are sometimes favored by those walking grouse, on the score of lightness, but for driving, it is hard to beat the killing power of the 12-bore. A leather or canvas full-length slip is a great advantage in avoiding damage to guns in Landrovers and other vehicles. For cartridges, modern thought suggests that 1 ounce (28 g) of shot will be perfectly satisfactory, particularly as today's crimp closure of cartridges is much more efficient than the former style of disk closure. Certainly, for anyone at a good day's driving and shooting 300 or more times, it will be far less fatiguing and headache-inducing to fire 1 ounce (28 g) than $1\frac{1}{8}$ ounce (32 g).

Other equipment includes, for walking up, a cartridge belt holding 20 or 25, although many traditional Scottish sportsmen still carry a dozen cartridges loose in each jacket pocket. A leather or canvas bag holding 100 is desirable, especially if someone else can be persuaded to carry it, for it weighs over 10 lb (4.5 kg) when full. A canvas game bag is necessary if you are shooting by yourself or on a small informal shoot lacking a keeper. For driving grouse, it is a good idea to carry a shooting stick, which aids the unfit up hills, when folded, and opens out to provide a rest for the legs when at the butts. Many Guns carry a plastic or paper chart marked in concentric circles, on which they can mark any prominent features around their butt, such as rocks or clumps of heather, and then pencil in the fall of their birds as they occur.

While grouse shooting has recently become a most expensive business if done on a full scale, there do exist a number of hotels in second- or third-class grouse country, whose guests can get permission to walk a moor with the chance of getting a brace or so by the end of the day. On an organized shoot, it would be a mistake to assume that the Gun may take home all the birds he shoots, for lairds nowadays rely on the sale of grouse to recoup part of the costs of running their moors, and a brace of birds per guest is the standard to take home; two brace would be extra generous.

The occasional sportsman may have the problem of tipping the keeper adequately but not over-adequately, and the best advice by far is to consult an experienced fellow-sportsman about the right amount, and whom to give it to. As with all such situations, of course, the most important thing is the warmth of your handshake and the thanks you give along with your money. [JMG]

Grouse in North America

Many North American hunters feel there is no finer shooting than for grouse in the woodlands. Fall is a special time for all hunters, but for hunters after forest grouse, it is extra-special. There are three North American species of forest grouse, the ruffed grouse, the blue grouse of the western forests, and the spruce grouse of the coniferous northern forests.

The ruffed grouse has acquired the disparaging name of "fool hen" in remote wilderness areas where it is little hunted and has no fear of man; offering little challenge, it is, when sitting, an easy target. Further south, by contrast, it has lost this innocence and flushes explosively with a thunderous whirring of wings. One needs lightning-fast reflexes to get off a shot before a ruffed grouse has vanished into the trees or disappeared in thick cover.

Ruffed grouse prefer edge cover near forest openings and young forests that are still in their early stages of growth. Plenty of saplings and brush are the keys to good habitat. The bird feeds on a variety of fruits, berries, grasses, and wild clover, which is primarily found in young forests and along the forest edges. Winter is the critical time for ruffed grouse, when their major foods are buds of white willow, catkins of hazel, and buds of male trembling aspen.

Pointing dogs are best for grouse, but a dog must have a keen nose so that it does not "bump" the birds—accidentally flush them. Some hunters use springer spaniels with good results.

The other species of North American grouse are those of the rolling prairies and open park-land forests. They are the sharptailed grouse, the sage grouse, and the prairie chicken.

The places to hunt sharptails are where grasslands are interspersed with trees and shrubs in semi-open country, with the best shooting occurring near clumps of poplar and brush that westerners call bluffs: hunters walk from bluff to bluff to try to find the birds. Sharptails also live in open woodlands, coniferous areas, large burns or cutovers, muskeg, and bogs; in consequence, they have a wide distribution. In agricultural areas, they visit fields of corn and other grains.

The sharptailed grouse holds very well for pointing dogs. It is a strong, fast flier, and, if it lived in such dense terrain as the ruffed grouse, not many would ever be shot.

The sage grouse is a large bird—cocks weigh as much as 8 lb (3.5 kg) and the hens rather less—of the sagebrush of the dry plains. It eats sagebrush, roosts and nests in sagebrush, and, in summer and winter, seeks shelter in the thickest stands of sagebrush; it also tastes of sagebrush!

As it is not a very fast flier, it does not provide particularly good shooting. But its plumage and size make it a rather spectacular game bird.

One hunts sage grouse usually by walking up or by pass-shooting. Walking up is generally the more popular, and hunters simply walk through the stands of sagebrush in the hope of finding and flushing the birds. Dogs are very useful—flushing dogs are better than pointers—for the birds tend to run ahead of the hunters. When pass shooting, one relies on the birds' habit of flying mornings and evenings to a stream or pond to drink; having first identified the water, the hunter hides behind bales of hay, brushy fence rows, or even behind fence posts, and waits for the birds to fly in.

Prairie chickens are birds of the North American West but, when the prairies were plowed and turned over to wheat, the prairie chickens lost their habitat, and their numbers plummeted. They became extinct in Canada, although they exist in shootable numbers in several western and midwestern states. The season is the fall. Hunting prairie chickens is similar to hunting sharptails. Weedy draws and grasslands near grain fields are the best covers. Like other game birds, they hold well early in the season, when cover is still thick. The young "birds of the season" hold better than the older ones, but, as a general rule, prairie chickens flush wildly, especially as winter approaches and they gather into large packs comprising of several coveys. As they flush, they cackle, a sound they also emit when running through thick grass; hunters should listen for this.

Walking the birds up is the favorite but probably the least effective method of hunting them. A better way is to hide in a field where the birds congregate regularly to feed. Bales of hay or straw, brushy coppices, or tall grass provide good cover. The birds fly in from the surrounding countryside to feed at dawn or in the late afternoon.

A good gun for all these grouse is a light 12-gauge. For ruffed grouse, the gun should be open-choked; for prairie chickens, full-choked at the end of the season, with a modified choke earlier. No. 7½ shot is suitable, but for prairie grouse, perhaps No. 6 shot may be better for late-season shooting. [JK]

Wild Turkey

Wild turkeys have become shy and secretive birds. They were first hunted by American Indians with bows and arrows, and are now hunted by hunters of all sorts with guns. Many North American hunters claim that the shooting of a big, wise, tom turkey is much more difficult than shooting a whitetail buck.

Turkey hunting in spring is done by calling the toms, in imitation of a rival for the hens or in imitation of a hen trying to attract a mate. In the fall, calling is employed, but with a different purpose: the hunter, having found a flock of turkeys, causes them to scatter, then calls in the manner of a lonely turkey seeking to regain its flock.

The gun most commonly used for wild turkeys is a 12-gauge, full-choked shotgun, loaded with No. 4 or No. 2 shot. Some hunters prefer a rifle, such as the .22 rimfire Magnum or the .222 Remington, if the use of a rifle is legal; the ordinary .22 rimfire is inadequate for turkeys and is illegal. Rifles are used chiefly in western states, where cover is rather open and shots tend to be long. [JK]

North American Quail

The bobwhite quail is the most common and most widely distributed of the six species of quail that occur in North America. More bobwhites are shot each fall than all the other quail species together.

Bobwhites need weedy fencerows, ditches, and brushy corners of uncultivated land for all aspects of their life: feeding, hiding, roosting, loafing, cover, and, particularly, shelter in the hard winter months. Clean farming, however, is destructive of this growth and, where it is practiced, bobwhites (and pheasant) have suffered. Bobwhite quail can also be found in grassy pine woods, but not in mature hardwood forests.

They are gregarious birds and live in coveys. During the season, in the early fall, hunting is most productive in the middle of the morning and the afternoon, when the coveys are out feeding. Bobwhites feed after rain, too, and when they are moving about then, their scent is more easily picked up by pointers.

A fine, fast brace of setters or pointers dashing with style and verve through the fields in quest of a covey of bobwhites is one of the classic experiences of North American hunting. The birds hold well, but a covey will scatter when flushed and a hunter is successful when he marks the single birds well. Hunting bobwhites without a dog is a frustrating business; the quail merely run ahead of the hunter, who can expect to bag only few of them.

There is no dyed-in-the-wool bobwhite hunter who does not have at least one bird dog. English pointers and English setters are the most popular, but more and more hunters are turning to Brittany spaniels and the German pointing dogs; the wirehairs are popular in country where there are lots of spiny brambles. The German dogs are used more as "singles" dogs, to hunt the scattered quail once the covey has been flushed; they work closer to the hunter and, being relatively easy to control, can be directed toward the spots where the hunter has seen single quail land.

The mountain quail and the California quail are two western birds, and the best hunting for both species is in California and Oregon. They can be confused with one another only if the hunter does not note that their plumes are different: the mountain quail's is straight, the California quail's curves forward. Both species are gregarious, and both run to escape danger.

California quail are to be looked for in tall shrubbery, brush interspersed with open areas, and grassy or weedy rows; any farming area that is not clean-farmed is thus likely to contain California quail. They eat weed seeds, grain in stubble, and wild fruits and berries. When a covey has been flushed, the individual birds scatter and rely on their coloration for protection, holding tight until the "all-clear" signal has been given by the older birds in the covey. It is this habit that gives the hunter his best chance to bag California quail, but he will still need a keen-nosed dog to find the single birds; they stay put until almost stepped upon.

The mountain quail is the largest of the North American quail, and the cock bird can weigh ¾ lb (350 g). The preferred habitat is highly diversified, ranging from chaparral thickets to humid hillsides. When the birds live near farmland, they feed on waste grains, including corn, but weed seeds make up the bulk of their diet.

Hunting mountain quail requires much walking over steep hillsides, centered around dense roosting and loafing cover and feed such as mountain rye, timothy, and wild oats. Water is another requirement, and, generally speaking, mountain quail are not found far from water. The key strategy is to approach the birds from higher up the hill, for they otherwise try to escape by running uphill, and if this direction of escape is closed, they will flush.

Scaled quail, sometimes also called blue quail, are birds of arid, brushy areas; thick stands of chaparral and mesquite with open spots are good hunting grounds for them. But such brush cover as scrub oak, greasewood, broomweed, and desert hackberry are all good habitat for scaled quail. Weed seeds are their principal item of diet, but, in farming areas, the birds feed also on corn and other grain. They need water, too, and any cover close to water holes or cattle-watering ponds is a good bet for them. Scaled quail do not hold well for dogs and prefer to run rather than fly. As they run at better than 15 mph (25 km/h), it is not so unsporting as it might sound to say that a fair number are shot on the ground, where they present a challenge similar to that of a running cottontail rabbit.

Gambel's quail are bird of the desert and live in drier habitat than other quail. They are capable of obtaining from their feed the water they need, but they prefer a daily drink if obtainable, and will even fly to a water hole or cattle-watering pond. Patches of hackberry are good ground for Gambel's quail. Grains are eaten in farming areas, but the birds eat a variety of seeds and wild fruits, including mesquite beans.

Gambel's quail are difficult to hunt because they prefer running to

flying; they do not hold well for dogs on point. Single birds hold better than coveys, but in the desert, where cover is sparse, coveys will not hold at all. The only technique that seems to work is literally to run at a covey, or have a dog do so, and then to concentrate on the single birds. Needless to say, this is a method suitable only for the fit; hunters who practice it wear light boots so as to be able to run a little faster. Apart from the strains of running, the desert country menaces the hunter and his dog with the risks of heat prostration, cactus spines, burrs, rattlesnakes, and so on.

Harlequin quail are birds of the dry grasslands and the best places to hunt them are grassy ridges and weedy fields; in very dry country, they are found near water holes. Harlequin quail nearly always prefer to sit rather than to run or fly, and, although this makes for good sport with a pointing dog, which will find birds that a hunter would otherwise walk past, they sometimes continue to sit even when a hunter is in plain view. For this reason, they have acquired the colloquial name of "fool quail."

A shotgun for quail should be light in weight and short-barreled. For bobwhite quail, the gun should be open-choked, with No. 8 shot. For the other quail, a modified or full-choked gun is the better choice, together with No. 7½ shot or perhaps No. 6. [JK]

Doves and Pigeons in North America

Of all the game birds in North America, none is harder to hit with a shotgun than the doves and pigeons. Their swift erratic flight makes mourning doves, the whitewing doves of the Southwest, and the band-tailed pigeons of the Pacific coast extremely elusive targets.

Bandtailed pigeons are normally hunted by pass-shooting when the birds are flying between roosting and feeding areas, or during migration. Hunters take stands on ridges or on high passes between hills, and gun the birds as they fly by. The higher ridge tops are generally best, because the birds are more likely to be within shotgun range there. Shooting is fast and extremely difficult. Bandtails fly faster than teal, and, if there is any wind, they slip and spin in the air currents with the agility of snipe. If a hunter has experience of shooting high-flying duck, or partridge or snipe driven as in Europe, he will probably shoot more pigeon than the average upland hunter.

A shotgun for bandtails should be full-choked but must be light and fast-swinging. Experienced bandtailed shooters advise leading the bird about twice as far as you would figure—and then doubling that.

The most popular method of hunting mourning doves is to take a stand behind cover on the edge of a recently harvested grain field where doves are known to be feeding. (It is sometimes said that mourning doves are hunted by telephone, for hunters find out in this way where the birds are feeding.) Dull-colored clothes are sensible, and gunners should be placed strategically so as to prevent the birds from resting or from slipping in and out of the field without presenting chances for a shot. In drier areas, water holes are a big attraction for mourning doves, which seem to choose one hole and water there in large numbers. The best hunting time is late in the afternoon, but hunters should never take a stand too near the water lest the birds be frightened off and abandon the hole altogether. Further, doves cupping their wings to land present unsporting targets. It is wise not to shoot near the same water hole for more than a day at a time; every fourth day is best.

Mourning doves can be hunted by jump-shooting. Hunters simply walk through fields where doves are feeding and shoot at those that get up within range; they are wary and seldom let hunters get very close. A retrieving dog is very useful, as downed doves can be hard to find, particularly in corn fields and lush soya-bean fields where the plants cover the ground.

Whitewinged doves of the Southwest are hunted in much the same way as mourning doves, but as whitewings live in drier terrain, shooting near

In northern Scandinavia, ptarmigan are hunted in winter by hunters on skis, who may also have the chance of taking capercaillie and hare. As the temperatures during the day can remain below -20°F (-30°C), the gun mechanism—and the day's supply of food and drink—can freeze solid. During the winter, the ptarmigan gather in largish numbers and are completely white except for a black band at the eye and at the tail. The hunter must be extremely fit to ski the distances necessary and should be familiar with weather conditions in the hills. Needless to say, he should never venture out alone. White clothing and a white-taped light rifle are usual, although if the hunter is extremely skillful, he can get within shotgun range.

water holes is practiced perhaps more than field shooting. In some places, it is possible to go pass-shooting.

Dove guns should have either full or modified chokes, because ranges tend to be long. Generally speaking, a 12-gauge gun is best, but smaller gauges can be used. The best shot sizes are No. 8 or No. 7½. [JK]

Pheasant

Pheasants have declined in number in North America since the mid-1950s. Many areas have only a marginal ability to sustain pheasants, and the onset of "clean farming," chemicals, and fall cultivation made matters worse. Mowing machines, for example, cut alfalfa but destroy pheasants' nests, and the harsh truth is that the pheasant population has fallen to the level that can survive in the face of these discouragements.

The British style of rough shooting is the way in which pheasants are usually hunted in North America. Typical places for hunting are weedy fields, overgrown ditches, fencerows, and small ravines. Corn fields are good if overgrown with weeds. In the late season, pheasants hide in the thickest cover imaginable—the edges of marshes and wetlands and even small woodlots.

What makes the pheasant such a fine game bird, apart from its qualities on the table, is its ability to hide: it can run, skulk, and take advantage of every bit of cover, and flies only when it has been compelled to do so. Without a good dog that can flush pheasants into the air, hunting them is a frustrating business. Springer spaniels are best, but they should also be good retrievers, for a winged pheasant will run off and be almost impossible for a hunter to trace on his own.

Pheasants are driven in the corn fields of the Midwest of the United States, somewhat in the same way as they are driven in Europe. A line of shooters walks through a corn field toward a line of blockers at the other end. The pheasants run ahead of the shooters and begin to flush as they near the end of the corn. The blockers tend to get most of the shooting, but the drivers do get some; when they reverse their roles in the next field, the balance is restored. In Europe, and in Britain, the shooters have the birds driven by beaters, and they themselves wait in a line, either in the open, at "pegs," or strung out along a clearing in woods, for example. In Britain, most pheasants are shot in organized drives, and a day's pheasant driving on a big estate is as much a social occasion as a sporting. The ladies, for example, will often stroll around and stand with the Guns during the drives; the shoot often involves a lunch for a couple of dozen gentry, and as many as forty or more beaters and keepers will be used to drive the birds over the waiting Guns.

Contrary to the opinion of uninformed laymen, the driven pheasant probably presents the most difficult target in all shooting, especially if the bird is still climbing, or turning right or left, when in range of the Gun. Very big bags—sometimes thousands of pheasants in a day—are achieved on the larger estates, where stock is bred specially for shooting and put out into the woods in spring and early summer.

In Britain, both cocks and hens are shot during drives, although by custom the last shoots, which are normally in January, are "cocks" only, since an excess of cocks during the breeding season merely makes trouble among the wild breeding stock. [JK, JMG]

Partridge

The gray partridge (*Perdix perdix*) of the European farmlands and the chukar partridge (*Alectoris chukar*) of the arid hills of the Middle East have both been successfully introduced into North America. Both offer fine shooting in areas where few other game birds can prosper. The gray partridge is commonly called the Hungarian partridge—or Hun—in North America, because the birds were first imported from the plains of Hungary.

In North America, the gray partridge is hunted almost exclusively over pointing dogs. It holds extremely well but, when it runs, it is trickier than the pheasant, even if slower, and only the keenest-nosed dog can follow a covey after it has twisted and circled around. The places to hunt gray partridge are grain stubbles, weedy fencerows, and fields near grain stubbles. Unfortunately, modern agricultural practices have not been kind to partridges, and the birds are less abundant than they once were. When cover is sparse, the birds flush far out, and shots may therefore be long.

Like pheasants, partridges fly unwillingly: when undisturbed, they have been estimated to fly voluntarily for no more than one or two minutes a day. They fly fast, however, and present a challenging target for the hunter.

The chukar partridge, which is slightly larger than the grey, prefers the rugged habitat of the deep-sided valleys and canyons of the eastern slopes of the Rocky Mountains, from southern British Columbia to Arizona. These areas are characterized by rocky debris at the foot of mountain slopes; vegetable growth is sparse, with cheat grass, sagebrush, juniper, or greasewood predominating. The birds move to slightly lower elevations in late fall, sometimes even to the farmlands on the valley floors.

In good cover, chukar partridge hold well for a pointing dog, but good cover is rare. Usually, they try to evade hunters by running first uphill and then flying downhill if need be; frequently, one can see a whole covey running away far ahead and out of range. Hunters who approach the birds from above, however, frequently get within shooting range before they flush and fly away downhill. They fly fast and are difficult to bag as a result.

The partridge (*Perdix perdix*) and the French, or red-legged, partridge (*Alectoris rufa*) are both hunted in Britain (the latter only in the south of the country). The normal method is walking in line across grain stubbles, and through fields of root crops such as potatoes and turnips. If coveys from grass and stubble can be maneuvered into roots, the coveys are often split up, the birds rise in ones and twos, and many can be shot.

The best partridge shooting occurs when there are enough birds for driving. The birds present a very fast and testing target, and a right-and-left of driven partridge will be remembered for a long time by the average shot. [JK, JMG]

Woodcock and Snipe

The North American woodcock is smaller than its European cousin but, apart from this difference, the birds resemble each other closely.

The woodcock's specialized habitat of moist woodlands dictates where it should be hunted, and it is quite easy to see if a particular woodlot has woodcock in it. When probing for worms, woodcock make small "drill holes"; their droppings are conspicuous, being white splotches about the size of a small coin. The birds are migratory, however, and can be present one day and gone the next; cold weather in fall causes them to move further south and weather forecasts of colder weather to the north arouse enthusiasm in woodcock hunters. Woodcock migrate more in north-south valleys than in those running in other directions. Light, sandy, or loam soils make for easier probing than heavy clays. These are two factors to be borne in mind when scouting for new coverts.

The woodcock has a nearly perfect dead-leaf coloration, and the birds can crouch down and often escape detection. A hunter without a dog should walk slowly, stopping every few steps, hoping to make the birds nervous. Woodcock flush wildly in windy weather, when natural noises mask the sounds of an approaching intruder. Woodcock hunting is most enjoyable and productive when using a good pointing or flushing dog. Either a springer or cocker spaniel is good for flushing—the latter acquired its name from its skill with woodcock. Some dogs, however, refuse to retrieve woodcock, perhaps because the small feathers loosen easily in the mouth or perhaps because the bird's taste or scent is unlike

that of other upland birds. But even a dog that will not fetch woodcock is valuable if it can find those that fall in tangled cover.

In Britain, if suitably moist ground is being driven, woodcock are occasionally shot during grouse drives, and less rarely during pheasant drives. Woodcock occur, too, in wooded country, where their twisting erratic flight can require quick evading action on the part of those not actually shooting. The story is told of a British gamekeeper who was celebrating his hundredth birthday. When asked to what he attributed his healthy old age, he replied, "I always threw myself on my face whenever I heard a shout of 'woodcock'."

Snipe should be looked for in moist meadows, mudflats, and on the edges of bogs and marshes: they are birds of open wetlands. The best way to hunt snipe is to walk through this sort of terrain with a flushing or pointing dog; one that retrieves is almost essential, for snipe that fall in or beyond pools of water are hard if not impossible to recover without wading. Like woodcock, snipe that are known to be present one day may have vanished by the next: a tidal flat with dozens of snipe on it may be empty within hours.

Snipe are fast on the wing and, when flushed, fly off with a characteristic zigzag flight that straightens out after a few seconds. A hunter who keeps his head and does not shoot at once is more likely to hit this elusive bird. To say silently, "Snipe-on-toast," before shooting has been held to induce the right delay...

A good woodcock or snipe gun should be light and open-bored, although a double bore, with one barrel of a tighter choke than the other, is even better because some of the shots can be long. The best shot size is No. 9, but No. 8 or even No. 7½ can be used. [JK, JMG]

Wildfowling

Wildfowling is the art of shooting water birds—above all, ducks and geese. Many methods are used; some of these originated long before the use of guns for hunting. Several thousand years ago, North American Indians lured ducks within range by laying out decoys and, probably, by using calls. These methods are used all over the world today.

Dabbling ducks can be stalked where there are enough ponds to make it worthwhile for a hunter on foot. Using whatever cover is available, the hunter gets as close as he can to the water before flushing the ducks into flight. Sometimes, it is possible to hear them quacking on a pond or marsh, so the hunter should be able to distinguish between the sounds made by the various species. Another stalking method is to use a canoe or a small rowing boat on a stream or smallish waterway; ducks are often not particularly disturbed by them as they float downstream.

Tolling for ducks is apparently practiced only in Nova Scotia, where the Nova Scotia retriever, a rusty-colored, fox-like animal, was developed for the sport. Ducks are inquisitive, if not distracted or alarmed, and they swim closer to investigate if they see a dog running up and down the shore, ignoring them and having a carefree time. This effect can be attained if the hunter hides himself and throws a ball or stick along the shoreline for the dog to retrieve. Once the birds are within range, they can be flushed and shot at. Tolling originated in Europe, when dogs were used to lure ducks into huge trap nets.

Bay, or diving, ducks include such sea ducks as eider and scoter, as well as scaup, canvasback, redhead, ringneck, and goldeneye. They generally are to be hunted on extensive lakes and estuaries. When taking off, they head into the wind and patter along the surface until airborne; their wings are smaller and less powerful than those of dabbling ducks, which take off with a spring from the surface.

The late fall is the peak season for shooting diving ducks, when bone-chilling winds sweep down from the north and the ducks fly south with the wind. Hardy and fast-flying, they always seem to come in with severe storms, as if they enjoyed them. The semi-darkness of the hours around daybreak, waves breaking on a lee shore, lots of ice-encrusted decoys—this is all part of the sport, which is a specialized, open-water business, requiring many decoys; sets of sixty are the minimum and twice that number is better, for diving ducks fly in large skeins. Once an area is found where ducks are seen or are known to feed, the decoys must be set out. This is done so that they float with plenty of open water between them and the hide, or blind, so that the ducks have room to land. The well-built blind will conceal the hunter(s) as completely as possible. It should be built and positioned before the ducks are due to arrive. This is important, because, if some ducks—such as scaup and redhead—will lure easily to decoys, others will not. Canvasbacks, for instance, are not easy to lure.

From the concealment of his hide, the hunter should watch the ducks as they approach. If they intend to land on the water, they will start trailing their feet while still some distance away. If their feet remain tucked up, the ducks will only "buzz" the decoys, picking up speed as they fly over; in such a case, it is important to give them plenty of lead, or forward allowance, to compensate for this. Different species approach in different ways, however.

Redhead come eagerly to large rafts of decoys, if hunting pressure has not been excessive; occasionally, they drop from great heights, plummeting down zigzag, but more often, they make several reconnoitering passes, descending gradually, and the hunter must be patient and not alert them too soon. Greater scaup seldom fly very high, but they sometimes frustrate a hunter by alighting on the far side of a decoy spread, just out of range; when they settle like this, they can be lured closer by an imitation of their call—a sort of mellow, feline purr—or by fluttering a cap or handkerchief above the blind or camouflaged boat. Greater scaup are intensely inquisitive of movement that is other than human. Lesser scaup, however, are not like this but are wary and suspicious.

Scoters are not wary and will be lured to just about any kind of decoy,

if they have not been intensely hunted. Wooden blocks are frequently used as decoys and, years ago, cork floats from fishing nets were used. Some hunters use silhouette decoys nailed in a row on a long board. If the hunter merely sits still in his boat, he need not otherwise disguise his presence—the birds sometimes even circle and drop in behind him, if he is in a boat.

A good place to hunt scoters is in a bay with a headland striking out to sea. If there are two or more hunters, they should moor their boats about 100 yards (90 m) apart, and each should set out his own decoys. Scoters are fast-flying birds that usually keep low, almost skimming the water and rising only to clear obstacles. They can be lured to one set of decoys and, when fired on, will fly to the next. Almost any kind of dully painted, stable boat can be used: experienced hunters often use old skiffs or dories. If two hunters share a boat, they should sit back-to-back and thus keep the whole compass covered. Even if one is shooting from the shore, it is necessary to have a boat to retrieve fallen birds.

Hunting for geese and ducks over fields of stubble after the grain has been harvested is a favorite North American method. The majority of geese shot in North America are bagged in this way, and so are many ducks; mallard, pintail, and widgeon all love grain. So do white-fronted and Canada geese, and they will feed on it in preference to anything else. The state of Maryland has fine goose shooting nowadays, for this reason; geese seem even to have altered their migration habits to take advantage of the grain production there.

Hunting Canada geese over stubble can be exasperating; the technique is the same as for ducks, but geese require greater care. Once a hunter knows where the birds are feeding, he must set up his decoys and dig his pit well ahead of the arrival of the flight, even the night before. For duck, it may be enough to use a low blind built of straw and weeds in a fencerow or at the edge of a shelter belt, but geese are too wise to land near fences or shelter belts. When digging a pit in which to conceal oneself from geese, it is necessary to remove all the freshly-dug earth

A hunter plants lesser snow goose decoys in a field where the geese like to feed. The lesser snow goose is an inland grazing bird, the greater preferring coastal feeding. Lessers come to much less sophisticated decoys, too—white rags or pieces of paper are just as effective. The hunter either shoots from a blind or he lies on his back, covered with a white sheet and, as the geese come in, he sits up and fires.

When preparing to shoot over decoys on water, set them out so as to resemble a raft of ducks, perhaps together with a few geese. Spread them out in a "fish hook" pattern (or in the form of a C, J, or V), for the incoming birds will tend to land in the space enclosed by your decoys. For this reason, the decoys farthest from your blind must not be more than about 50 yards (45 m) away: this should bring the ducks into easy range. When choosing or making decoys, remember that the hens of many duck species look rather alike—generally a dull brownish—and that, at the beginning of the season, the male birds are still in their eclipse plumage, which they will gradually molt later on. Over-sized decoys are good when you want to attract birds from a height. Your blind should be camouflaged with vegetation that is natural to the area in which you are hunting, and clothing should be as drab as possible. Keep your head low until ready to shoot.

from the vicinity of the pit, lest the geese see it and shy away. When they have been heavily gunned, they become extremely wary, avoid any flocks on the ground, refuse to decoy, and seldom feed in the same field on two consecutive days.

For a morning shoot, the hunter must be concealed in his hide well before the first hint of dawn. As the day begins to break, seemingly endless skeins of mallard fly out from the sloughs and marshes, and, occasionally, small flocks of other ducks—pintails, baldpates, or gadwalls—can be seen. When a flight begins to circle over his decoys, the hunter must wait patiently until the birds are within range and must restrain his dog from retrieving at once, for the flights can continue for some time. Only when they have ceased, or the hunter has shot his legal maximum for the day—perhaps five or six ducks—may his dog start to pick up and retrieve the birds. The last thing to do before leaving is to fill in the pit, unless the hunter has paid to use one provided by the landowner; some maintain permanent pits or blinds in or by hedgerows.

Goose decoys should imitate a flock of geese feeding: some of the decoys must have feeding heads, some resting heads, and a few upright, alert heads—but only a few: too many will send a message of unrest and caution to the birds to be decoyed. Once a flight of geese is in sight over the horizon, the hunter should begin calling but should stay concealed and, unless he is an expert caller, should fall silent as soon as the birds come close or start to head for the decoys; a false note can warn them off. Estimating their range is difficult, for they are larger and fly faster than inexperienced hunters realize; give them plenty of lead for this reason.

Hunting brant geese in North America is generally done over water in areas where these geese are known to feed. Scouting the shorelines for brant or stands of eelgrass, the plant they love to eat, is the best way to start. Brant decoys are almost always used, but the birds can be shot from passes, such as rocky points jutting out to sea.

Pass-shooting for geese in general is often chancy in clear weather, because the birds fly high until they come down into the fields, but, in foul or foggy weather, they do stay low and offer chances for shooting.

Geese generally spend the nights on big lakes or on rivers, and this is where one should look for them before finding a pass.

Pass-shooting is the hardest form of wildfowling; the birds are usually flying much faster than they would be when setting in to decoys, and ranges are considerably longer—60 or even 70 yards (55 to 65 m). It is a simple, uncluttered form of the sport, however, for no decoys are used. The hunter relies on his knowledge of the birds and the area; he selects a pass on a flyway which the birds can be expected to use, depending on the weather, between their feeding and roosting areas. A good pass can be a creek or a narrow neck of land or water between two marshes; the shortest routes between marshes and lakes and grain fields can give good positions. On the sea coast, reefs, breakers, or points of land can all be good passes if, once again, the wind is right and the birds are flying to feed in particular fields inland.

Other wildfowlers can pose immediate and other problems: an individual may have concealed himself in suitable cover sometime before dawn, only to find that he is too close to some other hunter for their separate comfort and sport. Even if this does not happen, a general increase in the level of shooting will cause ducks to change their flyways or to fly high; they may even fly to their feeding grounds long before dawn, which, in North America, is the earliest that shooting may be legally enjoyed. In some European countries, however, it is not illegal to shoot ducks and geese at night by moonlight. A good retrieving dog is a must for pass-shooting, if many ducks are not to be lost.

Pass-shooting requires a full-choked gun and heavy loads, and it is when the Magnums come into their own and enable the hunter to hit and kill wildfowl at the long ranges demanded.

Sculling is another method and is really a specialized form of stalking, but one that uses a small, extremely low-profiled scull boat in which the hunter lies down. He or a companion propels the boat with a single oar over the stern or a pair of small paddles held in the hands over the side of the boat. The art is to bring the boat into range of a raft of wildfowl, and,

as the boats are generally flat-bottomed and have a very low freeboard, it is a skillful business to man them if there is anything of a wind; even small waves can break over the gunwales. Punt-gunning is a variation of the sport pursued in the British Isles, mostly on the coast of East Anglia. It relies on an immense gun mounted over the bows of the punt—a bore of over an inch (2.5 cm) and a barrel length of some 60 inches (150 cm) giving a weight of 30 lb (14 kg); not merely the gun, but the entire boat, must be aimed at the birds. This sort of hunting is the preserve of a small, dedicated minority of wildfowlers. The shot is taken as the raft of wildfowl starts rising, so that wings will be clear of the more vulnerable flanks of the birds. As many birds are wounded by the one big bang of the punt gun, the gunner has to have a conventional shotgun with him to deal with those that are not killed outright.

Wildfowling in Britain is, apart from the punt-gunning already mentioned, usually a matter of solitary or nearly solitary expeditions on "saltings" and other maritime areas, walking through marshes and similar expanses of land between the low and high tide marks, to wait for morning or evening flights of ducks and geese.

Inland shooting in Perthshire, Scotland, is celebrated, for the area is exceptionally rich in geese. When resident between migrations, graylag and pink-footed geese spend the day feeding on grass and stubble and, at night, fly short distances to open water on various lochs, of which Carsebreck, Auchterarder, is probably the most famous. The water is privately owned and is shot only three or four times during the season. Invited guests are stationed in hides around the loch and on islands, and the bag of geese can reach several dozen in an evening. No decoys are used.

In areas like the Solway Firth, wildfowling almost brings the tourist industry a second season. Hotels organize shoots for their guests—for example, dawn expeditions to fields where geese are known to be feeding in large numbers. Guns hide behind stone walls and other natural cover, and silhouette decoys are used. [JK, JMG]

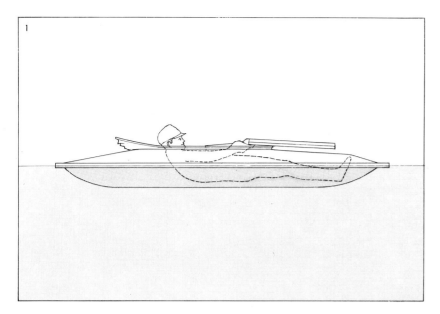

A sort of short, broad, shallow canoe, the layout boat enables a wildfowler to remain unobtrusively at water level far out from the shore. *(1)* The form of the boat is a little reminiscent of a punt-gunner's craft. Other means of hunting wildfowl include blinds built over water *(2)* or in reeds *(3)*. If well covered with local vegetation and allowed to weather, such a blind soon becomes accepted by waterfowl as part of the landscape.

Small game can be hunted in many ways. The biggest bags are usually shot during drives, a method common in Europe and rich in social tradition. Anything from twenty to a hundred beaters and hunters may be involved, and some of the game that may be expected includes *(1)* pheasant, *(2)* woodcock, *(3)* partridge, *(4)* fox, and *(5)* hare. The beaters with their dogs, often with a few shooters in the line, walk through the fields or cover toward the shooters, who must take care to aim well clear of those approaching. In the final stages of the drive, shooting is permitted only when game has passed through or over the line of shooters.

Chapter 3
Hunting Small Game

Rabbits and Hares

Methods of hunting rabbits and hares in North America are not elaborate, and the sport is one that can be enjoyed without lengthy journeys or expensive equipment. Rabbit hunting reaches its best when the hunter uses beagles or bassets to start the animals. The best rabbit hounds are relatively slow; too fast a pursuit will drive rabbits underground. If this does not happen, they run in large, irregular circles, as they try to return to their home ground, and the hunters must estimate which vantage point will give them the best chances of a shot.

If the hunter is without a dog, he must walk slowly through the sort of cover likely to hold rabbits, stopping every few steps to look around; this sort of overhanging threat makes rabbits nervous enough to break cover and bolt from where they have been crouching down almost invisibly. The wise hunter goes into every bit of thick cover—brush piles, for example, and clumps of thick grass—kicking as he goes. In the northern United States, cold winter weather forces rabbits to take shelter in woodchuck burrows and other holes, but the first warm days will bring them out. Rabbits can be stalked after a snowfall by a hunter who has the patience to walk very slowly, looking carefully and meticulously into thick cover to locate rabbits at rest; most frequently the hunter catches sight of a rabbit's eyes.

A good cottontail gun is an open-choked shotgun, from 20- to 12-gauge, loaded with No. 6 to No. 7½ shot. It should be light and fast-swinging. For swamp rabbits, many hunters prefer a bigger shot size: No. 5 or even No. 4. A .22 rimfire rifle is suitable when stalking in snow.

Swamp rabbits are best hunted with dogs. In the thick cover of wetlands, for example in south-central Tennessee, where swamp rabbits are plentiful, chases can last up to an hour or more. The rabbits run helter-skelter through the undergrowth but, when they come close to a hunter, they seem to know this, and then they sneak through the cover in an effort to keep out of sight.

Several species of hares are common in North America: the arctic hare of the northernmost tundra, the snowshoe hare of the northern forests, the three species of jackrabbits of the western prairies and the sagebrush deserts, and the European hare, which, after introduction into several areas of eastern North America, is still to be found there. Jackrabbits are regarded as pests in some states and may be shot as such; in others, they are protected by seasonal restrictions. When jackrabbits become numerous, drives are sometimes organized by hunters and ranchers: a group of hunters simply walks in a line, with gaps of about 100 yards (90 m) between each man, and the hares are shot at as they are started; a good choice for this sort of shooting is a full-choked shotgun loaded with No. 4 shot.

A couple of hunters can jump jackrabbits by walking slowly through areas where the animals lie up during the day, but the best time to hunt them is in the morning or evening, which is when they are most active. Once jackrabbits start running, they are difficult targets; they have been clocked at 40 mph (65 km/h), and whoever can consistently hit such a

Raccoon hunting with coonhounds is finest on a warm night in fall. The raccoon often patrols back roads looking for carrion left by automobiles, and hunters very often start their hounds along such roads.

When the hounds have put up a raccoon he will run for it, but inevitably, the chase ends with the raccoon up a tree. When the hounds bark "treed," the hunters recognize this from the change in voice and rush to the scene, for a raccoon will not always stay treed for long. Most hunters wear headlamps—"miner's lamps"—to leave both hands free. A .22 rimfire or a pistol is sufficient for this close-range shooting.

target will have little trouble with deer and antelope. The sportiest gun for this type of hunting is a light "varmint" rifle, such as a .222, with a scope of moderate power.

A few individuals in the West still practice the old and exciting sport of coursing hare with hounds. The animals traditionally used are greyhounds or whippets. The sport is common in the British Isles and is conducted in open country where hares are plentiful. Strictly regulated, the sport lays at least as much emphasis on the style of the pursuit as the kill—and kills are the exception, for most hares escape. After some forty-five seconds of chase, the hare, which is given a start of some 80 yards (75 m), starts gaining on the greyhounds, for its stamina is greater than theirs. Salukis, which are sometimes coursed in Britain and North America, cannot match greyhounds in pace, but have greater stamina.

In the Canadian province of Ontario, European hares are also hunted in drives, usually with five or six hunters. Some like to use hounds—foxhounds, black-and-tans, blueticks, or very large beagles. The European hare runs in a much larger circle than the cottontail and may cover 3 or 4 miles (5 to 8 km) before returning to its territory. Some hunters use full-choked shotguns with No. 4 or No. 2 shot; others prefer .22 rimfire Magnum or centerfire varmint cartridges in a .222 rifle.

Snowshoe hares can be hunted with hounds but, when this is done in deep snow, the hounds need to have long legs; larger beagles or hounds of some other large breed are best. Unless pursued by hounds, the snowshoe hare is apt to sense no great danger from a hunter and will not run at top speed; this is especially so in the remote wilderness areas. A .22 rifle is a good weapon for such hunting, but a handgun can be used, too. When hunting snowshoe hares in thick cover, such as young forests in logged-over areas or in old burns, ranges are likely to be short, and the best gun would be a 12-gauge, although 16- or even 20-gauge guns are sometimes used.

The arctic hare is rarely hunted for sport because few sportsmen venture so far north. These hares increase in population to an extraordinary extent every ten years or so—as lemmings do—and become an important source of food for Eskimos and northern Indians who, at one time, made blankets and clothing from hare skins.

Hares are shot as pests, not for sport, in Britain. The shooting does not take place in the season, and there are no social overtones. For many who work on the land, hare shooting is the only time in the year when they shoot in company (and legally!), and, for this reason, the hare shoot is considered a particularly dangerous business. Estate gamekeepers are often in charge. The hares do not move very fast, and shooting is easy, made slightly less so by the hunter's having to carry maybe 30 to 40 lb (14 to 19 kg) of dead hares in a gamebag while walking over the fields or moors. The hare is not eaten by the majority of the population other than the sophisticated classes. Many country people are inhibited by the remnants of old superstition—ill-luck and so on—from eating hare.

To farmers, the rabbit is a highly destructive and expensive pest, in extreme cases devouring a tenth of the crop. To sportsmen in Britain, it is a welcome addition to the bag of a day's mixed or rough shooting, although it is seldom the entire or even the principal quarry of a day's sport. The sole sport in England and parts of Europe in which rabbits are the only quarry is ferreting, a sport for a small team—ideally, two Guns, a gamekeeper to handle the ferrets, and an extra keeper who can be delegated for the job of digging out or otherwise apprehending a lost ferret.

The ferret is a mustelid, a relative of stoats, weasels, polecats, martens, and badgers. It is the right shape for going down rabbit burrows—long and thin—perhaps 12 by 2 inches (30 by 5 cm). Many are off-white, with evil-looking red eyes. Others, more nearly related to the polecat, are gray or gray-brown, and slightly larger. The ferret's instinct is to explore below ground and to attack anything it finds there. Its menacing

approach makes all but the boldest of rabbits immediately bolt from the burrow into the open air—where Guns and nets await them.

On a typical ferreting day, the Guns quietly station themselves so as to have a downhill and commanding view of the burrows, and the handler inserts a ferret into a likely hole. Five minutes later, the bleary white face of the ferret emerges at the same hole, and the ferret is taken to another possible entrance. The loud thump from the burrow is a rabbit stamping its hind legs in alarm. For a while, there is no more action but, without warning, a rabbit bursts from a hole, executes a quick right turn, and re-enters the burrow. Experienced Guns know not to shoot, for a wounded rabbit in the burrow is certain to be found by the ferret, who will then lie up for hours and probably have to be dug out.

The greatest drawback to ferreting is the delay caused by ferrets that lay up underground. Keepers have developed many ways of inducing them to come out—short of digging: gutting a rabbit and placing the entrails at the windward hole of the burrow; calling; imitating rabbit noises; even firing a gun down the burrow. To prevent the ferret from eating the quarry, it is often muzzled, or it can be withdrawn if a long line is attached to it by a shoulder harness. The latest development is an electronic bleeper which at least tells the owner exactly where to start digging.

Ferreting is a sport of the unexpected. In a classic instance, a sportsman seeking to entice a ferret out of a hole had his head at its entrance when a rabbit, having decided that guns were a lesser evil than the ferret, bolted with such force as to break the nose of the face blocking its exit. At the hospital, the patient was asked by a kindly nurse how the accident had happened. "I was kicked by a rabbit," he replied.

There is no pleasanter form of gun sport, however, when all goes well, and one has the satisfaction of ridding the farmer of vermin while providing someone with quite cheap food—and of excellent quality, too, if well cooked. Two Guns, with two keepers to handle the ferrets, can expect to have a day of fifty couple of rabbits on good ground.

Unlike hares, which benefit from several days of hanging entire, rabbits should be cleaned as soon as possible after shooting or being netted. In any case, before transfer to the gamebag, a rabbit should be held by the head while the hind quarters are squeezed in such a way as to expel any urine in the body; this is otherwise capable of souring the flesh. [JK, JMG]

Raccoon

The portly, low-slung, bushy-tailed, black-masked raccoon is not very glamorous game but is popular quarry in many parts of the United States and southern Canada.

Raccoons take a substantial amount of aquatic prey, but they are omnivorous; a chicken house or cornfield may attract more raccoons than a stream, but all the same, a good place to start a hound pack is near water. The presence of tracks, droppings, and obvious damage around poultry enclosures would make a start worthwhile there, too.

As raccoons are nocturnal animals, the best time to hunt them is at night. Hunters equip themselves with headlamps. Where raccoons are not an agricultural problem, a hunter may tree one just for the pleasure of watching his dogs at work and listening to their barking; if he does not want the meat or pelt, he hauls his dogs off and lets the raccoon go about its business. Some old raccoons become accustomed to this and seem to enjoy leading hounds on a chase through the woods. If the hunter wants to shoot the raccoon, an open-sighted .22 rimfire rifle or pistol is the best weapon and most often used, as a treed raccoon presents an easy short-range target. Shotguns put too many holes in a handsome pelt.

The dogs may be any of the coon-hunting breeds described in Part VI. Several dogs are better than one; the hunter can tell from their voices when their quarry is treed. Dogs that give tongue readily are better than

In some parts of Sweden, fox are shot at night over bait. This is mainly done in winter and at full moon, when the moon and the snow make for excellent visibility. Shotguns are used, very often equipped with telescopic sights with good light-gathering qualities. The bait—carrion of any kind will do—should be well weighted down with stones to prevent the fox from taking it away. It should be placed within easy shotgun range of a farm's outhouse or even of the farmhouse itself. A light on the outside of the building can be a help, if visibility is poor. A string from the bait to a muffled bell beside the waiting hunter will warn him when the fox has come to the bait.

silent ones, for one dog's barking will attract the others and, together, they have a better chance of keeping the raccoon treed.

In recent years, it has become popular to use a predator call, which emits a squeal as of a rabbit that is injured or, in some models, the cry of a small bird or rodent in distress. The hunter, usually wearing camouflage, remains hidden and lures the raccoon to him. Where hunting at night is not legal, success is greatest just after dawn and before dusk. Where hunting may take place at night, and calls and lights are legal, success is greatest. A headlamp with a red lens disturbs wildlife less than one casting a bright white beam. In addition to raccoons, a predator call lures foxes and, in some regions, coyotes and bobcats, and part of the enjoyment of this form of hunting is the knowledge that one must be prepared for the unexpected. In some regions, phonographic calls are legal for raccoons, but a mouth-operated call is more sporting and, with practice, can be just as effective.

Raccoons are very active in late fall, when they are feeding voraciously to put on winter fat: hunting is best then. It is good, too, in February, when the males are wandering about in search of mates. Some states permit hunting in late summer and, while this is a good time, many of the coons that are treed or lured will be young and small. [RE]

Foxes

There are several methods of hunting the foxes of North America—the red fox and the gray fox. There is the formal foxhunt, in which the hunters, dressed in scarlet and mounted, ride to hounds. This is very similar to foxhunting in the British Isles, where foxes are highly valued for the sport they afford; except as pests in suburban areas, where they cannot be hunted with hounds, foxes are not shot in Britain.

Another form of hunting in North America is practiced by farmers and country people, without formality, and mostly at night. The purpose of the hunt is to enjoy the "hound music," while the owners of the hounds sit around a fire and listen to the baying. Owners can identify their hounds' voices and so can tell when the hounds have lost the track, when they recover it again, and when the fox is going flat out. This type of chase is mostly practiced in the South, where there is a deep appreciation of hounds and hound music. Occasionally, the hounds may be followed by automobile.

Foxes can be hunted, after a snowfall, with only two or three hounds. Beginning in the early morning, the hunters start by looking for fresh tracks. The hounds are released, and the hunters try to intercept the fox so as to get a shot at it. Foxes run in irregular circles within their own territory, but shooting at them is not simple; they are too intelligent, sharp-nosed, and keen-eyed to let themselves be bagged easily. Some hunters prefer rifles, such as a .222, while others use a full-choked 12-gauge shotgun and No. 4 or No. 2 shot.

Other methods include walking through good fox country in winter, tracking the animals, while hoping to get a shot with a rifle. In clear weather, an even better method is to glass snow-covered hillsides for foxes sleeping in the sun. Particularly at dawn or dusk, gray foxes can be attracted with a varmint call that imitates the squeal of an injured rabbit. Gray foxes are not as clever as red foxes, which are not attracted in this way.

Occasionally, three or four hunters may conduct a small drive, when they know where a fox is likely to have bedded down for the day and where he will run when flushed. One or two of the hunters take up positions along fence lines or wooded ridges, where foxes are likely to cross, and the others drive or track the fox. It is, by the way, fairly easy to distinguish between the tracks of a gray and a red fox: the former has much larger toe pads, and the latter has so much hair between the toe pads that the prints of individual pads are sometimes almost obliterated. [JK]

Squirrels

Only the larger species of squirrel—the gray, the fox, and the tassle-eared—are considered as game animals. One of the finest ways to hunt them is to go into good squirrel woods at dawn. As soon as the sun rises, squirrels come out to feed, and the hunter must then keep quite still, with his eyes and ears open. On a still morning when squirrels are feeding, an experienced hunter can identify the sound of fragments and cuttings of nuts and acorns being dropped on dry leaves on the ground. Where a beginner will see a squirrel only when it is completely visible, the experienced hunter will spot a squirrel when all that is visible round the stem or branch of a tree is the squirrel's ear, paw, or tail, or when an odd silhouette on a bough indicates that a squirrel is lying outstretched there. This is sport for a good shot with a rifle: an accurate .22 rimfire with a low- or variable-powered scope is the best choice. Ranges can be up to 100 yards (90 m).

Another good technique is to walk very slowly through squirrel woods, listening and looking. A pair of hunters will fare better than one on his own, for squirrels dodge round the backs of trees, thus evading a single intruder. Once squirrels start moving through the trees and branches, a hunter needs a tight-choke shotgun; No. 6 shot is best.

Squirrels can be hunted late in the afternoon, too, and calm, warm, windless days are best. They are active after rain, especially if it is followed by sunshine. In cold or rainy weather, they do not come out.

The nuts and mast that squirrels feed on grow on trees that thrive in river valleys; for this reason, drifting downstream on small streams or rivers in a canoe is not only a pleasant way to hunt the animals, but also an effective one, being almost noiseless. Shooting from a moving boat may increase the demands on marksmanship, however. It is worthwhile, though, for the canoe-borne hunter to go ashore in promising territory and scour the woods; the rewards may include wildfowl and woodcock, to say nothing of pigeons or doves. Some hunters even take fishing equipment with them on such trips.

Squirrels can be called, if the hunter can get himself into a good squirrel wood without being noticed by the animals. Once he is concealed, he can begin calling; if he has been seen, he should wait for some ten minutes, and, during this time, the squirrels are likely to forget about him. A makeshift call can be produced by tapping a coin on the buttstock of the gun or rifle, or by clicking two stones together, but neither of these ways produces as good a call as that from a bellows device. Most manufactured calls are of this type and effectively reproduce the rapid "chucking" of a squirrel. Two long series of chucks are followed by several shorter sequences and, after a pause of about a minute, the whole call is repeated. The hunter then waits and listens for squirrels to appear or answer. If nothing happens within five minutes, he tries again, and keeps on for perhaps a quarter of an hour. If no squirrels show up then, he moves to another part of the woods. [JK]

Chapter 4

Hunting in Africa, Asia, and South America

African Lion

Lions can be hunted in a variety of ways: by baiting, by tracking in desert country, and by locating them from the sounds of their roaring. Baiting is the best bet, if it is legal.

The method of baiting is to hang the carcass of a zebra, buffalo, or wildebeest from a tree, well off the ground so that small carnivores cannot reach it, and then to wait in a blind some 60 yards (55 m) away, beginning two or three hours before sunrise. To be assured of a clear lane of fire, it may be necessary to cut grass and brush between the blind and the bait tree. Once a lion appears and there is light enough to shoot, one watches the lion until it is in a position that offers a good target.

Tracking, a very sporting method, can be done only in desert or very sandy terrain, unless a lion obligingly keeps to the bed of a dry watercourse. Expert trackers can follow spoor left in dew, but even they can see nothing once the sun has burned off the dew. When tracking, the chances of surprising a lion at close quarters are very good. On seeing the hunter, it either runs or charges. The hunter has only a few moments to decide if the lion is a good trophy; a clean killing shot is always desirable and sometimes essential.

In reasonably open plains, woodland, or savanna, a hunter out at night may hear a lion roaring, one of the greatest sounds in Africa. A very deep roar would indicate a big chesty lion. The hunter sets out on foot in the direction of the roaring, correcting his approach from successive roars; with luck, the lion will roar once more just before dawn, when the hunter has a 50–50 chance of finding him, provided the country is open enough.

On occasion, the hunter may see a pride of lions when he is cruising in the hunting car. He then leaves it unobtrusively and, as the lions watch it drive away, gets into position for a shot.

The ideal shot for a lion is on the shoulder about a quarter of the way up the body; this breaks at least one shoulder and pierces the heart. Other shots are more difficult: a brain shot between the eyes from the front, or at the base of the ear from the side. A frontal brain shot, however, is the only means of stopping a charging lion, which can move at about 60 mph (100 km/h); the hunter has almost no time at all to shoot.

In most African countries, the minimum caliber for hunting lions or any dangerous game is .375; the hunter is advised to use this or something heavier, with soft-nosed bullets. The Francophone countries of Africa permit 9.3×62mm or 9.3×64mm. [BH]

Leopard

Leopards are shot over bait. To attract a leopard, one ties the bait firmly to a sturdy, comfortable branch of a decent-sized tree in thick cover. The bait need not be large: a small antelope or baboon is the right size. The blind must be in thick bush, as close as possible to the bait, which should be silhouetted against the sky, for you shoot in poor light at dawn or dusk. While a distance of 30 yards (27 m) is about average, many leopards have been shot from as little as half that distance.

Killing shots for four of the big game of Africa: (1) brain shot, (2) heart shot, (3) shoulder shot, (4) neck shot. The frontal brain shot, the only remedy when one of these massive animals charges the hunter, must take account of the angle at which the oncoming beast holds its head. The buffalo's forehead armor is especially difficult to pierce.

107

The Cape buffalo is a difficult and dangerous animal to hunt. The dawn ambush is one of the most effective methods. Buffalo usually remain in cover during the heat of the day and move to watering places in the late afternoon or early evening. They drink and feed at night, returning at dawn to cover.

(Inset) The hunter, having established where the herd spends its nights and having picked out a suitable bull, makes his final approach on foot and in darkness. He positions himself where he will intercept the dawn movement of the animals. A range of 40 yards (35 m) is considered the maximum.

A shoulder shot, as with a lion, kills the animal outright. A wounded leopard is more dangerous than a wounded lion; even if a fallen animal is apparently dead, it may be merely stunned, and a second shot is only prudent. A wounded leopard takes cover and waits for his attacker; tracking requires a very cool head indeed, the help of a superb tracker, a 12-bore loaded with buckshot, and a fair measure of luck to survive and come home with a trophy.

Sometimes, you can surprise a leopard when you are out hunting during the late evening or early morning. It is a good rule never to shoot at a range of over about 80 yards (75 m), even under ideal conditions. Your rifle should be a .375 or larger, fitted with a scope sight.

It is sometimes possible, when out at night in the bush, to hear a leopard grunting as it approaches a kill (or a bait); the sound is similar to a throaty buck-saw, a sort of sawing cough, and, when you have heard it once, it is unmistakable thereafter. [BH]

African Elephant

The great fascination of hunting elephant in Africa has been the need literally to hunt the animals, usually by the now almost lost art of tracking, which is the only sure way to catch up with an elephant. As elephants cover great distances, a hunter has always had to be prepared to cover them too, most of all during the rains, when elephants scatter far and wide, and travel further than they do in the dry season.

To be worth following, an elephant's track must be both fresh and big—at least 20 inches (50 cm) wide. A smooth footprint indicates an older animal. Inspection of dung is a valuable source of information: if the dung is still not much attacked by dung beetles and other insects, it is fresh; the dung of older elephants contains undigested vegetable matter. Where an elephant rests, marks on the ground or on fallen logs and nearby trees may indicate the size of the tusks.

The hunter approaches the elephant from downwind, and, once close to the animal, it may be possible to hear the sounds it makes as it feeds: internal rumblings, sighs, and flapping of ears, which may be the only sound audible if the animal is resting. A herd at rest takes up positions like the spokes of a wheel; each animal faces outward.

An ideal range at which to shoot is 30 yards (25 m), or closer if possible. If the animal is in profile, the brain is about 3 inches (7.5 cm) in front of the ear on a line running to the eye. An accurate brain shot drops an elephant at once. A heart shot from the side is aimed about one-third of the way up the chest half behind the shoulder; an elephant so shot does not fall at once but goes at least 30 yards (25 m) before collapsing.

Elephants' tusks now seldom weigh more than 60 lb (27 kg), whereas weights three times as great were known about the beginning of the twentieth century. When the animal was hunted, rifles of a caliber of not less than .375 or .400 were used with solid bullets. Normally, the rifles were double-barreled or equipped with magazines.

Nowadays, the elephant is a threatened species, competing for its food with many other species in the national parks of Africa and constantly threatened by the farming needs of the growing population. Poaching is also creating great problems for the elephant and for those who want this magnificent animal to survive. [BH]

Rhinoceros

The white rhino is hunted only in South Africa, where the species is preserved on private property under strictly controlled conditions. The animals are located either by spotting or from a safari car; tracking is not required.

Black rhino are generally tracked, however, insofar as they are still legal game; tracks less than 8 inches (20 cm) wide are unlikely to indicate a trophy-sized animal. The first sign of a nearby, resting rhino is the raucous squawking of the oxpecker birds that exist symbiotically with rhino; their cries of alarm arouse the rhino, which either runs away or charges blindly toward the sounds or smell of the hunter. The animal dashes at full speed through whatever thick cover stands between it and the hunter, who will have to shoot at close range, perhaps 20 yards (18 m). The point of aim is the sloping forehead above the eyes and on one side or the other of the horn.

On a standing animal, a heart shot is aimed about a third of the way up the shoulder, and while this does not drop the rhino at once, it will at least not get very far. Rhino are, of course, thick-skinned: over the neck and shoulders, the skin is as thick as 2 inches (5 cm); elsewhere, it is more than an inch (3 cm). No caliber of rifle less than .375 should be used; bullets should be solid. [BH]

Cape Buffalo

Most hunters regard the buffalo as the most dangerous of all African game, as it has excellent sight, hearing, and sense of smell, as well as being immensely strong, alert, and cunning. These attributes make buffalo hunting exciting and unpredictable.

A hunter looking for a good bull scans a herd of several hundred animals or tracks a solitary bull or a group of perhaps only three or four bulls that have retired from the herd. In plains or savanna country, a hunter first spots a herd at a distance and then stalks it on foot. In forests, he must scout along trails or glades at dawn. Escarpments or hillsides provide vantage points from where he can glass the surrounding country. In miombo forests, which occur throughout much of the buffalo's range, the hunter may be able to track a single animal or a herd. He has to get very close—between 10 and 40 yards (10 and 35 m)—to the bull he wants to shoot. Anything much over 40 yards is too risky. Approaching from downwind is necessary to get within range. Each herd has several animals on watch the whole time, and if one of them is alerted, the chances of a trophy vanish. The odds of finding a trophy animal are greater in a herd of bulls than in a mating herd. A bull whose horns protrude more than 2 inches (5 cm) beyond his ears will qualify as a trophy.

Once the hunter has selected his bull and got within range, he settles down for a shot. The best shot is a heart shot, about one-third of the way up the chest, in line with the leg. Even if he is hit with a perfect shot, the animal will not drop at once but will jump slightly or rush off at full speed, moving the whole herd, and falling dead within about 40 yards (35 m). If a shot pierces the chest cavity, but neither strikes the heart nor breaks a shoulder, the buffalo goes a considerable distance and several shots may be needed to finish him off. A shot to the spine, at the point where neck and body meet, drops the animal at once but does not kill it outright, so that a second shot, to the heart, is needed. The frontal brain shot is the most difficult and should be attempted by a novice only to stop a charge, for nothing else will. When a buffalo is feeding, the point of aim for a brain shot is between the eyes at the edge of the boss of the horns. In the typical stance of enquiry, when the animal is looking down his nose, the target is just at the top of the nose. When a buffalo charges, he starts with his head up and ends with it right down (the victim's initial injuries are nearly always to the legs and thighs).

The dawn ambush is another method of hunting buffalo. During the early hours of the morning, the hunter must position himself near a trail that the herd will use to a nearby water hole. Great care must be taken to stay downwind of the herd at all times.

Following a wounded buffalo is difficult and dangerous. If he stays with the alerted herd, shots at ranges of up to 150 yards (135 m) might be necessary. If the animal is on its own, it makes its way through some of the thickest bush on hand and stops there, only to charge out suddenly and at short range. There will then be only a split second to get off a shot.

The right weapon and bullet are essential for buffalo hunting. Nothing under .375 is adequate. The .458 is excellent; so are the heavy doubles, from .450 up through .470, .500–.465. The bullet must be solid. Although a soft-nosed bullet would do for a body shot, it would be almost certainly useless in stopping a charge. [BH]

Asian Wild Boar

There are wild boar over much of Asia. They live in widely different sorts of terrain: snowy, open forests in Siberia; arid locations, such as those in India; and in tropical forests and jungles. The wild boar of India are almost hairless and are smaller and darker than the boar of Siberia or those of the tropical jungles. Wild boar that inhabit regions where rattan palms grow—mainly in the East Indies—are among the few animals that will attack man without provocation; they become bad-tempered from the thorns picked up while rooting under the rattans.

Shooting a trophy-class wild boar, especially in the deep forests, is usually a matter of following a spoor, which is often to be found along streams or in other rooting spots. When the marks of the fore hooves exceed a width of 2 inches (5 cm), the animal can be of interest; this size of hoof indicates a weight of about 250 lb (110 kg), and every additional $\frac{1}{4}$ inch (6 mm) indicates about an additional 100 lb (45 kg) in weight.

Tracking can involve many hours of difficult slogging through the bush in mountainous terrain. Great caution and alertness are always needed around grazing places and when tracking into dense underbrush and thick grasses, in which boar may have bedded down. With good luck, a hunter may see a boar early in the morning when it is still rooting and grazing; this would be his only chance of finding a boar preoccupied and possibly unaware of a human presence.

Wild boar of all regions have the peculiar habit of making beds of branches, twigs, grasses, leaves, and general debris. In mountainous regions, piles of this sort are usually formed on ridgetops; in open areas, they may be found under trees. When still fresh, leaves and grasses may be obvious and evidently out of place but, after some time, they may be difficult to detect. The boar beds down under all this vegetation and, when disturbed, erupts spectacularly, usually to head away downhill. It is prudent, therefore, for a hunter to approach a known bedding area from the top of the hill or slope.

Less permanent bedding places used by boar do not have this covering. The animals blend well into natural cover. Even when a boar is sleeping, its senses are still alert.

A boar's tracks zigzag about when they approach its bedding place and, on observing this, the hunter must move very carefully. A charging boar is very fast and agile, and it is only wise to select a 10- or 12-gauge double or repeating shotgun, loaded with heavy buckshot, when tracking wild boar. They are most formidable animals. [GY]

Tiger

Tiger were once hunted for pleasure by Asian potentates and their guests, who were borne through the jungles on the backs of elephants. Later, the great Jim Corbett won lasting credit for altering the sportsman's approach to the hunting of the big cats of Asia, so that the balance was made more even between the hunter and his quarry. Baiting, waiting in the vicinity of a kill, and tracking all became methods used by the visiting hunter; sometimes, local skills in imitating the squealing sounds of some small animal in distress were used to lure a tiger out of cover. Hunting was always dangerous, and the risks entailed in coping with wounded tigers were very real. It is now illegal to hunt tigers. However, if the conservation efforts that have been made since the mid-1970s prove successful, tiger hunting may be allowed again one day, as numbers will need to be kept within the limits set by supplies of wild game and an increasing human population. [GY]

Blackbuck and Nilgai

These two species are hunted in India, often in the same areas of open grasslands, on the fringes of the Gir and Sal forests; nilgai occur in cultivated areas, where they are agricultural pests. When near cultivation, both species are often extremely shy and wary. Stalking them is difficult, and great precaution must be exercised when shooting in such densely inhabited areas.

On open plains, both species either keep a distance from an approaching hunter or simply move out of sight. Driving may endanger beaters. The best bet is to circle round the animals, slowly getting closer until within range. Distances are hard to estimate in the absence of trees. The heated air distorts visibility, too, and shots at more than about 300 yards (270 m) should not be taken.

Less sporting but perhaps more effective methods are used by local hunters, who wait at or near watering-places. If suitable cover exists, a visiting hunter can employ such methods, arranging for the animals to be driven back from the water to the cover. Blackbuck in motion are hard to hit, for they move with a fast, bouncing gait and take great leaps when they want to go still faster. [GY]

Southern Asian Bears

In the tropics and deep forests, tracking is the basic method for hunting bears, especially when the rains have left the ground soft. The hunter should be accompanied by a guide; as they follow the tracks, the hunter should watch ahead and to the sides of the trail all the time. This is particularly vital when the tracks suddenly change direction, for this may mean that the bear has started looking for a place to bed down, or has become aware of being followed. In the latter case, it will be waiting in ambush. If it attacks, it will be silently and at great speed. All three Asian species of bear are dangerous, but the Tibetan black bear is by far the worst. Perhaps the best thing in dense jungle is to leave bears alone, unless the hunt is for a bear that must be shot because of its attacks on local people.

In drier regions and open mountain terrain, tracking is difficult, but bears may easily be spotted some distance away because visibility is relatively good. A hunter must aim carefully at a bear that is uphill of him, for, unless he kills it outright, it may tumble and roll downhill, only to halt itself on reaching him. The Tibetan black bear is frequently only wounded because of its peculiar anatomy and its habit of contorting itself into flatly-spread stances. More often, however, the animal will be only wounded because the hunter has shot in nervous haste; the hunter who goes after bear must be able to shoot well and calmly. [GY]

Asian Sheep and Goats

Hunting in the Asian mountains demands that the hunter is in very good physical shape and equipped for cool to cold mountain conditions. Rifles need to have scope sights and be low-caliber: the .270 Winchester or an equivalent is good. The .300 Magnums are excellent for sheep and goats. Rifles are zeroed at 250 yards (230 m) or used with matching loads that are at zero at 200 and 300 yards (180 and 270 m): the average ranges to be expected fall within these limits, although ranges may be longer in the Altai and Pamir regions.

The base hunting camp is established within an hour or two of the area inhabited by sheep or goats; this is usually below 10,000 feet (3,000 m) but at the beginning of the "thin air" zone; a hunter may need time to get used to this. The camp should be small and quiet, for mountain game can often be spotted without leaving the camp; many ibex, tahr, and markhor have been taken soon after a tent flap is opened in the morning.

Most animals of the high mountains, and especially sheep, have very keen eyesight and can spot an approaching man at a great distance. The hunter should, therefore, have taken up a good vantage point before dawn, so that he may rest, if need be, and glass at first light. Drab clothes blend in with the terrain. As few movements as possible lessen the risk of scaring the animals into immobility, which makes them all the harder to see. The hunter must be downwind of the animals; his scent would spook them at once. If they take themselves off, they are not likely to be seen again by the hunter. A quiet initial watch, constant alertness, and calm, unhurried walks pay dividends.

Before taking a shot, it is important to consider if the animal would fall into an inaccessible crevice, or suffer damage in falling, if it were hit. An animal can sometimes be induced to move to a "safer" place by a shout or a shot, provided it cannot see the source of the noise. This is an important tactic in the Himalayas and other similar regions. [GY]

Asian Deer

Asian deer are animals of deep forests and jungle, and the hunter must be prepared for jungle and forest conditions. He must expect to get wet, but his footware should repel both water and leeches; his personal equipment must include one or two canteens of drinking water. Furthermore, he must bear in mind that most shots are taken at relatively close range (under 100 yards) and that bullet deflection is a problem, most of all when bamboo is abundant. High-velocity cartridges are generally less effective than heavier, slower loads, or even shotgun slugs or buckshot. A telescope sight can hang up on jungle vines, while its lenses may fog up in the damp; the more streamlined a rifle is, the better.

European and North American concepts of fair chase may not be understood in many parts of Asia where, after all, the inhabitants hunt for meat and may not appreciate a hunter's regard for a trophy. A visiting sportsman needs to make sure that his guide understands his desire for sporting methods.

Tribal hunters themselves in some highland regions often employ very sporting tracking and stalking methods for deer. These demand stamina, patience, and skill. All Asian deer can be hunted by "pussy-footing" in search of the animals when they are feeding very early in the morning or late in the evening. During the rest of the day, the hunter should concentrate on selected tracks or walk slowly through areas known to contain bedded deer. Except for chital and barasingha, Asian deer bed deep in bamboo thickets and other dense forest growth; it takes much skill to surprise a bedded animal or to get close enough for a clear shot before it has run away.

Most deer commonly bed just off the ridgelines or on the slopes. The hunter keeps to the higher ground, somewhat behind his tracker, who moves noisily somewhat lower down the strip of hillside. They keep within earshot of one another, and the hunter knows where the tracker is. On wider slopes, an experienced tracker usually shows the hunter where to wait, while he "kicks up" the deer noisily from a direction that will move them toward the hunter. Such deer seldom move slowly, so the hunter must be ready to shoot at them on the run.

In some areas, the local people use whistles and calls to decoy the deer; such methods may be the only way for a hunter to see a deer in daylight. [GY]

Big Game Hunting in South America

South America has often been called the world's last frontier, yet, despite an abundance of relatively small creatures, it holds only a few species of big game, of which several have been introduced from Europe. The largest native creatures are the jaguar, the puma, the tapirs, and the Andean bear, which lives on the western side of the Andes. The big cats are now protected in one way or another, and no longer really the quarry of sporting hunters. Literally innumerable species of small animals, birds, insects, and fish, some of which have hardly been classified scientifically, inhabit the tropical rain forests, most of which are too thick for hunting.

The animals of major interest to the sporting hunter include those already mentioned and the European red deer, which has been introduced into Argentina. The world's largest rodent, the capybara, is a jungle species that is good to eat but not a very challenging target for a hunter. Central and South America are well known for their wildfowling and upland-bird shooting (notably doves).

It is not easy to go hunting in South America, even if one lives there. The forbidding jungle, transport difficulties, official attitudes that do not always tend toward an active encouragement of sport hunting: these prompt the caution that a hunter must not expect merely to arrive in the continent and go hunting. Arrangements must be made in advance.

Almost every South American country has a national hunting club through which the prospective hunter can get in touch with game agencies, organizers of hunting tours, guides, suppliers of equipment, and so on. This is the way to find out about hunting seasons, game limits, firearms, and other regulations, including those affecting species threatened with extinction. [LC]

Red Deer in Argentina

Argentina has fantastically good red-deer hunting. It is the only country in South America where there is a huntable population, and the chances of shooting a world-record rack are good. The deer are hunted on large ranches, many of which exceed 70,000 acres (29,000 hectares), called *estancias*; gamekeepers in full-time employment manage the herds of deer so as to breed the best possible trophy animals. Old and inferior animals are culled, and hunting is one of the means used to achieve this.

There are many ranches near Bariloche, a regional tourist center about 1,100 miles (1,800 km) from Buenos Aires. The town is dominated by the nearby Andes, which soar up to heights of 12,000 feet (3,500 m) to the west of the town. Hunters can call on the services of well-established guides who can ensure enjoyable and successful hunting.

Some of the ranches are private estates, to which the visitor could expect only to be invited. Others, however, are commercial ranches with ready access for hunters. A fee is paid for each animal shot, and a bonus may be charged for an exceptional trophy; this method of charging will be familiar to those who have enjoyed traditional continental European hunting.

Each hunter is provided with a guide; both of them must expect to do a lot of walking while searching the mountain meadows and alpine slopes. It is the guide's job to help spot the deer, before he and the hunter stalk it until they get within range. The hunter needs stout boots, warm clothes, and well-trained legs. [LC]

Hunting in the Jungle

Some hunters may be interested in adding tapir and capybara to the list of their trophies, but it must be doubtful if most hunters would travel a great distance to shoot only these rather innocuous jungle animals. But for a hunter who is alreday there, why not?

Tapir and capybara both provide good eating. The Indian villagers hunt them for this reason, and the visiting hunter, therefore, cannot reckon on finding either sort of animal near a village. In addition, tapir and capybara are shy: a tapir scurries back into cover at the first sign of danger, and capybara, being good swimmers, dive into the water, or run away into the jungle, when approached. Shooting from a small boat on a stream or river is perhaps the best method for capybara but, even so, shots are usually taken at relatively long ranges.

Tapir can be hunted with dogs, if a pack can be assembled, but tapir are elusive and can rush through thick undergrowth that is impenetrable for men and dogs, before vanishing from sight in the jungle or when they reach water or a swamp. [LC]

Bird Shooting in South America

Tinamous are the premier upland game birds of Central and South America. Various species are plentiful on the grasslands, where the hunting method is to get out in the open and walk. Pointing dogs are used in some areas, but, in the sandy areas of the pampas, the dogs get sand burrs between their toes and become incapacitated before long.

A species of tinamous occurs in the mountains of Ecuador, typical elevations being 10,000 to 12,000 feet (3,000 to 4,000 m).

Tinamous behave rather like pheasant, flushing with a furious beating of wings, then fly on, gliding from time to time on stiffly outstretched wings. The birds are found in coveys, but coveys do not flush together as do coveys of bobwhite quail, for example; tinamous rise one at a time, which can give good sport when a covey provides a succession of ten, twelve, or even more birds. [NS]

Wildfowling in South America

One of the world's greatest concentrations of teal is to be found in the huge marshes at the mouth of the Magdalena River in Columbia, on the Caribbean coast. Bluewing teal begin to arrive there in mid-October; some stay as late as mid-April. These marshes teem with birds and teal outnumber any other species in some parts of the delta. Hunters shoot over a dozen or so rubber decoys; they use dugout canoes or other suitable small boats, both to traverse the marshes and as a shooting platform. On some occasions, hunters need only conceal themselves in the rushes.

The Magellan goose provides hunting in the southern part of the continent. The birds fly north from Tierra del Fuego in April. In the Argentinean state of Chubut, local farmers welcome hunters, for the geese are very numerous and crop the grass intended for the farmers' sheep and cows. Hunters take up positions on the edges of swamps, lakes, or rivers, where the birds seek refuge at night. If there is no wind, newspapers can function as makeshift decoys in the pastures. Hunters conceal themselves as best they can, usually by wearing drab-colored clothes and standing still, for example by a large fence post. The geese often swing right into gunning range and even land among the decoys. The ashy-headed goose is less numerous than the Magellan, but it occurs together with it, sometimes even flying in formation with it. [NS]

III Reference

Hunter's Lexicon

Jerome Knap
Wilson Stephens

Action: The breech mechanism of a gun, by means of which it is loaded and which secures the cartridge in the chamber, preventing the cartridge from discharging to the rear. Also, a field-trial term describing the manner in which a dog moves in the field; the British term is "style."

Afon: A stream in Wales.

Aperture Sight: See **Sights**.

Autoloader: See **Semiautomatic**.

Automatic: Any firearm which continues to fire, to the extent of the capacity of its magazine, so long as the trigger is depressed. Sometimes erroneously applied to semiautomatic firearms.

Automatic Safety: See **Safety**.

Backing: An expression of a dog's pointing instinct, when a dog comes to point at sight of another dog's point, to "back" him, or "honor" his point.

Balance: In theory, the balance is that point between butt and muzzle where a gun balances when rested on a fulcrum. A gun balances properly when the point of balance is midway between the points where the hands naturally hold the gun in shooting. However, this is not the common understanding of the term. In most cases, balance is understood to mean the feel it gives the shooter in handling the gun—that is, whether correctly balanced or either muzzle-light or muzzle-heavy.

Ballistics: The theory of the motion of projectiles. The shooter loosely considers "ballistics" to mean data relative to the velocity, energy, trajectory, and penetration of a cartridge, and sometimes to related factors such as chamber pressure and a powder's burning characteristics.

Barrens: Flat wasteland with low, stunted vegetation. Also, a broad, flat marsh.

Bay: Second point of antlers, after the brow and before the tray; sometimes spelt "bey."

Bead: See **Sights**.

Beat (n): An area to be beaten or driven to flush out game.

Beat (v): To beat bushes etc., to drive out game.

Beater (n): One who beats, in order to send the game over the shooters at a covert shoot or grouse drive.

Beck: A stream in northern England.

Bed: Where big game—or even hares or rabbits—have been sleeping or resting. Another term for a rabbit or hare bed is "form."

Belted Cartridge: A cartridge, primarily of the heavy-caliber, high-velocity type, which is rimless but has a belt around the base.

Belton: A type of color formed in English setters when two colors blend so closely as to lose individual identity. Blue belton is a combination of black and white; orange belton a combination of orange and white.

Bench Rest: A wooden shooting bench, heavily constructed and firmly placed, with suitable "rest" for the muzzle or barrel, at which the shooter may sit to engage in accuracy tests of the firearm.

Bevy: A group of game birds, such as quail, generally a brood.

Big-bore: A rather loose adjective, normally applied in North America to rifles of calibers larger than .25, but applied in some countries only to much larger calibers. Also, large-bore.

Blind: A natural or man-made hiding place from which a hunter shoots ducks, turkeys, or other game. The British term is "hide."

Block: Colloquial word for a duck decoy.

Blowback: Automatic or semiautomatic action in which extraction, ejection, and reloading are accomplished by means of the force exerted rearward by the gas of the fired cartridge.

Blowdown: A thick tangle of fallen trees and brush, usually the result of severe winds.

Blown Primer: A cartridge case in which the primer was blown out during firing. Can cause serious injury, even blindness, to the shooter; one good argument for use of shooting glasses.

Bluebird Weather: Sunny, windless conditions which are the bane of the wildfowler's existence, as waterfowl normally do not move in such weather or else fly very high.

Boat-tail Bullet: A bullet with a tapered rear end designed to obtain greater efficiency at longer ranges.

Bore: The inside of the barrel of a shotgun, rifle, revolver, or pistol, the diameter of which is the caliber or gauge of the weapon. The term is also a synonym for "gauge" of a shotgun.

Brace: Standard term for two quail, partidge, pheasant, grouse, hares, or dogs.

Breech: The base (as opposed to the muzzle) of a gun barrel; the rear portion of the barrel, which, in a modern rifle, is chambered to hold the cartridge.

Breeding: The ancestry of a dog.

Brocket: A male red deer in his third year.

Broken: Term for a finished, completely trained bird dog.

Brood: All young together born or hatched by one female. See **Bevy** and **Covey**.

Brow: The first, or brow, point of antlers.

Browse: Branches of trees, small saplings, or low brush, which serve as food for members of the deer family and other ruminants.

Brush-cutter: A bullet, usually of large caliber and considerable weight, having enough velocity and weight to continue its original course without being deflected by light brush.

Brush Gun: A rifle or shotgun with a barrel shorter than average, designed for ease of movement through heavy brush.

Buck: American term for the male of various species, including antelope, goat, deer, and rabbit; in Britain, of non-native deer imported to Britain, and of the rabbit. Also, an accessory used in teaching retrieving, sometimes called a retrieving dummy.

Buckshot: Large lead or alloy shot used in shotgun shells, principally for big game such as deer.

Buffer: A biological term used to designate small forms of animal life upon which predators will feed, thus reducing the mortality of game. When enough "buffers" are present, predators eat fewer game animals.

Bugle: The sound a bull elk (wapiti) makes during the rutting (breeding) season to advertise his presence to the females and to issue challenges to the other bulls. The British term is "roaring" for stags of European red deer. In some regions, "bugling" is also used to describe the cries of hounds.

Bump: Slang for accidental flushing of game birds by a pointing dog.

Burn: An area which has been burned over by a forest fire; also, a stream in Scotland.

Burst: Generally, the first part of the run when hounds are close upon the fox; any fast part of a chase.

Butt (1): The rear part of a gun stock from the grip area rearward.

Butt (2): Camouflaged embrasure in which a shooter waits for the birds at a grouse drive. Also, the backing behind a target that stops the bullets.

Butt Plate: The metal, plastic, or hard-rubber plate covering the rear of a gunstock, usually checkered or corrugated to prevent slipping. See **Recoil Pad** or **Stock.**

Calf: Young, either sex, of the red deer until a year old.

Caliber: The diameter of the bore of a rifled arm in hundredths of an inch or in millimeters, usually measured from land to land (raised portion between grooves), which gives the true diameter of the bore prior to the cutting of grooves.

Caller: A hunter who does the calling when hunting ducks, geese, or turkeys, or other game.

Cape: The hide or pelage covering the head, neck, and foreshoulders of a game animal, often removed for mounting as a trophy. The British term is headskin.

Carbine: A short-barreled rifle, normally much lighter in weight than a standard rifle.

Carrier: The mechanism in a magazine or repeating firearm (other than a revolver) which carries the shell or cartridge from the magazine into a position to be pushed into the chamber by the closing of the breechbolt.

Carry the Line: When hounds are following the scent, they are "carrying the line."

Cast: The spreading out, or reaching out, of a pointing dog in search of game or of hounds in search of a scent. Also, in archery, the speed with which the bow will throw an arrow. Also, in falconry, a group or flight of hawks.

Centerfire: A cartridge of which the primer is contained in a pocket in the center of the cartridge base.

Chalk: White excreta of a woodcock, indicating the presence of birds in a covert.

Chamber: The enlarged portion of the gun barrel at the breech, in which the cartridge fits when in position for firing.

Charge: Load of powder and/or shot in a shotshell, or the load of powder in a muzzle-loading gun. Also, an old command, still occasionally used, to a hunting dog to lie down; it derives from the time when gun dogs were required to lie down while the guns were charged.

Cheeper: Game bird too young to be shot.

Chilled Shot: Shot containing a greater percentage of antimony than soft lead. All shot except buckshot and steel shot is dropped from a tower. Buckshot of the large sizes is cast, as are single balls.

Choke: The constriction in the muzzle of a shotgun bore by means of which control is exerted upon the shot charge in order to throw its pellets into a definite area of predetermined concentration. Degree of choke is measured by the approximate percentage of pellets in a shot charge, which hit within a 30-inch circle at 40 yards. The following table gives the accepted percentages obtained with various chokes:

Full Choke ....65 % minimum
Improved Modified ....60–70 %
Modified ....50–65 %
Improved Cylinder ....35–50 %
Cylinder ....25–35 %

Choke Constriction: The amount of constriction at the muzzle of various gauges, which produces choke, is as follows:

Gauge	Full Choke		Modified Choke		Improved Cylinder		Cylinder	
	inch	mm	inch	mm	inch	mm	inch	mm
10	.035	.889	.017	.432	.007	.178	0	0
12	.030	.762	.015	.381	.006	.152	0	0
16	.024	.610	.012	.305	.005	.127	0	0
20	.021	.533	.010	.254	.004	.102	0	0
28	.017	.432	.008	.203	.003	.076	0	0

Clip: Detachable magazine of a rifle or a pistol. A metal container designed to contain a given number of cartridges for a repeating rifle.

Cock (n): Male bird.

Cock (v): Make ready a firearm for firing by pulling back the hammer or firing pin to full cock. A firearm with a visible hammer usually has half-cock and full-cock positions.

Cold Line: The faint scent of the quarry.

Comb: The upper and forward edge of a gunstock against which the shooter rests his cheek.

Conseil International De La Chasse: An organization comprising members from various European countries, which assumes responsibility for the classification and measurement system employed in recording trophies of European big game.

Coon: A colloquialism for raccoon.

Cope: Muzzle for a ferret.

Couple: Two woodcock, snipe, waterfowl, shorebirds, or rabbits. Also used to describe two hounds.

Course: In fox hunting, to run by sight and not by nose. Also, the territory to be covered in a field trial for bird dogs and spaniels.

Cover: Trees, undergrowth, grass, or reeds in which game may lie. A place to be hunted.

Covert: In fox hunting, a place where fox may be found. Also, woodland. Also, the name for a place where any game may be found. Same as cover.

Covert-shoot: Pheasant shooting in which the shooters wait in line outside woodland from which the birds are driven by beaters.

Coverts: The wing feathers which cover the base of the flight feathers.

Covey: A group of game birds such as quail; a bevy. Also, a British term for a family group of grouse or partridge, generally four to sixteen birds.

Crimp: That portion of a cartridge case or shotshell, which is turned inward to grip the bullet or to hold the end wad in place, respectively.

Cripple: A game bird that has been shot down but not killed. This term is normally employed in duck shooting. (In upland shooting, the term "winged" is more often used.)

Cross Hairs: The cross-hair reticule or aiming device in a telescopic sight on a rifle. Wire or nylon is now used instead of hair.

Cry: The voice of a hound. The cry varies during the chase. By its tone, the other hounds can tell how strong the scent is and how sure the line is.

Dancing Ground: An area where such birds as prairie chicken, sharptail grouse, sage grouse, and black grouse perform their courtship dances in the spring.

Doe: Female of fallow, roe, or imported deer, and of the hare or rabbit.

Dogging: The shooting of grouse or partridges over pointers or setters.

Double: Any shotgun with two barrels, whether the side-by-side type or the over-and-under. Also, when a fox, raccoon, or other game animal turns back on his course to elude hounds.

Drag: Scent left by a fox as he returns to his den; or an artificial trail made by dragging a scented bag for hounds to follow.

Dram: Unit of weight, which is the equivalent of 27.5 grains. There are 256 drams in one pound avoirdupois (454 g).

Dram Equivalent: In the early days of black-powder shotshells, the powder charge was measured in drams. Dram for dram, today's smokeless powder is more powerful. The term "3 dram equivalent" means that the amount of smokeless powder used produces the same shot velocity as would 3 drams of black powder.

Drift: Deviation of any projectile, bullet, or arrow from the plane of its departure, caused by wind. Also, the deviation of the projectile from the plane of departure due to rotation. In all sporting firearms, the drift from the plane of departure due to rotation is so slight as to be of no consequence.

Drive (v): To move game toward the shooters.

Drive (n): A self-contained operation during a day's shooting in which the shooters remain stationary while game is driven from a particular direction.

Driven Game: Birds which are moved toward the shooters by beaters.

Driving: Method of hunting in which the hunters are divided into two groups. One group moves to an area to take up stands or watches covering a wide terrain; the other group moves toward the first, making sufficient noise to drive the game toward the group on watches. The individuals on watch are termed "standers" and those driving the game "drivers," or in Britain, "beaters."

Drop: Distance below the line of sight of a rifle or shotgun from an extension of this line to the comb and to the heel of the stock. See **Drop at Comb** and **Drop at Heel.**

Drop at Comb: Vertical distance between the prolonged line of sight and the point of the comb. The drop and thickness of the comb are the most important dimensions in the stock of a shotgun or rifle. They are affected by the drop at heel. If the dimensions are correct, the eye is guided into and held steadily in the line of aim. For hunting purposes, the best standard drop at comb on both rifles and shotguns is $1\frac{1}{4}$ to $1\frac{5}{8}$ inches (3.8–4.1 cm). Drop differs for target shooting. Ideal stock dimensions for field or target shooting are attained only by custom fitting.

Drop at Heel: The vertical distance between the prolonged line of sight and the heel of the butt. The amount of drop varies, depending upon the ideas and build of the shooter. Most shotgun hunters require a drop of about $2\frac{1}{4}$ inches (6.4 cm).

Earth: The hole of some burrowing animal, such as a woodchuck, appropriated by a fox. Also, the den.

Eclipse Plumage: The plumage of a male bird before the time when he takes on his full breeding plumage.

Ejector: Mechanism which ejects an empty case or loaded cartridge from a gun after it has been withdrawn, or partly withdrawn, from the chamber by the extractor. In a double-barreled shotgun, ejector often means extractor; "selective ejection" means automatic ejection of the fired shell only and is otherwise called automatic ejection.

Ejector Hammers: In a double-barreled shotgun, the driving pistons which eject the fired shells.

Elevation: The angle which the rear sight must be raised or lowered to compensate for the trajectory of the bullet and ensure the desired point of impact at different ranges.

Exotic: Any game bird or animal which has been imported.

Extractor: The hooked device which draws the cartridge out of the chamber when the breech mechanism is opened.

Fault: A check or interruption in a run by hounds caused by loss of scent.

Fawn: Offspring of the year of any deer other than red deer.

Field Dressing: The minimum dressing-out of a game animal in the field, merely enough to ensure preservation of the meat and the trophy, means usually the removing of the entrails and visceral organs.

Firing Pin: The pointed nose of the hammer of a firearm or the separate pin or plunger which, actuated by the hammer or the mainspring, dents the primer, thus firing the cartridge.

Firelighting: See **Jacklighting.**

Flag: The tail of a whitetail deer. Also, the long hair on a setter's tail.

Flat Trajectory: A term used to describe the low trajectory of high-velocity bullets which travel for a long distance over a flatter arc than other bullets. Scientifically an incorrect term, for no trajectory is truly flat. See also **Trajectory.**

Flighting: Ambushing duck or pigeon at their roosts or feeding grounds.

Fling: A period of aimless running before an enthusiastic bird dog settles to hunting.

Flush (n): The act of a questing dog putting game birds into the air, or an animal on foot.

Flushing Wild: Rise of game birds which have not been obviously disturbed, or birds that have been flushed out of shotgun range.

Flyway: Migration route of birds between breeding and wintering grounds. Also, the route waterfowl use between feeding and roosting areas.

Forearm: Synonymous with fore-end, although some use "forearm" when the butt stock and foregrip are separate pieces. See **Fore-end.**

Fore-end: Portion of the wooden gunstock forward of the receiver and under the barrel.

Forest: Open mountains, devoid of trees, on which stags are stalked in Scotland.

Fresh Line: Opposite of "cold line"— a fresh, or "hot," scent of game pursued by hounds.

Fur: All four-legged quarry.

Gaggle: A flock of geese. An old British term.

Game: In British law, pheasants, all partidges, all grouse, woodcock and snipe; by custom, also deer and hares.

Gang: A flock of brant. Also, an old British term for a group of European elk (moose).

Gas-operated: Said of a semiautomatic firearm which utilizes the gases generated by the powder combustion, before the bullet emerges from the muzzle, to operate a piston which extracts, ejects, and reloads the arm to the extent of the number of rounds in the magazine.

Gauge: The bore size of a shotgun. The number of the gauge has no relation to the linear measurement of the bore. Gauge is determined by the number of equal spheres, each of which exactly fits the barrel of the gun, which may be obtained from 1 lb (454 g) of lead. For example, a 12-gauge gun has a bore diameter the same as one of the twelve identically-sized spheres which can be made from a pound of lead. See **Bore.**

Gauge Measurements: The bore diameters of various gauges are as follows:

10 gauge	.775 inches (19 · 69 mm)
12 gauge	.725 inches (18 · 42 mm)
16 gauge	.662 inches (16 · 81 mm)
20 gauge	.615 inches (15 · 62 mm)
28 gauge	.550 inches (13 · 97 mm)
.410 gauge	.410 inches (10 · 41 mm)

Ghillie: Attendant, usually in charge of the pony, who accompanies a stalking party in Scotland. Also, an attendant on a fisherman.

Glass (v): To scan terrain with binoculars or telescope to locate game.

Grain: Abbreviated gr. Weight measurement. One ounce equals 437.5 gr. There are 7,000 gr in 1 lb (454 grams). In reference to gunstocks, grain indicates the direction of the fibers on the surface of the stock.

Gralloch (v): To field dress big-game animals immediately after shooting by removing the viscera and entrails. See **Field Dressing.**

Gram: Abbreviated g. Weight measurement. The equivalent of 15.43 grains.

Graze: Grasses, weeds, and similar low growths upon which deer and other ruminants feed.

Grip: That part of the stock of a rifle or shotgun which is grasped by the trigger hand when firing the gun. The two most common types of grips are the "pistol grip" and the "straight grip" found on some double-barreled shotguns.

Group: A series of shots fired at a target with a constant sight setting and point of aim. The diameter of the group is measured from the centers of the outer holes.

Group Diameter: The distance between centers of the two shots most widely separated in a group.

Gun: Any smooth-bore weapon projecting a charge of pellets; see also **Rifle**. Also, a participant in a British shooting party, as distinct from a helper or spectator.

Hair Trigger: A trigger requiring extremely light pressure for the release of the hammer.

Hammer: That part of a firearm, actuated by the mainspring and controlled by the trigger, which strikes either the cartridge rim or primer, or strikes and drives forward the firing pin so that it indents the primer or rim of the cartridge, to discharge the cartridge.

Hammerless: Of firearms having the hammer concealed within the breech mechanism.

Handgun: A firearm that is normally fired with one hand. A pistol or revolver.

Handloads: Cartridges loaded by hand for precision shooting, as opposed to commercial or "factory loads."

Hang-fire: Delayed ignition of the powder in a cartridge after the hammer has fallen and the primer has been struck.

Hard-mouthed: Of a dog that chews or crushes birds when retrieving.

Hart: The male deer. Usually used to refer to male red deer in Britain. A stag.

Head (n): The antlers of a deer, of any species and either sex.

Head (v): For a shooter to take post in advance of others to intercept birds flushing out of range of the rest.

Headspace: The space between the head of the bolt or breechblock and the base of the cartridge. Excessive headspace is exceedingly dangerous and can result in the bursting of the receiver.

Headstamp: The letters or number, or both, on the base of a cartridge.

Heel (n): Upper part of the butt of a shotgun or rifle. Also, a command to a dog to walk quietly beside or at the heel of the person giving the order.

Hide: Camouflaged embrasure in which a shooter waits for duck or pigeon. See **Blind**. Also, the skin of an animal.

High-base Shell: A shotgun shell furnished with high inside base wad, approximately $\frac{3}{4}$ inch (19 mm) thick before forming.

High-brass Shell: High-velocity shotgun shell on which the brass base extends a considerable distance up the plastic tube.

High Intensity: A term associated with a rifle or cartridge having a velocity of more than 2,500 foot-seconds (762 m/seconds).

High Power: A term associated with a rifle or cartridge having a velocity of more than 2,000 foot-seconds (609 m/seconds).

Hind: The female of the red deer.

Hochstand (Ger.): The seat at tree-top height from which deer are shot in woodland.

Hull: Empty cartridge or shell.

Hummle: A mature red deer stag which has grown no antlers.

Hunting: In British usage, the pursuit by a pack of hounds of ground quarry (fox, deer, hare) with followers mounted or on foot; gun sport is "shooting" in British idiom.

Imperial Bull: A bull elk (wapiti) that has seven points on each antler; a relatively rare and highly desirable trophy. Also, imperial stag in the case of European red deer.

Iron Sight: See **Sights**.

Jack: The male of the hare.

Jacklighting: The illegal practice of shooting game at night with the help of artificial light, which is reflected by the eyes of the game. Synonymous with firelighting.

Jump-shooting: A method of duck hunting in which the hunter stealthily approaches ducks by boat, or by stalking toward water, until within range and then flushes them.

Juvenile: A bird which, though having attained full growth, has not attained full adult characteristics or plumage. See also **Cheeper**.

Kentucky Windage: A term used by American riflemen to describe the process of "holding off" to the left or right of a target to allow for the effect of the wind on the bullet, but making no adjustment in the sight setting.

Knobber: Male red deer in his second year.

Lead (n): Term used to designate the distance it is necessary to hold ahead of any bird or animal to compensate for its speed of movement and the time required for the bullet or hot charge to reach it. The British term is forward allowance.

Lead (v): To cause a dog to follow under restraint, by means of a cord or leather thong attached to the dog's collar.

Leash: A group of three quail, partridge, pheasant, grouse, or hares. Also, a cord to lead a dog, a dog lead.

Length of Stock: The distance in a straight line from the center of the trigger to a point midway between the heel and toe of the buttplate, on the surface of the plate. Required stock length depends upon the build of the shooter, men of short stature or short arms requiring short stocks. The standard length for hunting arms is 14 inches (35.6 cm) for shotguns and $13\frac{1}{2}$ inches (34.3 cm) for rifles. Also called length of pull.

Line: The track or trail of an animal indicated by the scent the hounds are following. Also, the shooters deployed at a formal shoot, called "the line."

Line of Sight: The straight line between the eye of the shooter and the target. See **Trajectory**.

Line-running: Of a dog that casts in straight lines rather than hunts in places where birds are usually found.

Line Shooting: A form of scoter (sea duck) shooting along the North American Atlantic coast, in which several boats line up across a known scoter flyway to shoot at the birds as they fly past.

Live Weight: The computed or estimated weight of a game animal before it is dressed out.

Loader: Attendant who holds and re-loads the second weapon when a shooter uses two guns at a covert shoot where many birds are expected.

Loch: A lake in Scotland (also lough (Ireland) and llyn (Wales).

Lock: The combination of hammer, firing pin, sear, mainspring, and trigger which serves to discharge the cartridge when the trigger is pulled.

Lock Time: The time elapsed between the release of the hammer by the sear and the impact of the firing pin on the primer. Also called lock speed.

Lubrication of Bullets: Most lead bullets have to be lubricated with grease or wax on their surface or in their grooves to prevent leading the bore. Outside-lubricated cartridges have the lubricant placed on the surface of the bullet outside the case. Inside-lubricated bullets have the lubricant in grooves or cannelures on the bullet where it is covered by the neck of the case.

Lug: In a break-down, breech-loading shotgun or rifle, a lug on the barrel secures the barrel to the frame. Lugs on the front of a bolt or breechblock which rotate into slots to lock the action for firing are termed locking lugs.

Magazine: The tube or box which holds cartridges or shells in reserve for mechanical insertion into the chamber of a repeating firearm.

Magazine Plug: Plug or dowel placed inside or against the magazine spring of a slide-action or semiautomatic shotgun to limit the capacity of the magazine in order to comply with the law. (In the United States, waterfowlers may have no more than three shells in their guns; some individual states limit magazine capacity for other game.)

Mark: A call used to warn another shooter of the flushing or approach of a game bird. The term is often accompanied by a direction: "mark right" or "mark left."

Mark Down: To use some terrain feature to mark the location of a fallen game bird in order to facilitate retrieving.

Market Gunner: One who hunted for the purpose of selling the game he killed, a practice now illegal in North America. A market hunter.

Mask: The head or pate of a fox, raccoon, wolf, or coyote.

Match Rifle: A rifle designed for competitive shooting, a target rifle.

Minute of Angle: This is the unit of adjustment on all telescopic, and most aperture, sights, being indicated by a series of fine lines. One minute of angle is equivalent to the following distances at the ranges indicated:

British and American		Metric	
25 yards	$\frac{1}{4}$in	25 m	.69 mm
50 yards	$\frac{1}{2}$in	50 m	1.39 mm
100 yards	1in	100 m	2.78 mm

Moor: High, treeless land such as that inhabited by grouse.

Mounts: Metal bases used to secure a telescopic sight to the barrel or receiver of a firearm.

Muzzle Brake: A device on the muzzle of a shotgun or rifle which, by means of vents and baffles, deflects gases to the rear to reduce recoil.

Muzzle Energy: The energy of a bullet or projectile on emerging from the muzzle of the firearm that discharges it. Usually designated in foot-pounds or kilogram-meters.

Muzzle Velocity: The speed of a bullet or projectile at the moment of emerging from the muzzle. Usually expressed in feet or meters per second.

O'Clock: A means of indicating a location on the target or over a range or field, corresponding to similar locations on the face of a clock, 12 o'clock being at the top of the target, or at the target end of the rifle range. Thus, a shot striking the target immediately to the left of the bull's-eye is a hit at 9 o'clock, and a wind blowing from the right at a right angle to the line of fire is a 3 o'clock wind.

Offhand: Shooting in a standing position, without the use of a rest or sling.

Over-and-under: Double-barreled firearm with one barrel superimposed over the other.

Palmated: Of the shape of the antlers of moose, caribou, and fallow deer that is similar to the shape of the palm of a hand with fingers outspread.

Pass-shooting: A form of shooting in which the hunter places himself in position under a known flyway or travel route of ducks, geese, pigeons, or doves. The birds are shot as they pass, without the enticement of decoys.

Pattern: The distribution of a charge of shot fired from a shotgun.

Pattern Control: Control of the shot pattern by means of choke.

Peep Sight: See **Sights.**

Peg: The numbered stick indicating the position of a shooter at a covert shoot or partridge drive.

Pelage: The fur, hair, or wool covering of a mammal.

Pellet: Round shot, of any size, a given number of which make up the shot charge.

Picker-up: One who, helped by dogs, finds and gathers what is shot.

Piece: The mid-day meal carried by a shooter.

Piston: In an automatic or semiautomatic arm, a metal plunger which, when forced down a cylinder by powder gases, operates a mechanism to extract and eject the fired cartridge, and to reload and cock the arm.

Pitch: This can be observed by resting a gun upright beside a wall with the butt or butt plate flat on the floor. If the barrel is exactly parallel with the wall, the gun is said to have no pitch. If the breech touches the wall and the barrel inclines away from it, the distance between the muzzle and the wall is the "negative pitch." If the barrel inclines toward the wall, so that there is a distance between the breech and the wall, this distance is what is called, simply, the "pitch." A pitch of 2 to 3 inches (5 to 8 cm) is desirable on a repeating rifle because it causes the butt to remain in place at the shoulder when the rifle is fired rapidly.

Point: The motionless pose assumed by a dog which indicates the proximity of game birds.

Points: The horn features of an antlered head which determine its ranking as a trophy (e.g. "a twelve-pointer" is brow, bay, tray, and three on top of each antler).

Point of Aim: The bottom edge of the bull's-eye for a target shooter using iron sights; the center of the bull's-eye for one using a telescopic sight.

Pointing Out: A method of shotgun shooting in which the shooter selects a point ahead of the moving target at which to shoot so that the shot charge and target will meet. Opposite shooting style to "swinging past."

Post Sight: See **Sights.**

Pot-hunter: One who hunts primarily for meat rather than sport.

Powder: The finely divided chemical mixture that supplies the power used in shotgun and metallic ammunition, technically propellant powder. When the powder is ignited by the flash of the priming composition it burns with a rapidly increasing gas which develops a pressure of 6,000 to 55,000 lb per square inch (420 to 3,900 kg per square cm) in the chamber and bore of the gun. This gas furnishes the propelling force of the bullet or charge of shot. Originally, all propellant powder was black powder formed in grains of varying size, with the size of the grain determining the rate of burning and suitability for various cartridges. Modern powders are smokeless and their base is nitroglycerine or nitrocellulose or a combination of both, the product then being called double-base powder. The rate of burning is controlled by the composition, by the size and shape of the grains, and whether or not coated with some retarding substance called a deterrent. Those so coated are called progressive-burning.

Primaries: The outer and longest flight feathers of a bird; quill feathers.

Primer: The small cup, or cap, seated in the center of the base of a centerfire cartridge and containing the igniting composition. When the primer is indented by the firing pin, the priming composition is crushed and detonates, thus igniting the charge of powder. Rimfire cartridges contain the priming composition within the folded rim of the case, where it is crushed in the same manner. The British term is cap.

Pull: The distance between the face of the trigger and the center of the butt of the gunstock. Also, the amount of pressure, in pounds, which must be applied to the trigger to cause the sear to disengage and permit the hammer to fall. Also, the command given to release a skeet or trap target.

Pump Gun: Common name for the slide-action rifle or shotgun. See **Slide Action.**

Quartering: A hunting-dog term for the act of ranging back and forth across the course.

Quartering Bird: A bird which approaches the shooter at an angle, either right or left.

Rat-tailed: Lacking long hairs on the tail, as in the case of such dogs as the Irish water spaniel.

Receiver: The frame of a rifle or shotgun including the breech, locking, and loading mechanism of the arm.

Receiver Sight: See **Sights.**

Recoil: The backward movement, or "kick," of the firearm caused by the discharge of the cartridge.

Recoil-operated: Of a firearm which utilizes the recoil, or rearward force exerted by the combustion of the powder, to operate the action and extract, eject, and reload to the extent of the number of rounds in the magazine.

Recoil Pad: A soft rubber pad on the butt of a firearm to soften its recoil.

Reduced Load: A cartridge loaded with a lighter than standard powder charge, for use at a short range.

Reticule (or **Reticle**): The crossed wires, picket, post, or other divisional system installed in a telescopic sight to permit its use as a gunsight, or in a pair of binoculars to permit the use of a scale for estimating distances.

Retrieving: Dog's act of finding and bringing an object, generally dead or wounded game bird, to the handler.

Revolver: Any handgun embodying a cylindrical magazine, as opposed to a single-shot or semiautomatic handgun, either of which is usually called a "pistol."

Rib: The raised bar or vane, usually slightly concave on its upper surface and usually matted, which forms the sighting plane extending from breech to muzzle of a gun. It is used on all double-barreled shotguns.

Rifle: A firearm projecting a single rotating bullet. Also, as the Rifle, the member of a stalking party who will fire the shot (cf. the Gun).

Rifled Slug: A bullet-shaped projectile with hollow base and rifled sides used in a shotgun for hunting big game. Will not harm shotgun barrels and will not "ream out" any type of choke.

Rifling: Parallel grooves cut into the bore of a rifle or pistol, spiraling from the breech to the muzzle, causing the bullet to spin in its flight.

Rig: A setting of decoys in front of a boat or blind; also used to describe the entire hunting outfit.

Rimfire: A cartridge in which the priming compound is contained in a rim at the base.

Ring Hunt: A form of driving in which a large number of shooters and beaters form a ring and gradually close in, to drive the game toward its center. An ancient method, still used in Europe, primarily for hunting hares and foxes.

Rough-shooting: The pursuit and taking of game and other quarry by Guns who have no human assistants but are generally aided by spaniels. See also **Dogging.**

Royal: Fourth point, after the tray and before the fifth, of antlers.

Royal Bull: A bull elk (wapiti) that has six points on each antler. A very desirable trophy. Also, royal stag of the European red deer.

Run: In some regions, a game trail or path created by animals over a period of time.

Safety: The device which locks a firearm against the possibility of discharge; sometimes called a safety catch. In common practice, the term applies primarily to the button, pin, or toggle which, when set in the "safe" position, prevents the discharge of the arm by pulling the trigger. A safety which automatically resets itself in the "safe" position when the gun is opened during the reloading process is called an automatic safety. Such a safety is most common on double-barreled shotguns.

Scapulars: The feathers on each side of the back of a bird's shoulders.

Scope: Telescope or telescopic sight.

Sear: The device in the lock of a firearm which holds the hammer or firing pin in its cocked position. When the trigger is pulled to the rear, it depresses the sear, which in turn releases the hammer or firing pin.

Secondaries: The wing feathers inside the primaries.

Semiautomatic: Any firearm which will fire, extract, eject, and reload by means of pressure on the trigger, but requires repeated pressure on the trigger to fire each round.

Set: A "rig" or setting of decoys.

Set Trigger: A trigger, the sear of which is "set up" by a preliminary movement or by pressure on another trigger, permitting the sear to disengage the hammer at the slightest touch or pressure on the trigger.

Most set triggers are adjustable for the amount of pressure desired.

Sewelling: Cords carrying colored streamers which, when activated, cause birds to flush far enough back to ensure that they are flying high when over the Guns.

Shell: Empty case of any cartridge. Also, an American term for a loaded shotgun cartridge.

Shock Collar: A collar with an electronic device which can be set off by remote control to give a dog an electric shock to punish it when it does not obey or does something wrong. The shock collar is a dangerous instrument in the hands of a novice trainer because it can ruin a dog when used incorrectly.

Side-by-side: A double-barreled shotgun with the barrels positioned side by side, as opposed to the over-and-under configuration.

Sight Radius: The distance between the front and rear sights. The longer the distance the greater the accuracy of the firearm.

Sights: The aiming device on a firearm. On most rifles and handguns, the factory-installed sights consist of two elements called "front sight" and "rear sight," which together frequently are called "iron sights" because they are made of principally metal. The front sight, located on the barrel near the muzzle, is usually post-shaped or bead-shaped and hence sometimes called post or bead. The rear sight is usually located partway down the barrel, near the breech or on the receiver. If it consists of a V- or U-shaped notch in a flat piece of metal, it is called an "open" sight. An open sight with a deep U-shaped notch with protruding wings is called a "buckhorn sight." The rear sight can also consist of an aperture in a disk. It is then called an aperture, or peep, sight. When the aperture sight is attached to the receiver it is called a "receiver sight" and when it is attached to the tang it is called a "tang sight." When the aperture adjustments have micrometer settings, such a sight is sometimes called a "micrometer sight." A hunting shotgun usually has only one sight consisting of a bead near the muzzle, but most trap and skeet guns have a second bead halfway down the barrel. There are also telescopic sights for rifles and handguns.

Sign: Any indication of the presence of game. Sign may include tracks, droppings, marks on trees, or any other indication that the area has recently been visited by a game animal.

Silvertip: Colloquial name for the grizzly bear.

Singing Ground: An open area used by the male woodcock for its courtship display.

Six o'Clock, or Six-o'Clock Hold: A term for the aiming point indicating that a rifle or handgun has been sighted-in to place the bullet not at the point of aim on a bull's-eye but well above it, so that the shooter aims at the center of the bottom edge. If the bull's-eye is a clock face, the point of aim is at 6 o'clock, but the impact point is at the exact center, midway between 6 and 12 o'clock. Target shooters prefer to aim in this way, when using iron sights, as it permits them to "rest" the bull's-eye on the top of the front sight and center the bull's-eye in the rear-sight aperture. See **O'Clock.**

Slide Action: A repeating firearm action in which the breech is closed and opened and the action operated by means of a sliding fore-end that acts as a handle for sliding the breech into the opened or closed position. Also **Pump Gun.**

Small-bore: Specifically, of a .22-caliber rifle chambered for a rimfire cartridge. Sometimes applied to rifles chambered for centerfire cartridges up to .25 caliber and shotguns under 20 gauge.

Smoked Sights: Sights after they have been blackened by soot from a candle or blackening lamp, thus eliminating any shine or glare. Commercial spray blackeners are also available.

Smoothbore: A firearm without rifling.

Sneakbox: A term for the Barnegat Bay duck-boat.

Spike-collar: A dog-training accessory—a slip collar with small spikes on the inside, used to force obedience to commands.

Spook (v): To frighten game. A term used by a hunter to indicate that a bird or animal flushed or jumped from cover at his approach, or when it winded or heard him.

Spooky: Of any animal or bird that is extremely wary or constantly alert.

Spoor: Tracks or footprints of animals. Sometimes used to mean all game sign.

Spotting Scope: A telescope with sufficient magnification to permit a shooter to see bullet holes in a target at long range, and to permit hunters to see game and evaluate trophy animals at long range. The average sporting scope is 24 power.

Spread: The overall area of a shotgun pattern. Also, the inside distance between right and left antlers or horns at their widest separation or at the tips.

Spy: An interlude of halting, waiting, and watching in which a deer shooter observes his quarry and its movements before deciding the tactics of his approach.

Stag: The mature male of the red deer.

Stalker: The professional who guides and advises those seeking to shoot deer on open forests in Scotland; also, a shooter of deer in woodland who approaches the deer by stealth.

Stalking: A method of hunting in which the hunter locates game and then stealthily follows a predetermined route to arrive within shooting range of the quarry.

Stanch: Firm and decisive; describing a dog's style while pointing. The dog that establishes a point and holds it, without caution or admonition, until his handler flushes his birds, may be regarded as stanch. Also spelled "staunch."

Stand: The position at which the shooters are placed for each drive at a covert shoot (hence "first stand," "second stand," etc.).

Start: The moment when a hound first finds scent or a trail.

Steady: Of a dog's behavior after birds are flushed. The dog is "steady to wing and shot" when he retains his position after the birds are flushed and the shot is fired.

Still-hunt: A method of hunting in which a hunter moves very slowly and silently through cover in search of game, pausing frequently to scan the terrain. The word "still," in this context, means silent rather than motionless.

Stock (n): The wooden part of a shotgun or rifle, or the handle of a pistol or revolver. The butt section of a stock is called a buttstock.

Stock (v): In game management or preserve operation, to stock is to release game in suitable habitat.

Stop: An assistant tactically placed to prevent pheasants approaching the shooters too closely, or evading them, at a covert shoot.

Swinging Past: A method of shotgun shooting in which the target is overtaken and passed by the sight, and the swing with the target is continued as the trigger is pressed. See **Pointing Out.**

Switch: A mature male deer whose antlers have no points.

Take-down: Of a firearm in which the barrel and adjacent parts can be readily separated from the receiver or action, thus permitting the arm to be packed in a short container.

Tang Sight: See **Sights.**

Team: An old British term for a flock or group of ducks.

Telescopic Sight: A telescope with reticule, permitting an aim of greater accuracy and clearness than that of an ordinary sight.

Tertials: The wing feathers inside the secondaries that are closest to the body.

Throwing Off: Of a rifle that is performing erratically or failing to give reasonable accuracy. This often results from improper bedding of the barrel.

Timberline: The upper limit of forest growth at high altitude.

Toe: The lower part of the butt of a shotgun or rifle.

Tolling Dog: A dog once widely used in Europe, and used now only in Nova Scotia, to entice wildfowl to enter a trap or to lure them within range of the gun. The action of the dog in running back and forth on the shore stimulates the birds' curiosity. In Nova Scotia, these dogs are bred to resemble a red fox and are registered by the Canadian Kennel Club as the Nova Scotia tolling retriever.

Trade (v): Of game, to move back and forth over a given area: "The ducks were trading along the far shore."

Trailer: A dog which continually or frequently follows his bracemate.

Trailing: Act of following game. See **Tracking.**

Trajectory: The course described by a projectile in flight. It forms an arc due to the effect of gravity. Usually, measured in terms of height above the line of sight at midrange.

Tray: The third point of antlers of a deer, after the brow and bay (or bez). The word is sometimes spelt "trez."

Trigger Guard: A guard surrounding the trigger or triggers of a firearm.

Trigger Pull: The pressure required to bring about the release of the sear notch on the hammer, permitting the hammer to fall.

Tularemia: A virulent disease, known also as "rabbit fever." Rabbits are its major victims, and great care should be exercised when skinning rabbits. The disease can be communicated to humans if a cut or scratch on the hands or arms makes contact with an infected animal. The disease can be fatal. No harmful effects result from eating of an infected bird or animal, as thorough cooking destroys the virus.

Turkey Shoot: Originally, turkey shoots utilized a turkey as a target as well as a prize. The bird was placed behind a shield with only its head protruding. In early turkey shoots, contestants were permitted one shot in the standing position at 10 rods (55 yards/50 m); later, the ranges varied. At modern turkey shoots, a regulation target is used or clay targets are thrown from a trap, the turkey going to the shooter with the best score.

Turning to Whistle: A hunting-dog term for breaking the cast and turning the dog in response to the handler's whistle.

Twist: The angle or inclination of the rifling grooves off the axis of the bore. Twist is designated by measuring the number of turns or fractions of turns to the inch of barrel length. A "14-inch twist" means that the grooves make one complete turn inside the bore every 14 inches (35.6 cm).

Upland Game: A general term for all small game, including birds and mammals.

Various: In Britain, fair but unexpected quarry for which no category is provided in normal game records (e.g. jay, gray squirrel).

Varmint: A colloquial American term (stemming from "vermin") for a generally undesirable animal. Woodchucks and foxes are widely considered varmints. In some regions, the term is also used for predators such as bobcats. However, many predatory and non-predatory animals that were formerly classed as varmints are now protected or managed as game animals.

Varmint Cartridge: Cartridge designed to give exceptionally good accuracy, high retained velocity, and consequently flatter trajectory. Varmint cartridges are so called because they were originally developed for long-range shooting at woodchucks and prairie dogs.

Varminter: A rifle employed primarily for long-range varmint shooting. Many such rifles have long, heavy barrels for maximum velocity and accuracy.

Velocity: The speed of a bullet or shot charge, usually designated in feet per second or meters per second.

Velvet: Soft vascular tissue which covers the antlers of deer until they have attained their full growth and form, at which time membranous tissue dies and is removed when the animal rubs its antlers against brush and trees.

Ventilated Rib: A raised sighting plane affixed to a shotgun barrel by posts, allowing the passage of air to disperse the heat from the barrel which would otherwise distort the shooter's view of the target. Very useful on trap and skeet guns.

Vernier Sight: A rear sight, the aperture of which is raised or lowered by means of a threaded post with a knurled knob. A vernier scale on the frame indicates the elevation in hundredths of an inch.

Walk-up: A shooting method, chiefly for partridges and grouse, in which the shooters and their companions advance in line through a crop, stubble or heather, taking birds as they flush.

Wild Flush: The rise of game birds for no apparent reason, usually far from the gun.

Wing: All feathered quarry. See **Fur.**

Winged: A term indicating that a game bird has been hit but not killed. Used primarily by upland shooters. See **Cripple.**

Yard: An area, usually within a forest, in which a large number of deer, moose, elk, or similar mammals herd together, tramping down the snow and feeding on the browse supplied by the low branches. Used especially by whitetail deer when snow becomes deep enough to impede normal travel through browse areas.

Yaw: To vary from a straight course. A bullet which does not travel exactly "nose on" but wobbles slightly sideways is said to "yaw."

Yeld: A female deer without offspring; if a red hind, and barren, generally the leader of the herd.

Zero: The adjustment of the sights on a rifle to cause the bullet to strike a calculated impact point at a given range. A rifle with the sights zeroed for 100 yards will, under normal conditions, place the bullet in the center of the target at that range.

Bibliography

ACKLEY, P. O. **Home Gun Care & Repair.** Harrisburg, Pennsylvania, 1969.

ANDERSON, L. A. **How to Hunt Small American Game.** New York, 1969.

BAILLIE-GROHMAN, WILLIAM A. and BAILLIE-GROHMAN, F., eds. **Edward of Norwich: Oldest English Book on Hunting.** Repr. of ed. of 1909.

BARBER, JOEL D. **Wild Fowl Decoys.** New York, 1934.

BARNES, F. C. **Cartridges of the World.** Northfield, Illinois, 1972.

BERNSEN, PAUL S. **The North American Waterfowler.** Seattle, Washington, 1972.

BEST, G. A. and BLANC, F. E., eds. **Rowland Ward's Records of Big Game (Africa).** 15th ed. London, 1973.

BOUGHAN, ROLLA B. **Shotgun Ballistics for Hunters.** New York, 1965.

BOVILL, E. W. **The England of Nimrod and Surtees: 1815–1854.** London, 1959.

BRISTER, BOB. **Shotgunning: The Art and the Science.** Tulsa, Oklahoma, 1976.

BURK, BRUCE. **Game Bird Carving.** New York, 1972.

BUTLER, ALFRED J. **Sport in Classic Times.** Los Altos, California, 1975.

CAMP, RAYMOND R. **The Hunter's Encyclopedia.** Harrisburg, Pennsylvania, 1966.

CAPSTICK, PETER H. **Death in the Long Grass.** New York, 1978.

CARMICHEL, JIM. **The Modern Rifle.** Tulsa, Oklahoma, 1975.

CHURCHILL, ROBERT. **Churchill's Shotgun Book.** New York, 1955.

CONNETT, EUGENE V., III. **Duck Decoys.** Brattleboro, Vermont, 1953.

COYKENDALL, RALF. **Duck Decoys and How to Rig Them.** New York, 1955.

DALRYMPLE, BYRON. **Complete Guide to Hunting Across North America.** New York, 1970.

—**How to Call Wildlife.** New York, 1975.

DANIELSSON, BROR., ed. **William Twiti's the Art of Hunting.** Atlantic Highland, New Jersey.

DARTON, F. HARVEY. **From Surtees to Sassoon: Some English Contrasts 1838–1928.** Darby, Pennsylvania.

DA SILVA, S. NEWTON. **A Grande Fauna Selvagen de Angola.** Luanda, Angola, 1970.

DE HAAS, F. and AMBER, J. T., eds. **Bolt Action Rifles.** Northfield, Illinois, 1971.

DELACOUR, JEAN. **The Waterfowl of the World.** 4 vols. London, 1954–64.

DORST, JEAN. **Field Guide to the Larger Mammals of Africa.** London, 1970.

DUFFEY, D. M. **Bird Hunting Know-How.** Princeton, New Jersey, 1968.

—**Hunting Dog Know-How.** New York, 1972.

EDMAN, IRWIN., ed. **Socrates' Passages in Plato's "Dialogues."** New York, 1956.

ELLIOTT, CHARLES. **Care of Game Meat & Trophies.** New York, 1975.

ELMAN, ROBERT. **1001 Hunting Tips.** Tulsa, Oklahoma, 1978.

—**The Hunter's Field Guide.** New York, 1974.

ELMAN, ROBERT., ed. **All About Deer Hunting in America.** Tulsa, Oklahoma, 1976.

ELMAN, ROBERT and PEPER, GEORGE., eds. **Hunting America's Game Animals & Birds.** New York, 1975.

ERRINGTON, PAUL. **Of Men and Marshes.** Iowa City, Iowa, 1957.

FALK, JOHN R. **The Practical Hunter's Dog Book.** New York, 1971.

FITZ, GRANCEL. **How to Measure & Score Big-Game Trophies.** New York, 1977.

FORRESTER, REX and ILLINGWORTH, NEIL. **Hunting in New Zealand.** Wellington, New Zealand, 1967.

GATES, ELGIN T. **Trophy Hunter in Asia.** New York, 1971.

GREENER, W. W. **The Gun and Its Development.** London, 1881. Repr. 9th ed. New York, 1968.

GRESHAM, GRITS. **The Complete Wildfowler.** South Hackensack, New Jersey, 1973.

HALTENORTH T. and TRENSE W. **Das Grosswild der Erde und Seine Trophäen.** Munich, 1956.

HEILNER, VAN CAMPEN. **A Book of Duck Shooting.** New York, 1947.

HENDERSON, L. M. **Pocket Guide to Animal Tracks.** Harrisburg, Pennsylvania, 1968.

[HERBERT, W. H.] **Frank Forester's Field Sports of the United States.** New York, 1849.

HERNE, BRIAN. **Uganda Safaris.** Tulsa, Oklahoma, 1980.

HINMAN, BOB. **The Duck Hunter's Handbook.** Tulsa, Oklahoma, 1974.

HULL, DENISON B. **Hounds and Hunting in Ancient Greece.** Chicago, Illinois, 1964.

JOHNSGARD, PAUL A. **Waterfowl, Their Biology and Natural History.** Lincoln, Nebraska, 1968.

KNAP, JEROME. **Where to Fish & Hunt in North America: A Complete Sportsman's Guide.** Toronto, Canada.

KOLLER, L. **Shots at Whitetails.** New York, 1970.

KRIDER, JOHN. **Krider's Sporting Anecdotes.** Philadelphia, 1853.

MACKEY, WILLIAM J., Jr. **American Bird Decoys.** New York, 1965.

MARTIN, ALEXANDER C.; ZIM, HERBERT S.; and NELSON, ARNOLD L. **American Wildlife & Plants.** New York, 1951. MARTIN, ALEXANDER C., ed. Repr. ed. New York, 1961.

MELLON, JAMES et al. **African Hunter.** New York, 1975.

O'CONNOR, JACK. **The Art of Hunting Big Game in North America.** New York, 1977.

—**The Hunting Rifle.** Tulsa, Oklahoma, 1970.

—**Sheep and Sheep Hunting.** Tulsa, Oklahoma, 1974.

ORMOND, CLYDE. **Complete Book of Hunting.** New York, 1972.

ORTEGA Y GASSET, JOSÉ. **Meditations on Hunting.** New York, 1972.

OWEN, T. R. H. **Hunting Big Game with Gun and Camera.** London, 1960.

PETERSON, ROGER; MOUNTFORT, GUY; and HOLLOM, P. A. D. **A Field Guide to the Birds of Britain and Europe.** 3rd ed. London, 1974.

PETERSON, ROGER TORY. **A Field Guide to the Birds.** Boston, 1947.

—**A Field Guide to Western Birds.** Boston, 1969.

PETZAL, DAVID E., ed. **The Experts' Book of the Shooting Sports.** New York, 1972.

—**The Experts' Book of Upland Bird & Waterfowl Hunting.** New York, 1975.

REID, WILLIAM. **Arms Through the Ages.** New York, 1976.

REIGER, GEORGE. **Wings of Dawn.** New York, 1980.

RICE, F. P. and DAHL, J. I. **Game Bird Hunting.** New York, 1965.

ROURE, GEORGES. **Animaux Sauvages de Côte d'Ivoire.** Abidjan, Ivory Coast, 1962.

RUE, LEONARD L., III. **Sportsman's Guide to Game Animals.** New York, 1969.

SCOTT, PETER. **A Coloured Key to the Wildfowl of the World.** Slimbridge, England, 1957.

SPRUNT, A., IV and ZIM, H. S. **Pistols, A Modern Encyclopedia.** Harrisburg, Pennsylvania, 1961.

STEPHENS, WILSON. **The Guinness Guide to Field Sports.** London, 1978.

STEWART, J. and STEWART, D. R. M. "The Distribution of Some Large Mammals in Kenya." **Journal of the East African Natural History Society and Coryndon Museum** 24 (June 1963). Nairobi, Kenya.

SURTEES, R. S. **The Analysis of the Hunting Field.** New York, 1966.

TERRES, JOHN K. **Flashing Wings: The Drama of Bird Flight.** New York, 1968.

THOMAS, GOUGH. [GARWOOD, G. T.] **Gough Thomas's Gun Book.** New York

—**Gough Thomas's Second Gun Book.** New York 1972.

—**Shooting Facts & Fancies.** London, 1978.

TRENCH, CHARLES CHENEVIX. **The Desert's Dusty Face.** Edinburgh and London, 1964.

VILLENAVE, G. M. **La Chasse.** Paris, France.

WATERMAN, CHARLES F. **Hunting in America.** New York, 1973.

WELS, B. G. **Fell's Guide to Guns and How to Use Them.** New York, 1969.

WHITEHEAD, G. KENNETH. **Deer of the World.** New York, 1972.

WOLTERS, RICHARD A. **Water Dog.** New York, 1964.

WOOLNER, F. **Grouse and Grouse Hunting.** New York, 1970.

YOUNG, GORDON. **Tracks of an Intruder.** New York, 1970.

Index